A Female Activist Elite in Italy (1890–1920)

Elena Laurenzi · Manuela Mosca
Editors

A Female Activist Elite in Italy (1890–1920)

Its International Network and Legacy

palgrave
macmillan

Editors
Elena Laurenzi
University of Salento
Lecce, Italy

Manuela Mosca
University of Salento
Lecce, Italy

ISBN 978-3-030-87158-1 ISBN 978-3-030-87159-8 (eBook)
https://doi.org/10.1007/978-3-030-87159-8

This Palgrave Macmillan imprint is published by the registered company Springer Nature Switzerland AG
The registered company address is: Gewerbestrasse 11, 6330 Cham, Switzerland

Contents

1 **The Political Philanthropy of the Female Elites** 1
Elena Laurenzi and Manuela Mosca

Part I A Women's Network in Early 20th Century Italy

2 **Harriet Lathrop Dunham *alias* Etta de Viti de Marco** 31
Manuela Mosca

3 **Alice Hallgarten Franchetti: A Woman Beyond Barriers** 59
Maria Luciana Buseghin

4 **Cora Slocomb Savorgnan di Brazzà: An Artisan of Peace and Social Justice** 93
Idanna Pucci

Part II From Generation to Generation: A Case Study

5 **Harriet Luthrop Dunham and Carolina de Viti de Marco: Emancipation Through Lacemaking** 133
Elena Laurenzi

6 **The Second Generation: The Transmission of the Philosophy of Work and Assistance** 153
Elena Laurenzi

7 **The Present-Day Heritage** 175
Elena Laurenzi

Part III Arts, Politics and Transmission: Methodological and Historiographical Considerations

8 **The Signs of an Art** 191
Marisa Forcina

9 **Female Biographies and Family History: An Approach to Social and Political History** 207
Anna Lucia Denitto

10 **A Feminine and Feminist Story of Transmission** 227
À. Lorena Fuster and Fina Birulés

Index 245

Notes on Contributors

Fina Birulés is professor of Philosophy at the University of Barcelona. Her research lines are articulated around two main foci: political subjectivity, history and action; and questions of feminist theory and the study of feminine philosophical production.

Maria Luciana Buseghin is a cultural anthropologist, interested in artistic craftsmanship, textiles, fashion and costume. She has more than 70 publications to her name, mainly on the life and work of Alice Hallgarten Franchetti.

Anna Lucia Denitto is full professor of Contemporary History in the Department of History, Society and Human Studies, University of Salento (Lecce, Italy). Her main research areas are: the History of the South of Italy in the nineteenth and twentieth centuries, economic History, social analysis, territorial analysis.

Marisa Forcina is full professor of History of Political Thought at the University of Salento (Lecce, Italy). Her research focuses on Gender and citizenship, women's History and French thought from 1700 to the early 1900s.

À. Lorena Fuster holds a Ph.D. in Philosophy from the University of Barcelona. Her research focuses on the issue of imagination in contemporary women's thought and the subject of recognition and debt in transmission, with the aim of questioning the logic of recognition from a gender perspective.

Elena Laurenzi is professor of the History of Political Thought at the University of Salento (Lecce, Italy) and visiting professor at the University of Barcelona (UB, Spain). She has published articles in Italy, the USA, Spain and France on María Zambrano, Simone Weil, Iris Murdoch, Françoise Collin, on methodological and historiographical issues concerning the history of women's political thought.

Manuela Mosca is full professor of the History of Economic Thought at the University of Salento (Lecce, Italy) and visiting professor at the University of Bologna (Italy). Her main research interests are in the History of Economic Thought and in particular on Italian Marginalism.

Idanna Pucci published books on the Balinese culture, on the Central Africa's colonial past, on the courageous women who fulfil their aspirations in Iran's gender-apartheid regime and on Cora Slocomb, her pioneering activist American great-grandmother.

CHAPTER 1

The Political Philanthropy of the Female Elites

Elena Laurenzi and Manuela Mosca

1.1 Female Activist Elites

The book we are presenting in this introduction focuses on a number of emancipationist activists of different nationalities who lived and worked in Italy in the first decades of the 1900s. These women from the aristocracy and upper-middle class undertook economic and political initiatives that sought to transform society, especially the condition of women. The aim of the studies collected here is to bring into focus and discuss—also on a historiographical and methodological plane—a phenomenon that has barely been studied: the presence and the contribution to the history of the 1900s of women from the elite, and therefore rich and powerful, who were also activists, in other words, women who were motivated by

E. Laurenzi (✉) · M. Mosca
University of Salento, Lecce, Italy
e-mail: elena.laurenzi@unisalento.it

M. Mosca
e-mail: manuela.mosca@unisalento.it

E. Laurenzi and M. Mosca (eds.), *A Female Activist Elite in Italy (1890–1920)*, https://doi.org/10.1007/978-3-030-87159-8_1

the desire to influence reality, organised, connected to each other, and capable of producing visible results in politics and in the economy, despite not being in government.

Historiography has kept the presence of female elites in modern and contemporary history somewhat in the shadows.[1] J. M. Johnson (2017: 8) points out that 'the field of women's history has been reluctant to place wealthy women [...] in the spotlight' and underlines the reluctance of historians to connect 'women with wealth and power'. This disregard is partly due to the general approach of social history, which has focused its attention on the complex, variegated and changing reality of disadvantaged individuals and groups, with elites being depicted as 'an undifferentiated group of people who in one way or another were responsible for the exploitation and repression of those below them' (Beckert and Rosenbaum 2010: 13). Moreover, within the prevailing social-science approach, wealth and power, when referring to gender, are seen in mainly negative terms as female discrimination and exploitation. Without denying this situation, which is still widely suffered by women, this book sets out to examine the historical presence of the specific female elites who used wealth and power to implement the transformation of reality.

The public presence of female elites took on a specific relevance at the start of the twentieth century when, thanks to feminism, access to the public spheres was opened up to women of various social strata:

> Many Italian feminist activists were middle or upper class, although they did campaign for the rights of working-class women. Some of them, particularly those connected to the socialist movement, were lower middle class, including many primary teachers, but most were very much part of the social elite. (Willson 2009: 25)

[1] The interest in female elites—initiated in the pioneering studies of Daumard (1957) and Davidoff and Hall (1987)—has been given a boost by some recent works analysing women's presence in the public sphere in terms of elites, as in the study by Giammattei and Bufacchi (2018) on women scientists and writers in Naples between 1861 and 1943, by Holmes and Tarr (2006) on the *Belle Epoque* in France, by Larsen (2007) on wealthy single British women between 1730 and 1860, by Flanagan (2002) on Chicago from 1871 to 1933, or in the essays on female publishers, entrepreneurs and cultural agents in nineteenth and twentieth century Spain: Fernández (2019), Fernández de Alarcón (2015).

In this setting, the politically active female elites were agents of change, often endowed with avant-garde visions, who knew and promoted the most innovative approaches in various fields such as technology, education, medical theories and employment. They were cultivated, open-minded, curious women who kept up with the emerging movements and directions of thought, and they were interested in the international scene; they travelled and took part in cultural and political conferences and meetings. Often, as in the case of the figures presented in the first part of the book, they were foreign, belonging to different religious denominations (Jewish or Protestant), and married to Italian noblemen, intellectuals and politicians. These were the elites that brought new ideas to Italy, especially in the field of social assistance. Thanks to them, the Anglo-Saxon and central European culture of welfare made its way into the women's movement and into the political debate in general (Fossati 2010: 216).

In addition to the limitations of social history in accounting for these presences, we also find the shortcomings of political and economic history. In these sectors, studies ignore the specific nature of the effects exerted by women from the economic and cultural elites, and are therefore unable to focus on the contribution they made in terms of economic and political development. We believe that this is due to the restraints imposed by a limited methodological range. A large part of the historiography on female activism in the late nineteenth and early twentieth century revolves around institutions: the research has concentrated on examining associations, newspapers and journals, political parties, and trade unions,[2] shedding light on the epoch-making phenomenon of women bursting into the political scene. However, the limited nature of this approach, unless combined with other lines of research, maintains and even strengthens the political confines set by the traditional institutional (and male) framework. It therefore marginalises and fails to grasp a whole series of actions by women on the border between formal and informal, public and private, aimed expressly at having an impact on reality and transforming their world. As a result, the female contribution to political history is grossly underestimated and also demeaned since, as have been pointed out (Smith 2007), the institutional approach treats the presence

[2] Just to mention a few that are relevant to our topic, since they deal with contexts and associations close to the figures we are examining here: Bussey and Tims (1980), Greetings (2000), Taricone (2003), Gubin et al. (2005), Frattini (2008), and Paull (2018).

of women only as a numbers gap and makes them appear insignificant in terms of substance. The biographical studies of women who—through their work—had an influence on the public sphere represent another important line of research in political historiography. In this case, too, it is important to acknowledge the weight of these contributions, which finally show women as protagonists, as opposed to the stereotype that relegates them to the position of objects. In so doing, they give visibility to the processes of forming a female political personality and at the same time provide a genealogy of powerful figures that inspire the imagination of the present (Pomata 1990). Nevertheless, this individual-centred approach is also limited by the fact that women are seen in a 'monumental' perspective as mere exceptions to the rule, or as rational gender-neutral agents. Historiography, including feminist historiography, is largely indebted to this monumental vision that identifies the historical object-phenomenon with everything that leaves a lasting mark, identified with a name. This obliterates and undermines the contribution made anonymously, or in any event without identification, by those who have, however, left a trace, with actions that are instrumental in preserving but also transforming the world (Collin 1993).

1.2 The International Network: A New Methodological Approach

This book seeks to overcome the dichotomy between purely biographical and collective/sociological or institutional approaches, exploring instead the network linking the various figures through their shared participation in a range of political and economic initiatives, and their interests, readings, meetings, social events, collaborative endeavours and more or less informal ties. The possibility of tracing these connections (both on the contemporary level and on that of the transmission between generations) is fundamental for this research, since it is in itself an effective indicator of the power of the female elites to produce projects and collective actions through which they were able to influence their economic and political context.[3] It was in fact these bonds that transformed the action of individual figures into a collective action, the great impact of which, invisible

[3] See Harvey et al. (2004).

to the theoretical thought of the time, is actually essential for a more general historical, political and economic analysis.

The approach featured in the research studies gathered in this volume also goes deeper than the research based on political networks (see Di Meco 2017), which mainly examines only formal or institutional links, based on a corpus comprising official documents (statutes, bulletins, conference records, articles, reports and chronicles) or the public writings of outstanding women authors and/or leaders. We are convinced of the historiographic importance of investigating subtle ties that were not exclusively public and not always explicit—and which are therefore hard to identify with the categories and the documentary corpus usually used in studies of the political and economic history of women—but that take on special relevance in the case of women's public undertakings (see Ferrante et al. 1998). To examine these less obvious relations, which nonetheless produced powerful paths of influence and exercise of political force on the part of female elites, the studies collected in this book make an intensive use of materials from family archives and private papers. These enable us to bring out a female fabric composed of figures who did not always enjoy direct friendship or collaboration and who often did not belong to the same organisations, but who made up a clearly recognisable set. This highlights also the existence of a *milieu* that facilitated the circulation and transmission of a political and economic inventiveness that went also beyond explicit relations and actual collaborations.

The use of private papers for the history of women is an issue that has been extensively studied and discussed in feminist historiography (Varikas 1996; Guidi 2004; Soldani 2005). Using these sources is not only an unavoidable choice due to women's scarce public presence and the lack of consideration in which such presence is held (Soldani 2005); it also has repercussions for interpretation, since it allows us to reconsider some categories and assumptions of the prevailing historiographic approach. One of these misleading assumptions, as we have already said, concerns the separation between the formal sphere—institutional or semi-institutional—and the informal or private sphere, and the tendency to identify political action with the former. In the Italian context, for instance, studies focused on the female associationism that exploded at the beginning of the century and indicated it as both a signal and a cause of an authentic 'mental revolution' because it enabled the emergence and exercise of a spirit of female initiative (Taricone 2003). Nevertheless, a clear dividing line can certainly not be drawn between the formally constituted and recognised associations and those that Taricone calls as 'occasional networks of exchange',[4] including *salons*, workplaces and family and friendship settings. As the chapters of this book show, the spirit of initiative is expressed with great force and political drive also in the private domain, and the dividing line between the different spheres is often unstable.

1.3 The Legacy

The contrast between the type of private documentation that we have favoured in these studies, and the avenues it opens for examining the political relations between women, raises questions about the transmission of tradition and the way it takes root, a topic tackled in this book by Fina Birulés and Angela Lorena Fuster (Chapter 10). Reflecting on this crucial issue confirms the relevance of documents and elements that are seemingly devoid of political or theoretical significance, such as diaries, memories and stories about oneself. These materials often reveal the need to model one's figure and establish a style that can be a vehicle of freedom for subsequent generations, explaining the influence that one generation can have on subsequent ones, without there being a formal legacy.

The examination of the transmission of the female elite's heritage of ideas and experiences therefore brings into play an intergenerational aspect. The research presented in the second part of the book traces—starting with a case study—what the female elites were able to hand down, or, conversely, to inherit. In the specific case of Italian feminism, because of the trauma of the Great War, the radical post-war change of scene and fascism's rise to political power in the 1920s, many initiatives undertaken by women between the 1800s and the 1900s suffered an abrupt halt or suffered a rapid decline, and this resulted in much historiography writing off that experience as being over. In fact, feminist historiography records a waning of the initiatives and political presence of feminist activism as early as 1911, when the vote for women was rejected, and when political propaganda on the colonial war in Africa stifled the

[4] Unless stated otherwise, the translations of quoted texts are our own.

themes and voices of feminists. According to the historian Lucetta Scarrafia, this phase marked a break in the transmission of the legacy of early twentieth-century feminism:

> It really seems that in those years there was a breakdown in the sense of belonging to a recognised feminist tradition thus causing serious damage to the following generations, to whom the experiences that had led to profound changes in the culture and in individual and collective destinies were not handed down. (Scaraffia 1986: 5–6)

However, our study demonstrates that at times there was a transmission of ideas, values and above all of concrete experiences from some of these elites down to the following generations. It also shows that their ideas and experiences still persist today in some cases, or have re-emerged, though sometimes in very different forms since, as Collin (1993) has stated, history does not proceed by additions, but by renewals.

1.4 Political Philanthropy

The threads linking the various figures analysed in this book can be traced back to the philanthropic networks created and nurtured internationally within the emancipationist movement of the early twentieth century.

Throughout the industrialised world, traditional forms of charity gave way during the 1800s to initiatives that sought to establish and experiment with a modern model of social assistance. In the name of progress and expanding knowledge, the belief developed that it was necessary to move on from the individual dimension of charity and to establish an efficient system of collective organisation with interventions addressed to the population rather than to single cases. Traditional charity was accused of not reaching the social and systemic roots of poverty, of treating the symptom without tackling the cause, and of encouraging the beneficiaries to be dependent rather than giving them the means to become autonomous. A definitive turning point came at the turn of the twentieth century, coinciding with the accumulation of capital and the expansion of industrialisation. Urbanisation and the formation of urban suburbs marked by terrible living conditions and rampant poverty prompted the transformation of charity into social intervention.[5]

[5] See Burlingam (2004), Adam (2004), Zunz (2014), and Reich et al. (2016).

The first decade of the twentieth century saw an explosion of philanthropic activity, especially among women. This occurred in conjunction with the flourishing of women's organisations of various kinds (associations of crafts, sport, culture and politics, clubs and pressure groups), which often interacted with philanthropy. At the public level, women were generally involved in promoting social reforms and, reflecting the usual gender division, their activity focused mainly—though not exclusively—on the protection of women and children. However, it was precisely through philanthropic activity that they challenged traditional roles and broke into the political scene. As numerous studies have shown, philanthropy was the area of action that enabled women to master instruments and competences that they then transferred to use in the political sphere proper: familiarity with drafting programmes and announcements, public speaking skills, the ability to organise and coordinate actions, budgeting and book-keeping skills and so on. In this sense, philanthropy prepared the ground for the fight for rights and suffrage. It gave women the chance and the means to conduct political battles (Johnson 2017) and at the same time to try out new forms of entrepreneurial organisation (Capek and Mead 2006). It came to represent a strategic significance for feminist battles (Beillard 2009).

In the light of these considerations, some feminist historians object to the distinction between philanthropic activism as apolitical or pre-political, and an activity recognised as fully political. As the Italian case analysed in the studies collected in this book shows, many important philanthropic actions were created and developed in the incubator of political organisations. The work of feminist philanthropists was motivated by the desire to bring the female masses out of their marginal state and to equip them with an effective instrument of autonomy. Furthermore, they understood their work as a profession and specialisation, and not as an idle pastime, thus developing, through philanthropic action, a political subjectivity. It is no coincidence that an acute observer such as the feminist writer Sibilla Aleramo, writing at the turn of the century, referred to philanthropists as 'the most notable figures of female intellectuality' (Aleramo 1910/1978: 160). In this sense, Buttafuoco (1988a) spoke of 'political philanthropy' underlining the discontinuity of these initiatives from traditional charity, which kept the women involved—both in the role of the beneficiaries and of the benefactors—in a subordinate, marginal position.

In Italy, the philanthropic activity of the feminist elites we deal with was concentrated mainly—though not exclusively—in rural areas. It should be borne in mind that in this country industrialisation was delayed compared to other countries in northern Europe, and it mainly involved the regions in the north of Italy, while most of the territory and the economy had a predominantly agricultural character (Salomone 2016). The corporativist trade unions and those of socialist inspiration were active among factory workers, but country areas were largely ignored, with peasant families and farm labourers, who lived in miserable conditions, not getting the benefit from any social assistance policies. The women doubled or even tripled their working hours: besides working in the fields and at home for their family, they often did weaving or embroidery piece-work in their homes, commissioned by middle-men who then sold their products to the textile industry (Pescarolo 1997, 2019). They only received a paltry payment for this work, which was often done at night.

This was the setting of the philanthropists' activity: taking advantage of the women's skills, they organised their work and optimised their products, offering them a means not only of making money, but also of empowerment. Many aristocrats and landowners, as in the case of Alice Hallgarten Franchetti or Cora Slocomb di Brazzà, who are studied in this volume (Chapters 3 and 4), opened workshops or schools on their land; others, such as Etta de Viti de Marco (Chapters 2 and 5), travelled around Italy in search of ancient craft techniques and traditions to be recovered, encouraging workers to join together and organise themselves and promote their products internationally. One of the exemplary manifestations of this unprecedented philanthropic activity was that of the Italian Female Industries, which are extensively analysed in the essays of this volume since they directly or indirectly involved all the protagonists.

1.5 The Italian Female Industries

The Italian Female Industries (Industrie Femminili Italiane: IFI) was a cooperative company set up and run entirely by women from the labour section of the National Council of Italian Women (Consiglio Nazionale delle Donne Italiane: CNDI); it could be seen as one of the richest and most emblematic experiences of pre-WWI feminism in Italy.[6]

[6] On IFI see Rosselli (1905), Bisi Albini (1905), Melegari (1907), AA.VV. (1906), Ponti Pasolini (1922), Taricone (1996), Gori (2003), and Palomba (2009).

The foundation of the cooperative was part of the increasing prominence of women in different fields of knowledge and creation, spurred on by the women's movement. It had a precedent in an exhibition called 'Beatrice', devoted to the world of women,[7] and later in another exhibition called 'Operosità femminile' (Women's Works) held in Rome in 1902 (Amadori 1902; Soldi 2015). These exhibitions revealed the vigour of artisanal lacework, which was spreading across the whole of Italy at that time. Several schools and workshops had sprung up in various regions since the end of the nineteenth century on the initiative of highly placed women who were curators and collectors of this ancient art and at the same time committed to women's liberation, as we will see in the first part of this volume. Bringing these dispersed enterprises together in one cooperative linked to the CNDI represented a shift towards more strictly political values, since its aim was to steer the economic and social strength of these companies towards the promotion of active citizenship. Cora Slocomb di Brazzà, a woman who was gifted with a sharp entrepreneurial spirit and moved by a strong political and moral sympathy towards the weakest members of society, was elected president of the IFI (see Chapter 4). Etta de Viti de Marco set up the cooperative with Cora and had a chair on the first board of directors. She was accompanied on this by a number of women from the aristocracy and *haute bourgeoisie*, representatives of a pluralistic milieu which was open to theories of civil society development and growth: Lavinia Taverna (1924–1997), a writer noted for her publications on botany and gardening (Taverna 1982, 1997, 2011); Liliah Nathan (1868–1930), Jewish sculptress and philanthropist[8]; Bice Tittoni Antona Traversi, philanthropist and wife of the parliamentary deputy Tommaso Tittoni, foreign minister in the Italian governments from 1903 to 1910 and Giuseppina Bakałowicz-Aloisi (who died in 1940), volunteer nurse and wife of the Armenian-Polish painter Stefan Bakałowicz.

The IFI brought together some four hundred schools and workshops spread across the entire Italian peninsula. These multifarious organisations were grouped into regional committees headed by a patroness, who was responsible for supervising and promoting the workshops and individual

[7] It was organized by Angelo De Gubernatis in Florence in 1890.

[8] She was the niece of the Mazzinian patriot Sara Levi Nathan and Ernesto Nathan, mayor of Rome from 1907 to 1913.

lacemakers in her area, studying traditional patterns, reconstructing their history where possible and training the craftswomen in lacemaking techniques. Often a school was set up next to the workshop for the workers to receive a basic education in reading, writing, mathematics and elements of general culture, law and rights. The products of each workshops were sent to the head office in Rome, where they were exhibited and sold. Sales exhibitions were held in large hotels, tourist resorts and spas, and a proportion of the products was exported to America, where outlets were set up in New York, St. Louis, Baltimore, Washington and New Orleans. An exhibition centre was soon established in Rome, and in the following years the cooperative showed its products at the Universal Expositions of Rome, Milan, Paris, London, Brussels and Berlin.

The commercial fortune of the IFI was related to a large extent to the lace market, which had grown exponentially in Europe and the USA since the mid-nineteenth century. The fashion had been launched by the Arts and Crafts movement, inspired by John Ruskin and William Morris, which had a strong influence on the cultural world at the turn of the twentieth century. This movement had rediscovered lacemaking and restored its value as an art that preserved and handed on an extremely rich cultural heritage. Spurred by this historical and philosophical interest, the lacemaking sector saw rapid growth, with a huge increase in production and sales, and a reorganisation of manufacturing. At the same time, and also thanks to the showcases of the international exhibitions where prices were agreed and fixed, lacemakers came under the scrutiny of researchers and collectors (Ricci 1911; Carmignani 2005; Fontanesi 1992).

Thus, lacemaking took on a 'polyvalent character' (Carman 2014: 93) in these years. It was an interweaving of cultural, aesthetic, social and political factors, and a wide range of different figures were involved: promoters, workers, master craftswomen, researchers, purchasers, collectors, philanthropists and activists. It was one of the few manufacturing sectors in which women were not simply employed as cheap labour but were able to achieve positions of prestige as skilled workers, master craftswomen and entrepreneurs.

This dynamism goes against the common sense of our times, where lacemaking seems emblematic of gender stereotypes and the exaltation of 'the female values of patriarchal society: […] patience, domestic reclusion, refinement' (Guidi 1992: 171). In the historical and cultural context of the early twentieth century, these crafts appear instead as the cornerstone of a comprehensive redefinition of gender relations. Entrepreneurs, master craftswomen and even workers often owed their success to having made a series of breaks with the female role. Amelia Rosselli, the Italian Jewish writer who was the first secretary of the IFI, published a series of articles at the time that revealed her clear awareness of the transformational power represented by this apparently traditional enterprise, defining the IFI as 'one of feminism's greatest successes' (Rosselli 1905: 9). This women-only enterprise, Rosselli argued, constituted a challenge to the codes and prejudices that saw women as incapable in administration, and which served to legitimate and perpetuate their dependence on and subjection to men. In the IFI, women found not only a source of income, but also the chance to show that they were 'able to organise, manage and regulate the complex financial mechanism without which even the highest ideals cannot become reality today'.

The experience of the IFI was also innovative in terms of the relationships between the women taking part, which in many cases defied barriers of age, provenance and social class. In some schools and workshops, there was an unprecedented process of communication between women of different classes on the basis of their respective capacities and experience. Amelia Rosselli (1903: 146) described the workshop as a 'neutral terrain' where relationships among women were taken out of the vertical hierarchies of charity and instead inspired by shared research and study:

> no longer expressed in the act of the hand that gives and that which receives, but by two heads bowed in unison over arabesques of old lace, together working out their secret. (Rosselli 1903: 492)

The most immediate objective of the cooperative was to tackle the serious problem of the over-exploitation of women's domestic craft production. The IFI tried, wherever possible, to turn women into their own bosses. Its statutes enabled workers to receive 65% of the proceeds, and they could become shareholders with full rights by donating the first ten liras they earned to the cooperative. The statutes also empowered the board to provide raw materials and advances on sales to particularly impoverished workers. Furthermore, needlework was seen as an outstanding example of the 'traditional industries' and as such an alternative to the 'machine industries' (Ponti Pasolini 1930). This contrast referred primarily to the higher quality of craft work over mass production, and secondly to the aesthetic sense advocated by John Ruskin, whose works were highly fashionable in Italy and much valued in women's movement circles (Ruskin 1857; Lamberini 2006). Amelia Rosselli (1903: 483) also argued that needlework countered the alienation of production-line labour because it 'tears women away from slavery to machines, leaving them free to infuse their own work with feeling'. Finally, lacemaking provided an alternative means of independent subsistence to factory work, which for women was oppressive both in terms of class and gender. As the contemporary trade unionist Ines Oddone observed, women workers were the victims not only of the greed of industrial interests but also of men's corporate unions, which enabled them to monopolise the best-paid jobs, 'with the cruel indifference that stems [...] from their traditional position of domination'. The factory, therefore, perpetuated women's 'servile status', taking them from paternal and marital dominion only to make them 'slaves to work, without being offered an adequate recompense' (Oddone 1902: 58).

1.6 Practical Feminism

The political philanthropy of the emancipationist elites corresponded to a change of strategy that was widespread in Italian feminism. After Italian Unification (1861), pioneering feminists like Anna Maria Mozzoni and Paolina Schiff had raised their voices to demand universal suffrage and the reform of the Civil Code which kept women under the control of men.[9] At the end of the nineteenth century, the Leagues for the Defence of Women's Interests were formed, pursuing the same aims (Mancina 1993). Journals like *Vita femminile* ('the mouthpiece of the women's movement in Italy') were founded, and intense lobbying was begun along with campaigns to raise awareness in public opinion and among the political class.

In the passage to the new century, however, the women's movement weighed up the challenges still open and saw that the goal of political rights not only came up against the hostility and closure of political circles, but had also made little headway with women, who seemed to be wary or fearful of joining the movement. The new generation of feminists therefore decided to work more proactively, carrying out more practical actions. Instead of calling for equality, they insisted on the value

[9] See Conti Odorisio (1980), Buttafuoco (1997, 1988b), Pieroni Bortolotti (1975), Rossi Doria (2007), and Willson (2009).

of the difference that women made; rather than aiming at assimilation and conquest of the spaces reserved for men, they appealed to the virtues and knowledge traditionally reserved for women, seeing them in a positive light, interpreting them as a value and no longer as a shortcoming or inadequacy.

> Unlike the feminism of the suffragists, early twentieth-century feminists did not emphasise the issue of equality but tended to couch their demands in the language of gender difference and equivalence. (Willson 2009: 24)

Winning their rights certainly remained a central goal, as is shown by the effort some of these activists put into the battle for the vote. However, emancipation in the broader sense was now to be achieved through a set of initiatives ranging from education to publications and to social assistance, which embodied a double strategic value: on the one hand, they would serve to attract the masses of women who were indifferent to, or wary of the suffrage battle, while on the other, they would demonstrate to the official powers and society in general that women were capable of dealing with the management and control of crucial sectors of national life such as healthcare, vocational training and the preparation for employment.

This pragmatic shift did not concern only the initiatives of political philanthropy we are examining in this book. It marked a more general tendency in the Italian feminism of that time, with an expansion of operations of social support reflecting different ideological positions and having different features.[10] Feminist historiography records the specificity of this age, labelling the feminism of the early 1900s with the term 'practical feminism' (Conti Odorisio 1980), which was already a widely used formula at that time. In an article published in 1907 in the journal *Vita femminile italiana* and explicitly titled 'Femminismo pratico e femminismo teorico' (Practical feminism and theoretical feminism), Amelia Rosselli gave a clear formulation. She identified two tendencies in feminism, not in contrast but distinct in their priorities. Theoretical

[10] The best known of these initiatives was *L'unione femminile* (The female union), founded by Ersilia Majino, of socialist inspiration (Buttafuoco 1985, 1986). Its welfare initiatives included numerous training courses (ranging from literacy to domestic science and childcare to professional development), employment agencies for domestic staff, assistance to poor mothers and the Information and Assistance Offices (Willson 2009: 31).

feminism stressed suffrage, summing up the aspirations of women in 'a single aspiration (the highest of all), the right to vote' (Rosselli 1907: 18). It therefore neglected the cultural and social condition of the masses of women, and above all the fact that the majority of women did not have economic independence, the 'first condition to participate properly in political life'. As a result, 'a group of highly intelligent women demand on behalf of women a reform of which they alone are able to understand the importance and the meaning'. Practical feminism, on the other hand, acted concretely to promote the conditions of the female masses, so that they could develop political awareness, together with material autonomy and cultural stature. Under the banner of practical feminism, Rosselli outlined a real political movement with its own profile, its goals and its own agenda, even if these did not appear as well defined and detailed as in the case of suffragism, since it was difficult to 'make propaganda of simple, modest ideas, which cannot unfurl any flag of revolt to the wind'.

On the value and political significance of the philanthropy promoted by the early twentieth century feminist elites, subsequent feminist historiography has expressed diverging opinions. The historian Franca Pieroni Bortolotti (1975) argues that converting the goals and strategies towards practical feminism was a step backwards compared to the first-generation feminists' demands for equal rights, and she denounces the bourgeois, elitist, conservative nature of the initiatives undertaken. The historians of the later generation—of the 1980s—have however reviewed this negative assessment, seeing those initiatives of political philanthropy, seemingly regressive, moderate, or even minimalist, and superficially irrelevant, in a different light. They reinterpret practical feminism as a vast movement of political and social action that sought to redefine the concept of citizenship and to construct the welfare state. However, despite this admission, most scholars have not corrected their judgement on the moderate, conservative character of that movement. Annarita Buttafuoco, for instance, who as said was the first to recognise the innovative political character of the philanthropic action of the female elites, observes at the same time that they made their own demands and slogans related to traditional gender structures, so ultimately these protagonists presented themselves as preserving the social structure, indeed, with their rationalising action, they compensated for its distortions and dysfunctions without actually questioning its foundations (Buttafuoco 1988a). This conservative label is one of the factors leading to the oblivion into which women's works of political philanthropy fell for many years, not deserving the interest of male or female historians. Some young Italian scholars have only recently rediscovered the interest in early twentieth century feminism, also proposing a different historiographic approach: shifting the axis of analysis onto processes of subjectivation, they have studied the formation of political consciousness in the female philanthropist elites, through the study of correspondence and documents from family archives (Gori 2003). This reopening of the archives has also made it possible to recognise the newness of these women's projects and their avant-garde character, which undermined the logic of the industrial capitalist system from within, promoting, for example, corporatism as opposed to the logic of capital and profit, or creating local development opportunities as opposed to the theory of emigration as a source of development.

As Marisa Forcina's essay in this book (Chapter 8) clearly shows, the practical aspect and sense of reality in these experiences of political philanthropy appear to be closely intertwined with the ideal of a renewed society, regenerated from within. Practical feminism was a movement projected towards the future, but at the same time proud of the past and its legacy. It promoted the profile of the 'new woman' (De Giorgio 2014), without acquiescing in the myths of progress and modernity; rather it attempted to enhance the skills acquired in the sphere of female action (motherhood and care work), as meaningful and useful for the construction of the nation, and to raise traditionally female jobs to levels of excellence. Work thus became the driving force of political action aimed at affirming full female citizenship; this citizenship was no longer completely projected into the future and identified with equal voting rights and equal access to male professions, but was claimed by virtue of the existing contribution, already effective, that women made to the common good with their work. Alongside the issue of work, mention must be made of education. While in nineteenth-century feminism the interest in this issue was entirely centred on the demand for female education in order to bridge the gap with the male gender, now instead women became the promoters of a revolution in the field of education and training. Education was placed at the heart of the project for the renewal of society and became the fulcrum of many actions—circulating or rural libraries, vocational schools and popular schools, rural and infants' schools—for developing and testing the new pedagogy of freedom, in the style of Montessori or Steiner (Pironi 2010; Kramer 2017). Last but not least, the pluralist, inter-faith, international character of this movement must be highlighted. The participants were lay women, Jewish, Catholic (mainly innovators, close to Modernism), Protestant, Orthodox, women from the north and south of the world, socialists and liberals: a world that was no longer provincial, but cosmopolitan, pluralist and cohesive at the same time (Fossati 2010). It revolved around networks of female relationships and its 'lively eclecticism' enabled diverse cultures and experiences to be drawn on and justified alliances and attempts to reconcile differences.

1.7 The Contributions

The first part of the book reconstructs the women's network that linked three paradigmatic figures of American women based in Italy who exhibit the liberal, inter-faith and international profile of an early twentieth-century political elite. It exemplifies their practical feminism, which went beyond the mere demand for rights to undertake significant experimental and entrepreneurial initiatives. At national level, the network involved the whole country, as one of the three American women acted in the South, one in the Centre, and one in the North of Italy.

In Chapter 2, the author Manuela Mosca reconstructs the life, thought and activity of Harriet Lathrop Dunham (New York 1894—Rome 1939), known in Italy as Etta de Viti de Marco. This chapter does not deal with her activism in the struggle for women's emancipation, as this issue is dealt later in the book (Chapter 5). Rather, it outlines her biography, which has never been studied before, focusing mainly on her cultural and political interests. The chapter describes her social commitment, and her patronage of artists and writers. It also reconstructs her involvement in the political battles in support of free trade and the development of the South of Italy. She fought them between the 1890s and 1920s with her husband—the economist and politician Marquis Antonio de Viti de Marco (1858–1943)—and the group of Italian liberals. In particular, Etta de Viti de Marco took care of the relations of the Italian radicals with the Anglo-Saxon liberal world. Like most of the enlightened elite of that generation, she believed in education, democracy and civil progress, topics on which she wrote articles published in prestigious journals.

In Chapter 3, Maria Luciana Buseghin examines the activism of Alice Hallgarten Franchetti (New York 1874—Leysin 1911), a Jewish American woman of German provenance, already educated to philanthropy by her family of origin. She married Baron Leopoldo Franchetti from Tuscany. Like Antonio de Viti de Marco, he too was a politician, and they both defended the rural masses and struggled for the development of the agricultural sector of the country. In her beautiful Umbria region, in the centre of Italy, Alice founded in 1908 the Tela Umbra's cloth company which produced canvases and laces: it was intended as an instrument of emancipation for peasant women. The quality of life, the original conception of the work and of its organisation were of primary importance for her: for instance, a kindergarten was attached to the laboratory, and flexible hours were introduced. In 1909, she also started a vocational school for women, where home economics, the care of infants, elementary sociology and pedagogy were taught. The author also describes the Rural Schools founded by the Franchettis, with their innovative experimental courses.

Chapter 4 should be read as a precious testimony written in the first person, both from its author (Idanna Pucci), and from her maternal great-grandmother Cora Slocomb Savorgnan di Brazzà (New Orleans 1862—Rome 1944): the long quotes from the latter give the reader the impression of hearing her voice. This American woman, who married Count Detalmo Savorgnan di Brazzà in 1887, introduced the art of lace-making in order to improve the conditions of peasant women in the northern Italian region of Friuli. She founded several Cooperative Lace Schools which achieved the highest level of quality and succeeded in her struggle to abolish American tariffs on foreign lace. Designer and producer of dolls and toy animals, she transformed the fortunes of a small shop that produced biscuits, turning it into a big factory that is still in operation today; she also bred a new white violet that received important awards. As we have already said, Cora was the first president of the Italian Female Industries, the extraordinary organisation that we have just described. Through her rules of life, spread out in her schools and also applied within her own family, we understand her philosophy and the ideals to which she aspired. In 1895, she launched an American campaign against capital punishment, in order to help a young woman immigrant to the USA from Southern Italy, and she succeeded. Two years later, she designed the peace flag, and actively contributed to the first international peace movement. Sadly, since 1906 Cora lived in isolation for 37 years because of a mental illness.

Taken together, the international network described in these three chapters is amazing: the three women had a lot in common, besides moving to Italy from America because of their marriage to wealthy Italian noblemen. They had the same sources of inspiration, common ideals, similar entrepreneurial skills, an incredible activism and a huge social commitment.

The second part of this volume investigates an example of transmission of ideas and experiences through the study of one extraordinary case from the extreme southeast of Italy, which has had wide international resonance and repercussions. The author of the whole part, Elena Laurenzi, follows the journey of two generations of highly active women from the same family, and demonstrates the endurance of, and changes in a wide-ranging political-entrepreneurial project that has continued up to the present day.

Chapter 5 starts with the reconstruction of the political and social project of two sisters-in-law: Harriet Lathrop Dunham (*alias* Etta de Viti de Marco), who we have already met, and Carolina de Viti de Marco (1863–1965). The partial portrait of the former, outlined in the second chapter of the book, is now completed with an analysis of her activism in the struggle for women's emancipation. The author shows that her most outstanding and original contribution to feminism was in the field of political philanthropy, thanks to her innovative vision of social assistance, and her active participation in the Italian Female Industries. Together with her sister-in-law, Carolina de Viti de Marco, in 1901 she set up a pioneering enterprise, the Casamassella School of lacemaking, where old embroidery techniques were taught. Their project intended to fight poverty and foster the autonomy of local women. Their enterprise grew during the first decade of the twentieth century and became so internationally known and renowned that their products received twice a gold medal in exhibitions (in 1906 and 1910). Carolina de Viti de Marco was also asked to run the female section of an Art School Applied to Industry, in a period in which women's technical and professional training was very scarce in Italy, particularly in the south of the country. The hostility of the local aristocracy and the effect of the Great War put an end to their lacework production.

In Chapter 6, the author highlights the legacy received by the second generation of the De Viti de Marco family. Carolina's two daughters (Lucia and Giulia Starace), together with one of Harriet's daughters (Lucia de Viti de Marco), continued the social and political commitment of the previous generation, developing it in different directions. In 1908, Lucia Starace (1891–1983), then eighteen, moved to Koppies, a village in South Africa, to pass on the culture of lacemaking and the ideals of female emancipation and autonomy to Boer women. Living and teaching in corrugated iron shacks, travelling on horseback to reach the students' homesteads, she replicated the experiences of her Italian forerunners. Once back in Italy, Lucia Starace opened a new lacemaking school and workshop, spreading and transmitting techniques, entrepreneurial spirit and values. On their side, the two cousins Giulia Starace (1895–1984) and Lucia de Viti de Marco (1900–1989) inheriting and reinterpreting the philanthropic spirit of their mothers, created a Steiner community where they treated children suffering from polio. In the meanwhile, they pursued the project of creating a centre for the promotion of a holistic vision embracing healthcare, non-alienated labour, respect for the environment and organic farming. In the end, this project took the shape of a foundation that they succeeded in setting up, and that is still working today.

Chapter 7 is focused on the present situation of the said foundation, in which the original message is still alive. Conducting field observations and interviews with some key witnesses, the author describes the estate and the manor house in which Le Costantine foundation is located. It shows the attention given by the founders to the Steinerian principles of balancing fullness and emptiness, and their openness towards the guests, materialised in the structure of the house. Today the foundation has textile workshops which combine tradition and innovation, production and research. It also produces biodynamic products, offers courses to the population and provides education for children, mainly from refugee minorities. The principles behind the organisation of the activities succeed in combining profit-making with the common good.

At the end of this journey through the generations, the author reflects on the real content of the transmission that occurred from the first pioneers of the beginning of the twentieth century to the present day: 'a completely feminine awareness of reality and freedom [...] a practical awareness that pits the idea against the roughness [...] a political awareness that bringing someone or something into the world means letting it live its own life' (below, p. 186).

The third and final part of this book uses an interdisciplinary approach to present some methodological and historiographical considerations in which the political dimension of the activity of the female elite studied in this volume emerges in different shapes. It emerges as the value of subjectivity in the study of women's political thought, or in the historical study of families and its implications for the political history of women, and in the possibility of delineating a hidden feminine political tradition.

In Chapter 8, the author Marisa Forcina sheds light, from the point of view of the history of political thought, on the most salient aspects of the experiences created by the female elites studied in the book. She focuses on the art of work well done, seen as a symbol of emancipation for women, but also as a revolutionary project for the whole society. Through the concepts of Kant's subjective happiness and Arendt's public happiness, she finds in the history of political thought the roots of the idea that work can be the basis of a new model of women's liberation: whether it was needlework or social work, for the female protagonists of this book it became the art of cultivating themselves. Thanks to a search in undeservedly little known writings, she shows that the art of work well done was seen as a revolutionary political project by writers of the period, such as Nikolaj Chernyshevsky, with his vision of equality and happiness reached through work; Charles Péguy, with his insistence on art as an exercise of marvellous precision as well as the basis of a project imbued with history and culture; and William Morris, with his idea that 'good work' can bring excellence and personal fulfilment. By recalling the philosopher Françoise Collin's claim that every woman artist is a feminist, the author of this chapter highlights, in a perceptive and evocative way, the political meaning of the actions undertaken by the women studied in the present volume, not so much in their explicit engagement in social movements, as when they acted in their pre-political domains.

In Chapter 9, the author Anna Lucia Denitto analyses women's history from the perspective of family stories, and social and political history. She deals with different historical methods to approach the history of women, and indicates the most productive and useful ones both for interpreting the stories reconstructed in this book, and for studying women's political history in general. By examining the internal analysis of the family and its relations with civil society, she shows that the relationships between women and men can be reinterpreted in the sense of complicity and/or otherness. Through the stories of the women reconstructed in this volume, she highlights the groundlessness of the separation between the public/political sphere on the one hand and the private sphere on the other. She also applies the perspective of world history to this book's research, which brings together the multiple interconnections between the different worlds in which our protagonists acted for promoting emancipation, work and support for the weak. Moreover, the author notices that the results of this book help in overcoming the stereotypes linked to the dualism backwardness/development: indeed, all the women dealt with in this volume operated in poor rural areas; nevertheless, they promoted innovative initiatives for the economic development of their regions. They also overcame the *cliché* linked to the tradition/modernity dichotomy, as our female elite gave the new meaning of a means for emancipation to a pre-modern activity such as embroidery. The relation between history and memory is finally reconsidered in the light of the crucial importance of archives, testimonies and interviews for the reconstruction of the history of women.

The point of departure of Chapter 10 is the ground recently gained by the task of recovering the presence of female figures in all areas of knowledge: the main aim of this chapter is to construct an intelligible narrative of how this current situation has been reached. The key concept on which the authors À. Lorena Fuster and Fina Birulés focus is that of the transmission of the past. By using tools that they have previously elaborated for the study of female philosophical thought, they show that women were not absent from the canon of the various disciplines, nevertheless their names have not been transmitted. They point out that in general, when the canon includes women, it is as an exception to the norm; in this case 'the way of telling history does not change, but rather ... this simply adds an appendix of excellent women to the usual way of transmitting the past' (below, p. 232). The authors also claim that women of the past were aware of their non-central position, and that to overcome this limitation they found original channels to become visible and transmit their knowledge. To discover their valuable legacy, and in general to reconstruct the lines of continuity and transmission of female thought and gesture, the authors urge historians to turn to the archives. Finally, they show that, by giving a political meaning to the female tradition of lacemaking, the women dealt with in this volume, taken as a collective entity, created the conditions for transmission—both practical and theoretical—among generations, allowing us to include them in history.

1.8 Our Aims

With this book, we wish to achieve the aims of:

1. presenting a network of representative figures from the early twentieth-century female elites in Italy and tracing their individual careers and the contacts, ties and relationships among them;
2. highlighting the existence of a shared political culture focused on emancipationism and philanthropy as a political tool for promoting women's interests, which also converged with some of the major currents of the European political and cultural scene of the first half of the twentieth century, such as the Arts and Crafts movement, Modernism and religious reform, innovative healthcare and educational theories (such as those of Steiner or Montessori), anti-colonialism and pacifism;
3. tracing the paths and modes of transmission of this elite's ideas and practices down to our own times, mainly through the study of private letters from family archives;
4. reflecting critically on the ideal historiographical and methodological instruments for studying these figures and analysing their value and significance both for women's political history and for history in general.

References

AA.VV. 1906. *Le industrie femminili italiane*. Milan: Pilade Rocco.

Adam, Thomas. 2004. *Philanthropy, Patronage, and Civil Society: Experiences from Germany, Great Britain, and North America*. Bloomington: Indiana University Press.

Aleramo, Sibilla. 1910/1978. Appunti sulla psicologia femminile italiana. In *Sibilla Aleramo: la donna e il femminismo. Scritti 1897–1910*, ed. Bruna Conti. Rome: Editori Riuniti.

Amadori, Rosi, ed. 1902. *Operosità femminile italiana*. Rome: Federazione Italiana delle opere Femminili.

Beckert, Sven, and Julia Rosenbaum. 2010. *The American Bourgeoisie: Distinction and Identity in the Nineteenth Century*. New York: Springer.

Beillard, Corinne. 2009. *L'émancipation des femmes à l'épreuve de la philanthropie*. Paris: L'Harmattan.

Gubin, Eliane, Leen Van Molle, Leen Beyers, and Els Flour. 2005. *Des femmes qui changent le monde: Histoire du Conseil International des Femmes, 1888–1988*. Brussels: Racine.

Bisi Albini, Sofia. 1905. Le industrie femminili italiane. *Rivista per signorine*, November.

Burlingame, Dwight F., ed. 2004. *Philanthropy in America: A Comprehensive Historical Encyclopaedia*. Santa Barbara: ABC-Clio.

Bussey, Gertrude, and Margarethe Tims. 1980. *Pioneers for Peace. Women's International League for Peace and Freedom 1915–1965*. Oxford: Alden Press.

Buttafuoco, Annarita. 1985. *Le Mariuccine. Storia di un'istituzione laica, L'asilo Mariuccia*. Milan: Angeli.

Buttafuoco, Annarita. 1986. *L'Audacia insolente. La cooperazione femminile, 1886–1986*. Venice: Marsilio.

Buttafuoco, Annarita. 1988a. La filantropia come politica. Esperienze dell'emancipazionismo italiano nel Novecento. In *Ragnatele di rapporti: Patronage e reti di relazione nella storia delle donne*, eds. Laura Ferrante, Maura Palazzi and Gianna Pomata, 166–187. Turin: Rosenberg e Sellier.

Buttafuoco, Annarita. 1988b. Straniere in patria. Temi e momenti dell'emancipazione femminile italiana dalle Repubbliche giacobine al fascismo. In *Esperienza storica femminile nell'età moderna e contemporanea*, ed. Anna Maria Crispino, 91–124. Rome: Unione Donne Italiane.

Buttafuoco, Annarita. 1997. *Questioni di cittadinanza. Donne e diritti sociali nell'Italia liberale*. Siena: Protagon.

Capek, Mary Ellen, and Molly Mead. 2006. *Effective Philanthropy: Organizational Success Through Deep Diversity and Gender Equity*. Cambridge: The MIT Press.

Carman, Jillian. 2014. The Users of Lace. A Socio-political Case Study. *Image & Text* 23: 93–109.

Carmignani, Marina. 2005. *Tessuti, ricami e merletti in Italia: dal Rinascimento al liberty*. Florence: Electa.

Collin, Françoise. 1993. Histoire et mémoire ou la marque et la trace. *Recherches Féministes* 6 (1): 13–23.

Conti Odorisio, Ginevra. 1980. *Storia dell'idea femminista in Italia*. Rome: ERI.

Daumard, Adeline. 1957. Les relations sociales à Paris à l'époque de la monarchie constitutionnelle d'après les registres paroissiaux des mariages. *Population* 12 (3): 445–466.

Davidoff, Leonore, and Catherine Hall. 1987. *Family Fortunes: Men and Women of the English Middle Class, 1780–1850*. Chicago: The University of Chicago Press.

De Giorgio, Michela. 2014. Madri del "secol novo". Sfide, lotte, scelte. In *Di generazione in generazione. Le italiane dall'Unità a oggi*, eds. Maria Teresa Mori, Alessandra Pescarolo, Anna Scattigno and Simonetta Soldani, 139–166. Rome: Viella.

Di Meco, Lucina. 2017. Women's Political Networks. Defining Leadership, Breaking Barriers, and Fostering Change. *Wilson Center*, 7, available at www.wilsoncenter.org/publication/womens-political-networks-defining-leadership-breaking-barriers-and-fostering-change (22 June, 2021).

Fernández, Pura. 2019. ¿Una empresa de mujeres? Construir la re(d)pública de las letras: Editoras iberoamericanas contemporáneas. *Lectora. Revista De Dones i Textualitat* 25: 11–41.
Fernández de Alarcón, Roca. 2015. La mujer de élite del siglo XIX como transmisora de la cultura. *Opción* 31 (6): 245–260.
Ferrante, Laura, Maura Palazzi, and Gianna Pomata, eds. 1998. *Ragnatele di rapporti. Patronage e reti di relazione nella storia delle donne*. Turin: Rosenberg & Sellier.
Flanagan, Maureen A. 2002. *Seeing with Their Hearts: Chicago Women and the Vision of the Good City, 1871–1933*. Princeton: Princeton University Press.
Fontanesi, Harriette. 1992. Dalla Storia il merletto ci parla della storia. *Alla Ribalta* 23 (4): 24–25.
Fossati, Roberta. 2010. Attiviste sociali di primo Novecento. Un mondo coeso? In *Politica e amicizia. Relazioni, conflitti e differenze di genere (1800–1915)*, ed. Emma Scaramuzza, 115–130. Milan: Angeli.
Frattini, Claudia. 2008. *Il primo congresso delle donne italiane, Roma, 1908. Opinione pubblica e femminismo*. Rome: Biblink.
Giammattei, Emma, and Enrica Bufacchi. 2018. *Potere, Prestigio, Servizio. Per una storia delle élites femminili a Napoli (1861–1943)*. Naples: Guida.
Gori, Claudia. 2003. *Crisalidi. Emancipazioniste liberali in età giolittiana*. Milan: Angeli.
Greetings, Joyous. 2000. *The First International Women's Movement, 1830–1860*. Oxford: Oxford University Press.
Guidi, Laura. 1992. Maestre e imprenditrici nell'industria manifatturiera meridionale dell'Ottocento. In *Operaie, Serve, Maestre, Impiegate*, ed. Paola Nava, 166–177. Turin: Rosenberg & Sellier.
Guidi, Laura. 2004. *Scritture femminili e storia*. Naples: Clio Press.
Harvey, Charles. 2017. *Art, Enterprise and Ethics: Essays on the Life and Work of William Morris*. New York: Routledge.
Harvey, Robert, Ann Kaplan, and Françoise Noudelmann. 2004. *Politique et filiation*. Paris: KIME.
Holmes, Diana, and Carrie Tarr. 2006. *A Belle Epoque? Women and Feminism in French Society and Culture 1890–1914*. London: Berghahn Books.
Johnson, Joan Marie. 2017. *Funding Feminism: Monied Women, Philanthropy, and the Women's Movement, 1870–1967*. Chapel Hall: The University of North Carolina Press.
Kramer, Rita. 2017. *Maria Montessori: A Biography*. New York: Diversion Books.
Lamberini, Daniela, ed. 2006. *L'eredità di John Ruskin nella cultura italiana del Novecento*. Florence: Nardini.
Larsen, Ruth. 2007. For Want of Good Fortune: Elite Single Women's Experiences in Yorkshire, 1730–1860. *Women's History Review* 16 (7): 387–401.

Mancina, Claudia. 2003. Anna Maria Mozzoni. In *Italiane dall'Unità d'Italia alla Prima guerra Mondiale*, eds. Eugenia Roccella and Lucetta Scarrafia, 135–139. Rome: Dipartimento per le Pari Opportunità.

Melegari, Dora. 1907. Un avvenimento femminista. *Vita Femminile Italiana* 1 (2): 179–185.

Oddone, Iris. 1902. La donna operaia. In *Operosità Femminile Italiana*, ed. Rosi Amadori, 58. Rome: Federazione Italiana delle opere Femminili.

Palomba, Ivana. 2009. *L'arte ricamata. Uno strumento di emancipazione femminile nell'opera di Carolina Amari*. Maniago: Le Arti Tessili.

Paull, John. 2018. The Women Who Tried to Stop the Great War: The International Congress of Women at The Hague 1915. In *Global Leadership Initiatives for Conflict Resolution and Peacebuilding*, ed. Andrew H. Campbell, 249–266. Hershey: IGI Global.

Pescarolo, Alessandra. 1997. Il lavoro a domicilio femminile: Economie di sussistenza in età contemporanea. *Annali Della Fondazione Giangiacomo Feltrinelli* 33: 173–195.

Pescarolo, Alessandra. 2019. *Il lavoro delle donne nell'Italia contemporanea*. Rome: Viella.

Pieroni Bortolotti, Franca. 1975. *Alle origini del movimento femminile in Italia. 1848–1892*. Turin: Einaudi.

Pironi, Tiziana. 2010. *Femminismo e educazione in età giolittiana. Conflitti e sfide della modernità*. Pisa: ETS.

Pomata, Gianna. 1990. Storia particolare e storia universale: In margine ad alcuni manuali di storia delle donne. *Quaderni Storici* 25 (74): 341–385.

Ponti Pasolini, Maria. 1922. *Le industrie femminili italiane. (Cenni storici sulla società)*. Rome: Tipografia del Senato.

Ponti Pasolini, Maria. 1930. Intorno all'arte industriale. *Nuova Antologia* 272: 109–120.

Reich, Rob, Chiara Cordelli, and Lucy Bernholz, eds. 2016. *Philanthropy in Democratic Societies: History, Institutions, Values*. Chicago: University of Chicago Press.

Ricci, Elisa, ed. 1911. *Antiche trine italiane. Trine ad ago e trine a fuselli. Raccolte e ordinate da Elisa Ricci*. Bergamo: IIAG.

Rosselli, Amelia. 1903. Una buona iniziativa. Esposizione e vendita del lavoro femminile nazionale. *Nuova Antologia* 187 (4): 483–492.

Rosselli, Amelia. 1905. Le industrie femminili Italiane. *Unione Femminile* 5: 9–10.

Rosselli, Amelia. 1907. Femminismo pratico e femminismo teorico. *Vita Femminile Italiana* 1 (3): 16–20.

Rossi Doria, Anna. 2007. *Dare forma al silenzio. Scritti di storia politica delle donne*. Rome: Viella.

Ruskin, John. 1857. *The Political Economy of Art*. London: Smith, Elder & Company.

Salomone, A. William. 2016. *Italy in the Giolittian Era*. Philadelphia: University of Pennsylvania Press.

Scaraffia, Lucetta. 1986. I luoghi della memoria femminile. In *Donna o cosa? I movimenti femminili in Italia dal Risorgimento a oggi*, eds. Maria Linda Odorisio, Anna Rossi Doria, Lucetta Scaraffia and Monica Turi, 3–16. Turin: Milvia.

Smith, Hilda L. 2007. Women Intellectuals and Intellectual History: Their Paradigmatic Separation. *Women's History Review* 16 (7): 353–368.

Soldani, Simonetta. 2005. Memoria delle donne e presenza politica. In *Carte di donne, Per un censimento regionale della scrittura delle donne dal XVI al XX secolo*, ed. Alessandra Contini and Anna Scattigno, 59–64. Rome: Edizioni di Storia e Letteratura.

Soldi, Manuela. 2015. Esporre il femminile. L'Esposizione Beatrice (Firenze, 1890). *Ricerche di S/Confine* 6 (1): 24–36.

Taricone, Fiorenza. 1996. *L'associazionismo femminile italiano dall'Unità al fascismo*. Milan: Unicopli.

Taricone, Fiorenza. 2003. *Teoria e prassi dell'associazionismo italiano nel XIX e XX secolo*. Cassino: Università degli studi di Cassino.

Taverna, Lavinia. 1982. *Un giardino mediterraneo*. Milan: Rizzoli.

Taverna, Lavinia. 1997. *La compagnia di un giardino*. Grosseto: Tipografia Ombrone.

Taverna, Lavinia. 2011. *Un giardino mediterraneo: Un'amante della natura ci racconta come trasformare un terreno incolto in un vero paradiso: I giardini della Landriana*. Bologna: Pendragon.

Thompson, Edward Palmer. 1974. *William Morris: Romantic to Revolutionary*. New York: Pantheon Books.

Varikas, Eleni. 1996. L'approccio biografico nella storia delle donne. In *Altre storie. La critica femminista alla storia*, ed. Paola Di Cori, 349–369. Bologna: Clueb.

Willson, Perry. 2009. *Women in Twentieth-Century Italy*. New York: Palgrave Macmillan.

Zunz, Olivier. 2014. *Philanthropy in America: A History*. Princeton: Princeton University Press.

PART I

A Women's Network in Early 20th Century Italy

CHAPTER 2

Harriet Lathrop Dunham *alias* Etta de Viti de Marco

Manuela Mosca

2.1 Introduction

This chapter reconstructs the life, thought and activity of Harriet Lathrop Dunham—known in Italy as Etta de Viti de Marco—in the context of the political battles that marked the so-called liberal era.[1] Her biography is outlined, providing as much information as possible on her life, which has never been studied,[2] and highlighting her culture and her many intellectual pursuits. Her social involvement is reconstructed along with the shared activity in support of the political work of her husband, the economist Antonio de Viti de Marco. A short mention will be made of her

[1]The liberal era refers to the period from Italian unification (1861) to the rise of fascism in the early 1920s.

[2]The sources used in this chapter are all primary, or very indirect secondary sources, such as the few references to Etta present in the literature on figures who came into contact with her.

M. Mosca (✉)
University of Salento, Lecce, Italy
e-mail: manuela.mosca@unisalento.it

E. Laurenzi and M. Mosca (eds.), *A Female Activist Elite in Italy (1890–1920)*, https://doi.org/10.1007/978-3-030-87159-8_2

activism in the struggle for women's emancipation, which was certainly at the heart of her interests, and which will be examined in depth in the second part of this book.

2.2 The Origins

Harriet Lathrop Dunham was born on April 1, 1864, in New York. Her parents were James Harvey Dunham[3] and Harriet Winslow Lathrop.[4] Her mother died at the age of forty-five, when she was fifteen. Her father, the owner of the Manhattan corporation James H. Dunham & Co.,[5] was on the board of directors of the Central National Bank of the City of New York (Anonymous 1901). On his death, she received a large inheritance, the management of which she often discussed in letters to her four sisters, all younger than her. They were Lilian Howland Dunham, Helen Bliss Dunham, Catherine Skinner Dunham and Grace Louise Dunham.[6] Little is known about their education. They were Episcopalians,[7] and Etta was not educated at home but certainly attended a real school[8]; one of her sisters studied pianoforte with maestro Paderewski (Ryan 1997: 29–10),[9] and they had their portraits painted by the American artist Singer Sargent.[10] They loved Europe, especially England, where they went to stay for long periods.[11] Like Harriet, they too were active in social life

[3] Born in New York in 1832 and died in 1901.

[4] Born in 1834 and died in 1879.

[5] The street numbers of the Corporation on Broadway are: 340-342-344.

[6] The dates of birth and death are respectively: Lilian (1867–1939), Helen (1868–???), Catherine (1871–???), Grace (1876–???). There was also a fifth sister, Elisabeth Howland, Catherine's twin, who died soon after birth.

[7] Etta's wedding was celebrated by an Episcopalian pastor. The same religion was attributed to her sister Grace in Eilish Ryan (1997: 29–30).

[8] In the letter to Umberto Zanotti Bianco of September 6, 1933, Etta says that a certain Lucy Lee was her schoolmate. Archive of Associazione Nazionale per gli Interessi del Mezzogiorno d'Italia (ANIMI), folder Umberto Zanotti Bianco (1889–1963), Rome.

[9] Ignacy Jan Paderewski (1860–1941) was a Polish pianist, composer, politician and diplomat. He was obviously very young when he taught James H. Dunham's daughters.

[10] John Singer Sargent (1856–1925) is considered one of the greatest portrait artists of the 1800s.

[11] In 1908 Etta wrote in a letter that her sisters were all in England. The *New York Times* of September 3, 1910 reports of her sister Helen that 'Of late years she has spent her time principally in London' (Anonymous 1910). Her sister Grace is described as one

and in philanthropy, especially Grace who was involved in the schooling of African American children.[12]

We know little else of Harriet's life prior to her arrival in Italy, nor why she moved here and stayed. Her future sister-in-law Carolina de Viti de Marco wrote that when her brother met her in Rome, she was in Italy 'for pleasure – and not for the first time'.[13] We know that in 1894, before marrying Antonio de Viti de Marco, she took part in a hunting party on horseback in the company of Lombard high society. The friend who provided this account already called her Etta (Anstruther-Thomson 1904: 273–276), the pet name that was also used in the announcement of her marriage. We believe that when she was in Italy, she lived in Florence, and that by 1895 she could not have been here long, as the Italian of her early letters is very basic. Let us now take a look at the person she was about to marry.

2.3 Antonio de Viti de Marco

Much has been written about the thought of the great Italian economist and parliamentarian Antonio de Viti de Marco, from both the economic and the political points of view.[14] Born into an aristocratic family in 1858 in Lecce, Apulia, and specifically in Salento,[15] he studied law in Rome with his close friend Maffeo Pantaleoni. After several years working at different Italian universities, in 1887 he transferred to the University of Rome. From 1885, when his first book was published (De Viti de Marco 1885), he combined his academic work with the administration of the family estate, made up of large landholdings that he had inherited in the meantime. From 1890 to 1912 he was the editor of *Giornale degli*

of those 'Americans of the sort found in the pages of Henry James's novels, who annually spent some time in England and finally decided to settle there' (Ryan 1997: 29–30).

[12] This information comes from a post by Miller (2018).

[13] Carolina de Viti de Marco, *Annales*. The reference is to a series of notes that she had drafted later in life in chronological order. Archive Carolina de Viti de Marco and Giulia Starace. The archive—currently being organised—is located at the Le Costantine Foundation, Casamassella (Lecce). Unless stated otherwise, the translations of quotations are our own.

[14] The secondary literature on Antonio de Viti de Marco is very wide. For a general description of his activity see Mosca (2016) and the literature cited there.

[15] The Salento peninsula is in the south-eastern most part of Italy's heel, in Apulia.

economisti, a leading journal in Italy and abroad, which was both one of the instruments for the development and international dissemination of the new economic theory and a forum for political discussion designed to establish the liberal and free-trade doctrine and put it into practice. For him, the English model was always a source of inspiration for the customs and tax reforms on which he worked constantly. In 1901, he was elected to the Chamber of Deputies and joined the radical party. In 1904, he founded the Anti-protectionist league, an experience he repeated in 1914, becoming the leader of anti-protectionism in Italy. Starting from this period, he set up a winery in the south of Italy which he managed using ultra-modern methods. In favour of Italy's intervention in the Great War, which he interpreted as a European war of liberal democracies against authoritarian states, he promoted the Italian-British League. De Viti's democratic and anti-nationalist interventionism was strengthened in 1917 when the United States entered the war. After the conflict he gave up his political commitment and his parliamentary activity to devote himself to writing his own manual of public finance (De Viti de Marco 1928); then, in 1931, having decided not to swear allegiance to the fascist regime, he also withdrew from his academic activity. Focusing his theoretical investigation solely on the economic functions of the state, De Viti outlined a contrast between two ideal types of political organisation: the absolute state and the democratic state. In the first type, the ruling class has a monopoly on decision-making in public revenue and expenditure. In the second, the possibility of voting enables the alternation in power of the rulers and the ruled which, according to De Viti, makes the interests of the two classes coincide. In De Viti's view, the practical achievement of this sameness of interests required the maximum participation of citizens in public decisions, and for this reason he was always in favour of universal suffrage. This theoretical system allowed De Viti to place the themes of public finance in a coherent structure for the first time, and he thus became the founder of the pure theory of public finance. The years of the fascist dictatorship were for him a period of gloomy retreat, interspersed with the reedition of some of his previous works and with sporadic contacts with those students who by choice considered him their master, such as Luigi Einaudi, Gaetano Salvemini and a few others. He died in Rome in 1943. Now, let us go back to the years when he first met Etta.

2.4 The Marriage

During their courtship, Marquis Antonio, who already had a considerable inheritance, went to visit her in Florence,[16] which is where they were married on June 4, 1895. The wedding was also reported in the *New York Times* (Anonymous 1895). She was 31 and he 37 years of age. As their 'party favour'[17] they published the book by the economist Ugo Mazzola *L'imposta progressiva in economia pura e sociale* (Progressive tax in pure and social economics) (Mazzola 1895), for private circulation in a limited number of copies. On the title page we read: 'Marriage of Marquis Antonio de Viti de Marco to Miss Etta Lathrop Dunham', not exactly a romantic idea![18]

Between the end of the 1890s and the First World War the couple enjoyed an intense social life between Rome, Salento and the Tuscan Apennines in marvellous houses with dozens of tastefully furnished rooms.[19] In Rome, they lived in a villa that had been renovated by Antonio, who had a talent for architecture (Chirilli 2016: 23), in fact, he even had a medieval style castle built in Salento in 1902.[20] When in the South, they also spent time in the authentically medieval family castle at Casamassella, where Antonio had spent his childhood. In the Apennines, on the other hand, the couple owned a villa to which Etta was very attached.[21] They spent long periods in London, in a 'little refuge', as Etta

[16] This is mentioned by, among others, his friend Maffeo Pantaleoni in a letter to Napoleone Colajanni dated April 12, 1895: 'I cannot immediately ask Deviti [sic!], because he is in Florence staying with his fiancée', in Ganci (1959: 323).

[17] Party favours, originally called *nuptialia*, were pamphlets or even books dedicated to the bride and groom which, in the period under consideration, could deal with any kind of topic.

[18] We thank our colleague Massimo Paradiso for pointing this out.

[19] A witness said: 'Their rooms are very fine, one hung with beautiful crimson damask', from the letter of Julia Ward Howe dated May 4, 1898, in Richards (1915/2018: 432).

[20] In a letter to Angelica Pasolini dall'Onda dated 28 October 1902 Etta wrote: 'Antonio is building a house on his plantation I Veli, near Brindisi. He has been his own architect, and seems to be a very successful one!'. Archive Pasolini dall'Onda, Gabinetto Vieusseux, Florence. We were told that this was the castle where the King slept on 9 September 1943 when fleeing from Rome.

[21] Shortly after Etta's death, her daughter Lucia wrote to Zanotti Bianco on 30 September 1939 from the house in the Apennines: 'The more I stay here the more I feel that this is where we should bring Mamma, that this would be her dearest personal

called it.[22] The couple also went to New York for long periods, staying in her father's grand house[23]; from August to December 1896 on their arrival in the USA their presence was recorded in both the local press in the column 'Return from Abroad of Many Well-Known Persons', and in the city's *Social Register* (Anonymous 1896, 1897), which confirms that Etta's family was prominent in New York high society.

Between 1896 and 1900 their three children were born, one every two years: James (named after his maternal grandfather), Etta (with her mother's pet name) and Lucia (called after her paternal grandmother). English was spoken at home.[24] Details on the organisation of their home life as a couple with young children, devoting their energy to work and social life, emerge from Etta's letters to Angelica Rasponi,[25] whom she frequently asked for help in hiring domestic staff. The children were at school in England, and in 1911 we find Etta as a visitor at Heathfield School in Ascot, which was attended by the two girls,[26] while James was studying in Norfolk, also in the UK.

2.5 Culture and Patronage

Etta had hundreds of books and the remains of her library today are worthy of a separate study.[27] Her correspondence often contained knowledgeable critical references to her reading. Many were history books

wish. Everything here speaks of her'. Archive Associazione Nazionale per gli Interessi del Mezzogiorno d'Italia (ANIMI), folder Umberto Zanotti Bianco (1889–1963), Rome.

[22] Etta uses this expression in a letter to Camillo Pellizzi on 23 March 1923. Ugo Spirito and Renzo De Felice Foundation, folder 19 Camillo Pellizzi. Etta's house was at 40 Oakley Street, Chelsea SW3.

[23] The house address was 37 East 36th Street.

[24] Their son James recalls this in his memoir, and the letters between siblings are also in English. Archive Carolina de Viti de Marco and Giulia Starace, Le Costantine Foundation, Casamassella (Lecce).

[25] Archive Pasolini dall'Onda, Gabinetto Vieusseux, Florence.

[26] Her name appears among the visitors in the *Heathfield School Magazine* in 1911 and 1914.

[27] At the Le Costantine Foundation in Casamassella (Lecce), where the Archive Carolina de Viti de Marco and Giulia Starace is located, they are only just starting to open the boxes of books from the house at Boscolungo Pistoiese, in Tuscany.

linked to the places she was in (from the history of Europe[28] to that of the Apulian castles[29]). Her comments on the books she read were detailed and critical and sprang from the contrast between the arguments they put forward and her own convictions. In her husband's filing cabinet, which is still found today in the family castle,[30] there are some catalogue cards for books that we think may be linked to Etta's interests: works on China, divorce, education, philanthropy and other social issues. Furthermore, Etta followed Italian politics closely. For example, in 1914, she asked her friend Gugliemo Ferrero[31] for his articles, especially one in which he compared official diplomatic documents (*Official White Book*, *Official Orange Book*, etc.).[32] She was also interested in political news from the Anglo-Saxon world: we know she collected articles from the *Times* and the *Manchester Guardian*.[33]

Her cultural interests are also revealed by the people she frequented, the events she organised and her patronage of the arts. In the magnificent houses mentioned earlier, her *salon* was judged 'le plus intéressant de Rome' by the French writer and winner of the Nobel Prize for Literature Romain Rolland.[34] The personalities she welcomed included the American poetess and activist Julia Ward Howe[35] and the dramatist and

[28] As one of the examples, see the letter of August 6, 1897 from Courmayeur addressed to Angelica Rasponi in which Etta makes many brilliantly perceptive observations on her reading of Mandell Creighton (1882–1894). Archive Pasolini dall'Onda, Gabinetto Vieusseux, Florence.

[29] In a letter to Umberto Zanotti Bianco dated December 10, 1932 from Salento, Etta says she has read Ross (1889), then Bacile di Castiglione (1927) and also Tea (1932).

[30] A study on De Viti de Marco's filing system by the author is in press.

[31] Guglielmo Ferrero (1871–1942) was a sociologist, historian and writer, and worked closely with the radical newspaper *Il Secolo*.

[32] Letter from Etta to Ferrero dated December 13, 1914, Guglielmo Ferrero Papers, box 56, New York, Columbia University, Rare books and manuscript library.

[33] Letter from Etta to Luigi Einaudi dated April 3, 1918, Archive Luigi Einaudi, Turin, Einaudi Foundation.

[34] Letter from Romain Rolland dated August 25, 1907, in Séché and Rolland (1962). Romain Rolland (1866–1944) was a French writer and dramatist, winner of the 1915 Nobel Prize for Literature.

[35] See Richards (1915/2018: 432). Julia Ward Howe (1819–1910), known mainly for writing the American patriotic anthem *The Battle Hymn of the Republic* in 1861, fought for the abolition of slavery and women's suffrage.

librettist Modest Tchaikovsky,[36] brother of the famous composer. In 1910, Emily Hobhouse,[37] the British reformer working in South Africa, who, as we will see in Chapter 6, would play a major role in the affairs of the family, was her guest and reported also meeting, in that salon, the German foreign minister Baron Gottlieb von Jagow.[38] In 1912, we find Etta in the home of the entrepreneur and literary figure Marco Besso,[39] for an evening of Dante. Two figures in particular are worth remembering among Etta's countless social contacts. One was Maria Montessori (1870–1952): in 1913, she hosted the first international Montessori training course, held by the pedagogist in the presence of 'the Ambassadors of the United States and Great Britain, as well as the Italian Ministers of Public Instruction and of the Colonies'.[40] Then, in 1914, she helped Montessori by interpreting for her in meetings with the American delegates of the International Council of Women, which was holding its conference in Rome that year (Kramer 1976). We will return to Maria Montessori and to this Council in the following chapters. The other figure worth mentioning was the actress Eleonora Duse (1858–1924), who was Etta's

[36] Tschaikowsky-Gesellschaft, Sodener Str. 45a, D-61462 Königstein im Taunus, Mitteilungen 18 (2011), S. 204–215. Modest Ilic Tchaikovsky (1850–1916) devoted his life to pedagogy, music and literature.

[37] Emily Hobhouse (1860–1926) fought to improve the conditions of women and children in the concentration camps in South Africa during the Second Boer War. We will return to her in Chapter 6.

[38] In a 1916 letter addressed to Gottlieb von Jagow (1863–1935), Emily Hobhouse writes that she had met him five or six years earlier at Etta's home in Rome. Hobhouse (2015: 94).

[39] Online Historical Archive Foundation Marco Besso, file 13, other correspondents (1912). Besides being president of Assicurazioni Generali, Marco Besso (1843–1920) was a member of the board of the Banca Commerciale Italiana; a great Dante enthusiast, and member of the Accademia dei Lincei.

[40] Susan Feez also writes that 'those who participated in the course attended three lessons a week, two lectures and one practical lesson, given by Dr Montessori herself. The introductory lecture was delivered during a welcome reception organised by Dr Montessori's great friend and supporter, Marquise Maria Maraini Guerrieri-Gonzaga, and held at the grand house of the Marquise de Viti de Marco [...]. The subject of this lecture was: *General Review of the Montessori Method as Introducing a New Experimental Science*' (Feez 2013: 10–13).

guest on multiple occasions: it was a deep and lasting friendship which appears to have started before her marriage to Antonio.[41]

From her correspondence, on which she spent many, many hours each day,[42] we also learn about her social relations with artists and literary figures: we find the English poetess Violet Fane[43], the American writer Hamlin Garland[44] and other leading figures.[45] Letters from the theologian Paul Sabatier[46] attest to the family's affinity with the Modernist movement, an attitude that, as we will see, was shared by other figures presented in this book. Etta was also in contact with the Webbs, whom she invited to lunch in Rome on 2nd April 1909 with Ferrero,[47] an episode recorded in Beatrice Webb's diary.[48] It was a lasting friendship

[41] On February 5, 1917, Duse wrote to her daughter about Etta: 'Je la connais depuis quelque 28 ou 30 ans' (Biggi 2010: 161).

[42] At the end of a very long letter to Duse, Etta implied that she spent an exaggerated amount of time on her correspondence, saying 'Etta and Lucia have come to send me to bed'. Eleonora Duse Archive, Istituto per il Teatro e il Melodramma, Giorgio Cini Foundation, Venice.

[43] Violet Fane is the pseudonym of Lady Mary Montgomerie Currie (1843–1905), English poetess and writer. See for instance Etta's letter of January 25, 1899, Special Collections, University of Reading, Violet Fane, RUL MS 2608/1, 158–159.

[44] Hannibal Hamlin Garland (1860–1940), known for his descriptions of the harsh working conditions on farms in the Midwest. See the letter from Etta of July 12, 1906, University of Southern California, Digital Library 2017-06-08.

[45] Between 1909 and 1919, there were many letters to Hellen Buchanan, who lived with Etta's daughter in Rome. She was the daughter of the military officer James A. Buchanan and the wife of Walter McJones, founder and first mayor of Villalba in Portorico from 1917 to 1919. Helen Buchanan papers, University of Michigan, Manuscript Division, William L. Clements Library.

[46] Archive Paul Sabatier, Romolo Murri Foundation, Centro Studi per la Storia del modernismo dell'Università degli Studi di Urbino Carlo Bo. Charles Paul Marie Sabatier (1858–1928) was the French historian who started modern Franciscan historiography; a Calvinist pastor, he was part of Christian theological modernism. We will also meet this figure in later chapters.

[47] Letter from Etta to Ferrero on 26 March 1909. Guglielmo Ferrero Papers, box 56, New York, Columbia University, Rare books and manuscript library.

[48] From the diary of Beatrice Webb on April 20, 1909, written immediately after a six-week journey to Italy: 'A pleasant little circle of Italians – the Scipio Borgheses, Countess Pasolini, Conte Balgani, Marquise de Viti, the Godivinis, various monsignori and other cultivated men and women, belonging to the 'White' and the 'Black' Sets, just gave the touch of intimacy with native things that prevents one from sinking into the guide book attitude and feeling the mere tourist'. *Diary of Beatrice Webb, Typewritten Transcript, vols. 21–27, 2 January 1901–10 February 1911*, 540. LSE Library, Ref. No PASSFILED/1.

because Etta invited them again almost fifteen years later, in 1923, this time to her house in London.[49] Her correspondents included figures connected to her husband such as his economist colleagues and the editors of the journals to which he contributed, which we will discuss later, and with whom she interacted both on her own account and on his behalf.

To facilitate this intense network of relations, they used letters, postcards, telegrams and at times the telephone, the number of which was printed on the letterhead. The phone was not used for conversations; telephone appointments were fixed by letter, announced with a note and served only to confirm invitations and arrange meetings. Communicating by notes in that era even seemed more convenient and... faster! This opinion seems to have been shared by others in that period, for instance by Marcel Proust, who described his initial misreading of the immediacy of telephone communications as follows: 'I found not rapid enough [...] the admirable sorcery for which a few moments are enough to bring before us, invisible but present, the person to whom we have been wishing to speak'.[50] This situation gives credibility to a statement by Antonio in a well-known article on the telephone industry, which sounds somewhat odd today, in which he says that competition with the telephone in the city comes from 'messenger boys' or 'servants' (De Viti de Marco 1890/2001: 522).

See also Etta's letter to Ferrero of March 26, 1909 (Guglielmo Ferrero Papers, box 56, New York, Columbia University, Rare books and manuscript library).

[49] Letter to Camillo Pellizzi dated 23 March 1923: 'Next Tuesday, 27 c.m., the Sidney Webbs will come to me for lunch'. Ugo Spirito and Renzo De Felice Foundation, folder 19 Camillo Pellizzi.

[50] However, the depth and complexity of the emotions aroused by the telephone call to his grandmother described by Proust in the *Recherche* indicate a very different use from that described here (Proust 1920–21/1925: 86).

2.6 Social Commitment and Philanthropy[51]

To her companion, the socialist leader Filippo Turati,[52] Anna Kuliscioff[53] described Etta thus:

> an intelligent lady, very cultured, active and with some inclination towards socialism. She is very involved in the female industries[54] and was the organizer of the exhibition of Abruzzese[55] lacework recently held in London. In other words, she is one of the most serious and modern feminists in Rome, perhaps precisely because she is not Roman or even Italian.[56]

An article in an Italian newspaper linked her to 'a group of idealistic women gathered around Miss Meysenbug', [57] the German writer who was a friend of Giuseppe Mazzini—one of the fathers of Italian unification—and of Nietzsche, and who 'devoted her entire life to an ideal of man's inner education' (Geraldini 1953). The correspondence reveals that education was also very close to Etta's heart, an attitude typical of a vision of the world based on democratic ideals, like that of the De Viti de Marcos. We will see later how much effort she put into the embroidery school at Casamassella (from 1901 to 1911), founded and run by her as a means of achieving female emancipation through work. This will be dealt with in greater detail in the second part of this book.

In the first decade of the 1900s, we find her actively involved in the female emancipation movement. In 1906 she was among the founders of

[51] Etta's activism includes many more aspects than those examined in this paragraph. For a detailed study of Etta's activity in this field, see the second part of this book, Chapter 5.

[52] Filippo Turati (1857–1932) was an Italian politician, journalist and political expert, the leader of the reformist group of the Italian Socialist Party, which he helped found in 1892 with Anna Kuliscioff.

[53] Anna Kuliscioff (1957–1925) was a Russian revolutionary, physician and journalist, naturalised Italian, one of the founders and main exponents of the Italian Socialist Party.

[54] She refers to the Italian Female Industries (IFI), on which see Chapter 1.

[55] Abruzzo is a region of central Italy. For a detailed description of this episode, see the next chapter.

[56] Quoted in Cardini (1985: 178).

[57] See Geraldini (1953). On Baroness Malwida von Meysenbug (1816–1903), see Mezzomonti (1934). As we shall see, other figures treated in this book also followed the model of the German philosopher and writer.

the National Council of Italian Women (CNDI). In this important organisation, which will be examined in depth in the coming chapters, Etta became the director of the 'City Life' section and, with 'virile energy', [58] implemented a plan to reorganise charity work in Rome. To carry out this task, she had discussions with the President of the Women's City Club of New York and was inspired by the most advanced models in Europe and the United States, especially the Charity Organisation Society operating in London and New York (Anonymous 1907: 288). In March 1906, Etta was a board member of the Anti-Begging Society, and in 1908, she became head of the Social Support and Welfare Section, set up by the National Council of Italian Women prior to its First Conference, held in Rome from April 23 to 30, 1908.[59] The programme she drew up and presented to the conference was impressive, as we shall see in Chapter 5. The journal *Vita femminile italiana* commented thus:

> Marquise Etta De Viti De Marco, the intelligent and extremely active President of the *Information Office and Guide to Charity* in Rome, who manages to perform an indescribable amount of good, also organized and chaired the *Social Support and Welfare Section* of the 1st Conference of Italian Women, presenting a broad, complex program that was handled masterfully.[60]

It provoked lively sessions where the participants voted to approve the need to require women's participation on the boards of Charity congregations and of Houses for the support of the disadvantaged, as well as to coordinate charity organisations and to find an urgent solution to the unemployment problem. This last issue had been the subject of interesting

[58] A quality recognised in the bulletin of the National Council of Italian Women (Anonymous 1907: 291). The use of the term 'virile', very fashionable at the time, sounds paradoxical in this feminist context.

[59] 'The National Council of Italian Women has appointed a Commission composed of Marquise Etta De Viti De Marco, president - donna Sofia Cammarota - Countess Lisa Danieli - Mrs Alda Orlando - Countess Maria Pasolini - Miss Maria Roesler Franz - Mrs Elisa Vannutelli - Mrs Alina Wollemborg, with the task of organizing the Social Support and Welfare Section of the first Women's Conference to be held in Rome from April 23 to 30, 1908' (Anonymous 1908).

[60] *Nota della direzione*, first footnote on page 1 of the article by De Viti de Marco (1908: 620).

correspondence between Etta and Gina Lombroso[61] in which the two activists discussed whether a female association should deal also with male unemployment. They agreed that this should be done but Etta added:

> the danger I fear most in these discussions by women with a philanthropic spirit, but inadequate scientific knowledge, is the failure to recognize the natural forces that, in this field too, frustrate the best intentions, and cause unexpected side effects.[62]

As is clear from the rest of the letter, she was talking about the 'natural' laws of the economy, to which we will return.

Among Etta's other activities, it must be mentioned that in 1906 she was part of a women's committee that draped the Italian athletes leaving for Athens for the Intercalated Olympic Games in tricolour sashes.[63] In January 1915, following an earthquake in Abruzzo, she organised 'one of the most useful and merciful of all the provisions for relief [...] for finding mothers of lost children' (Page 1915). In May of the same year, the enthusiasm for Italy's entering the war brought her onto the streets of Rome with her car loaded with oranges, cigars and cigarettes to distribute to the soldiers leaving for the front (Anonymous 1915).

2.7 The Mobilisation of the Liberals

In 1930, Antonio wrote in his own hand on the title page of his newly published book *Un trentennio di lotte politiche* (Thirty years of political battles): 'To Etta to remember shared ideas and ideals' (De Viti de Marco 1930).[64] The couple's political partnership did coincide with his thirty

[61] Gina Lombroso (1872–1944), daughter of Cesare, the well-known anthropologist, wrote about psychiatric and criminological issues, political questions and the condition of women. She was married to Guglielmo Ferrero.

[62] Letter of January 25, 1907. Contemporary Archive 'Alessandro Bonsanti', Gabinetto Viesseux, Florence, Archive Angelica Pasolini Dall'Onda.

[63] In *La Stampa sportiva* of 18 March 1906, on page 16, we read that 'In Rome, under the presidency of donna Emilia Doria Pamphili, a women's committee was formed to send off our champions on their way to Athens, draping them in special rich tricolour sashes'. Etta was in fact a member of the Committee of Patronesses for the Italian participation in the Athens Olympics (Anonymous 1906).

[64] On their alliance, Cardini writes: 'she shared his political positions and collaborated with her husband's journals' (1985: x); and again: 'the two shared actually identical views

years of battles, but unlike the unemotional coldness of the Marquis,[65] his wife had an 'impatient' temperament.[66] The year 1898 was one of great mobilisation for the group of Italian liberals[67]: in the midst of economic crisis and the protests of workers and peasants,[68] they decided to carry out a programme of talks and articles to be disseminated abroad to denounce the wrongdoings of the Italian government. Etta played an active part: she wrote a letter illustrating the programme but the famous economist and sociologist Vilfredo Pareto, though judging the contents right, advised against making it public so as not to reveal their plan to the government.[69] As the press was the only way of conveying ideas and stirring up public opinion in those decades,[70] the liberal group was deeply involved in founding journals and supporting newspapers, and Etta was just as keen. In 1901, having come into the inheritance from her father, she decided to invest part of it in a newspaper in support of the liberal group.[71] And again in 1915, a series of letters from her to Prezzolini[72] reveal that she intended to contribute her own money to cover the losses

and the same idealistic motives' (126–127). Zanotti Bianco, too, in the biography of Antonio, writes: 'She supported and agreed with him in many of his initiatives especially in those closest to her spirit, like the Italian-British League, promoted by her husband, the battle to defend Wilsonian principles and to make the League of Nations, of which he was briefly the Italian delegate, an effective supranational body' (1962/1964: 354).

[65] Gaetano Salvemini in 1948 recalled him thus: 'He was a seemingly cold man, of few words, who rather kept one at a distance. His spirit was a volcano under the ice, a thoroughbred kept in check by an iron hand' (1949: 2).

[66] A word she used to describe herself, complaining about the moderation of men: 'with my impatient temperament I do not trust their actions, for they are too measured, moderate and reflective, while I would like them to jump in'. Letter to Ferrero of February 26, 1905. Guglielmo Ferrero Papers, box 56, New York, Columbia University, Rare books and manuscript library.

[67] On the rise and fall of the liberals in Italian history, see the classic study by Vivarelli (1981).

[68] We are referring to the peasant protests in the South, followed by the riots in Milan in May 1898 against the government because of the rise in the price of bread.

[69] Letter from Pareto to Pantaleoni of November 7, 1898, in Pareto (1960: II, 248).

[70] See Castronovo et al. (1979). For the way the economists of the time used the newspapers as a means of mobilisation, see Augello, Guidi and Pavanelli (2016).

[71] Letter from Edoardo Giretti to Luigi Einaudi, November 15, 1901. Archive Einaudi, Correspondence, folder Edoardo Giretti, Einaudi Foundation, Turin.

[72] Giuseppe Prezzolini (1882–1982) was a journalist, writer and publisher who founded *La Voce* in 1908.

of the newspaper *La Voce*, for which her husband had been editor for a short while.[73] Then, in 1916, she was trying 'to scrape together a bit of money' to reopen a similar paper, which she hoped would be 'run by Salvemini, Giretti, De Viti de Marco, Zanotti Bianco and…?'[74] These were in fact the ones who in the previous decades had been the strongest supporters of the idea of creating a movement with a clear liberal and free-trade character.[75]

Political battles can be tough, and Etta was often on the warpath supporting and defending Antonio's friends and radical colleagues, as in the case of the accusations directed at Maffeo Pantaleoni in 1902,[76] or in that of the attacks on the International Agricultural Institute which was 'under the control of Antonio, Maffeo, Montemartini',[77] or again when she insisted on Pantaleoni writing the preface to the reprint of 'Cronache' (Chronicles) by Francesco Papafava[78] for the anniversary of his death in March 1913.[79] Antonio's political career, with almost twenty

[73] De Viti replaced Prezzolini as editor of *La Voce* because the latter was leaving for the war, but the experience was short-lived due to contrasts between the old editor and the new one. Etta's intervention however enabled the last issue of the year to be brought out, containing articles that were ready for printing. The episode is also mentioned by Antonio Cardini (1985: 280–281): 'she tried to heal the rift and partly covered the debt from her own funds'.

[74] Original punctuation. Etta's letters to Zanotti Bianco of March 10, 1916, and April 8, 1916. Archive of Associazione Nazionale per gli Interessi del Mezzogiorno d'Italia (ANIMI), Rome, folder Umberto Zanotti Bianco. Edoardo Giretti, silk producer and radical politician, was very close to De Viti in his anti-protectionist battle. We have already encountered the name of Umberto Zanotti Bianco, archaeologist, politician and anti-fascist, who was a good friend of the De Viti de Marco family.

[75] See Tedesco (2002), Felice (2006), and Cardini (2009).

[76] Letter from Etta to Ferrero dated 19 October 1902. Guglielmo Ferrero Papers, box 56, Columbia University, Rare Book and Manuscript Library. In that year, Pantaleoni was involved in a banking scandal from which he emerged unscathed.

[77] Letter from Etta to Ferrero dated 26 February 1905. Guglielmo Ferrero Papers, box 56, Columbia University, Rare Book and Manuscript Library. Giovanni Montemartini (1867–1913), a student of De Viti de Marco and Pantaleoni, was a marginalist economist and a reforming socialist.

[78] Francesco Papafava (1864–1912) was the author of 'Chronicles' in *Giornale degli economisti*, from 1899 to 1909. See in particular the letter of 1902 reported by Antonio Cardini (1985: 122–123).

[79] Letter from Pantaleoni to J. Régis dated January 26, 1913: 'J'ai eu d'abord les assauts de Madame De Viti […] pour que je faisse une préface à la réimpression de ses 'Cronache' […] pour l'anniversaire de sa mort en mars' in Pareto (1960, III: 387).

years as a member of Parliament, found solid backing in his wife's activity: in 1913, she wrote to their great friend Gaetano Salvemini,[80] hoping that the results of the elections—the first to be held with almost universal male suffrage—would be favourable for him, as well as obviously for her husband. But this was not to be. Salvemini was not elected,[81] and nor was Antonio, who had been in parliament since 1901 and was defeated in 1913,[82] but only for a short time: he returned to the Chamber in the 1915 by-election for six more years. Still thinking of Antonio's political career, in 1915, Etta asked Salvemini to do something to get her husband called into the government, underlining 'that he was the first and the clearest supporter of the war, among the radicals'.[83] But we will return to the question of the war shortly.

Another issue on which they 'shared ideas and ideals' was that of the South of Italy, which was the focus of Antonio's electoral campaign, and which would continue to be crucial throughout his political career.[84] The first year he stood for election in the college of Gallipoli (in Salento, Apulia), Etta had asked their good friend Guglielmo Ferrero to help her husband give national exposure to the issue of the moral and material conditions of the South. She was in love with the South,[85] and—partly through the pioneering venture we will describe in the second part of this volume—took part in the battles for 'the progressive economic and moral improvement of the whole country, and especially for the revival and renewal of the South',[86] as she wrote to her friend Salvemini. Her letters

[80] Gaetano Salvemini (1873–1957) was an Italian historian, politician and anti-fascist.

[81] Letter from Etta to Ferrero dated October18, 1913: 'I hope the fight goes well for Antonio and for poor Salvemini!' but the latter was to be defeated. Salvemini had stood for election in 1913 in the constituency of di Molfetta, Bitonto and Terlizzi, but was defeated. Guglielmo Ferrero Papers, box 56, Columbia University, Rare Book and Manuscript Library.

[82] Defeated by his socialist rival Stanislao Senape De Pace.

[83] Letter from Etta to Salvemini dated May 24, 1915. Archive Salvemini, Istituto storico toscano della resistenza e dell'età contemporanea, folder De Viti de Marco, box 88. On the close relationship between Salvemini and De Viti de Marco see Cardini (1986).

[84] On De Viti de Marco's policy for the southern Italian regions (called *Mezzogiorno*) see, among others, Denitto (2008) and Mosca (2008).

[85] Her letters from Salento were full of a rapturous sense of the beauty of the countryside, and of a proactive concern for the conditions of the local population.

[86] Letter to Salvemini of November 9, 1913. Archive Salvemini, Istituto storico toscano della resistenza e dell'età contemporanea, folder De Viti de Marco, box 88.

to the latter deal with the economic problems of the South, showing a detailed, in-depth knowledge of the economic and political issues related to the situation of Southern Italy,[87] and embracing her husband's free-trade line, in opposition to the interventionist alternative proposed by other Italian economists and politicians.

As well as the battle for the South, Etta openly supported the fight against customs barriers, which her husband—the Italian leader of the anti-protectionist movement[88]—saw as connected to the former in his vision of an Italian path to economic development, convinced that free trade also offered the antidote to the pressure exerted by industrial groups to obtain privileges from the state. In this context, one must remember the moralising function that De Viti de Marco's leadership attributed to the Italian free-trade movement. Etta accompanied Antonio during his talks in favour of free trade, and she did her best to ensure that more of these talks were held all over Italy. In 1914, she told Salvemini of the great response to her husband's rally in Bari (in Apulia), where he was finally able to explain his position against duties on grain, which had previously been distorted and obscured. She said she wanted to push Antonio to get his ideas across to the population and therefore asked Salvemini to reprint and circulate her husband's old articles against grain duties; she also enclosed 100 lire and suggested giving some of the readers free subscriptions to the newspaper.[89] Again, for the anti-protectionist cause, in 1915, on behalf of her husband, she asked the future President of the Italian Republic, the economist Luigi Einaudi, to make some pamphlets to be distributed in Italy and England through a contact from the Cobden Club. She added that she had been asked by the *Commercial Supplement* of the *Times* for figures on trade between Italy and England.[90] Another issue concerning free trade that was important to Etta was the conditions of Italian migrants in America: between 1902 and 1907, she wrote

[87] See footnote 87.

[88] On De Viti de Marco's leadership of the Italian anti-protectionist movement, see Cardini (1981) and Tedesco (2008).

[89] Letter from Etta to Salvemini dated January 12, 1914. Archive Salvemini, Istituto storico della resistenza della Toscana, box 88.

[90] Letter from Etta to Einaudi dated December 26, 1915. Archive Einaudi, Corrispondence, folder De Viti de Marco, Einaudi Foundation, Turin.

two letters[91] to Luigi Bodio[92] about this matter, putting him in contact both with Archbishop Corrigan[93] and, on behalf of the U.S. Ambassador Griscom, with the members of an American commission for immigration then visiting Europe.[94]

The question of the war burst into the letters from Etta, who shared the ideas of the group of democratic interventionists,[95] embracing their anti-nationalist, pro-Entente position. In 1914, she was mainly campaigning for the Italo-British League, founded that year by her husband in an initiative by 'those who propounded the need for us to intervene alongside the Entente and saw and declared from that moment the ideal democratic nature of our war'.[96] Etta, an Anglo-Saxon, threw herself into involving as many well-known people as possible; among others, she asked Leone Caetani[97] to contact also the 1909 winner of the Nobel Prize for Physics Guglielmo Marconi[98] With her husband, she was extremely busy taking care of the League's *Rassegna mensile* and its distribution, also in England. Italy's declaration of neutrality, which the couple attributed to an agreement between 'socialists and clerics', was a disappointment for the interventionists: in March 1915, she repeatedly asked Salvemini to go to Salento to be with her husband, who at that moment thought he had chosen the wrong direction in life and was not

[91] One letter is undated (but must be prior to 1902), the other is dated June 17, 1907. Pinacoteca di Brera, Biblioteca Nazionale Braidense, Milan.

[92] Luigi Bodio (1840–1920) was an Italian economist and statistician, firstly general secretary and then president of the International Insitute of Statistics.

[93] Michael Augustine Corrigan (1839–1902) was Catholic archbishop of New York.

[94] Lloyd C. Griscom was ambassador to Rome from 1907 to 1909. 'In the summer of 1907, Commissioners Dillingham (chairman), Latimer, Howell, Bennet, Brunnett, and Wheeler visited Europe for the purpose of making a general survey of emigration and conditions in countries which are the chief sources of the present immigration in the United States'. Reports of the immigration commission, *Emigration Conditions in Europe*, presented by Mr. Dillingham, December 5, 1910, 3.

[95] On the affiliation of the De Vitis and Salvemini to the group of democratic interventionists, see Martelloni and Mosca (2018).

[96] See de Viti de Marco (1914). The footnote cited was added in 1918.

[97] Letters from Etta to Leone Caetani in December 1914. Archive Leone Caetani at Accademia Nazionale dei Lincei, Rome. Leone Caetani, duke of Sermoneta e prince of Teano (1869–1935) was a historian, Islamist and orientalist.

[98] Apparently, she succeeded, as Marconi is among the members of the Economic Committee of the Leauges' *Rassegna mensile*.

cut out for politics.[99] Another letter contained a bitter accusation against Germany, and against those in whose interests it was to 'sell Italy to the German sword', with a paean to democracy and the masses.[100]

In 1915 she lavished praise on the young, full of will power and moral energy, and on the heroic Italian soldiers. The officers in 1916 also included her son James, who really was heroic, being awarded a silver medal. However, with surprising foresight, in August 1915 Etta wrote to Salvemini, who was about to leave for the front, saying that victory would not be happy because the good would leave and their place would be taken by profiteers.[101] This is what actually happened, disproving the democratic interventionists' initial belief that the war would have a moralising effect on the Italian population.

2.8 Democracy, Free Trade and Civil Progress

Eleonora Duse described Etta thus: 'she works and writes, never resting, from morning to night'.[102] Apart from taking care of her correspondence, she published articles on various topics, some of which appeared in *Giornale degli economisti*, the prestigious journal of which her husband was editor for a long period, and to which Etta and the previously mentioned Maria Pasolini Ponti were the only female contributors. In 1915, she contributed to *La Voce* with an article signed E.L.D. and entitled 'Giustizia militare … o giustizia tedesca? Il caso di Edith Cavell' (Military justice … or German justice? The case of Edith Cavell) (De Viti de Marco 1915a). Edith Cavell was an English nurse in Belgium, who, when the country was invaded by Germany, took care of both Germans and Belgians, as well as sheltering British soldiers and helping them to escape. For this she was tried and sentenced to death. The article condemned the brutal methods of German military courts, which still used force instead of law, ignoring the moral considerations of civilly advanced peoples.

[99] Letter from Etta to Salvemini dated March 5, 1915. Archive Salvemini, Istituto storico della resistenza della Toscana, box 88.

[100] Letter from Etta to Salvemini dated March 6, 1915. Archive Salvemini, Istituto storico della resistenza della Toscana, box 88.

[101] Letter from Etta to Salvemini dated August 3, 1915. Archive Salvemini, Istituto storico della resistenza della Toscana, box 88.

[102] Letter from Eleonora Duse to her daughter, July 31, 1915, in Maria Ida Biggi (2010: 62).

In most of her articles, Etta typically reported and commented on the news from Anglo-Saxon countries, providing Italians with official information or figures on current affairs. In 1898, for instance, she wrote a short article on telephones in England, signed E.d.V. (De Viti de Marco 1898a), commenting on the report of a parliamentary enquiry into the telephone service that had just been conducted in England. Then, in 1915, she wrote a letter to the daily paper *Resto del Carlino* in response to an article which seems to have rekindled her memories of childhood and youth. The article, entitled 'America e civiltà' (America and civilisation) was about the American pioneers and their ideals. With reference to the War of Independence and the Civil War, she described America as 'the refuge of the oppressed, the realm of a free people [...] the same justice for all. Self-government'. For Etta, these principles represented 'the continuation on the new continent of the battle already fought in England [for] constitutional government', and for the 'democratic principles at the base of the American Constitution' (De Viti de Marco 1915b).

Then there were her articles of political analysis, like the one in 1898 about 'Rivalità internazionale in Cina' (International rivalry in China), published in the *Giornale degli economisti* (De Viti de Marco 1898b). Starting from the fact that the extraordinary development of the means of communication made the 'unity of the world become a political and economic fact' (547), the article analysed the attitude of the great powers towards China, whose economic development was, according to Etta, 'of worldwide relevance' (548). From a non-Eurocentric perspective, she demolished some of the clichés about the Chinese,[103] seeing them not only as 'capable of becoming civilized' (549), but also as being able to generate a democracy and open to 'modern industrial development' (550) while she accused the Chinese leaders of being immobile and isolationist. In 1903–04, a long article entitled 'Imperialismo, protezionismo e liberismo in Inghilterra' (Imperialism, protectionism and free trade in England) signed D. (De Viti de Marco 1903–04) also appeared in different issues of the *Giornale degli economisti*. We cannot be sure that the article was written by Etta. It could have been written by her husband or more probably by both of them, as it features characteristics that can

[103] Though using, at the same time, many others about other nations.

be linked to either of them: the style is that of the 'Chronicles' in *Giornale degli economisti* that Antonio had written on a monthly basis from 1897 to 1899, and at the same time it reminds the reader of the typical pieces written by Etta commenting on documents and figures from the Anglo-Saxon world. The article intends to give a 'first-hand' account of the positions taken by protectionists and free-traders in the English debate and to analyse their arguments.[104]

2.9 After the Great War

After the Great War, the hopeful enthusiasm of the years we have so far described was replaced by disillusionment. Etta followed Antonio's last electoral campaign,[105] but there was no longer any sign of personal activism: in 1920, the Italian Chamber passed a bill to grant women the vote, but she seemed to be absent from this new battle; then, before the bill went to be examined by the Senate, Parliament was dissolved due to the early closure of the chambers, and nothing more was heard of female suffrage in Italy until 1945. As we have said, her husband gave up his political activity and withdrew from public life in the early 1920s, but she had actually done so years earlier: we have already seen the conclusion of her entrepreneurial activity in the 1910s. However, she continued to cultivate their social life, as attested by her friend Zanotti Bianco (1962/1964: 354):

> In the years of 'retirement', she often tried – by inviting to lunch or dinner their closest friends with whom he [Antonio] loved to converse – to lessen the impact of the detachment from the activities to which he had devoted so much of his life.

So, the invitations continued, while Antonio increasingly devoted himself to the wine-making business and to the books he was still working on. From her correspondence in the Twenties 1920s and 1930s with the

[104] In its index by year, *Giornale degli economisti* attributes it to her husband. Antonio Cardini (1985: 126–127) attributes it to her. Antonio usually signs V; this is the only article signed by D. If our hypothesis of co-authorship is right, it may refer to both their surnames (De Viti de Marco and Dunham).

[105] Letter to Eleonora Duse from the South of Italy, January 14, 1920, Archive Eleonora Duse, Istituto per il Teatro e il Melodramma, Giorgio Cini Foundation, Venice.

political scientist Gaetano Mosca, with Luigi Einaudi and Zanotti Bianco, we learn that the journeys to her house in London continued,[106] and that her interest and cultural curiosity had not died. In 1934, Etta offered to help get reviews of the books launched by the publisher Giulio Einaudi published in the *Manchester Guardian* or the *Times Literary Supplement*. A message sent to Gaetano Mosca raises a wry smile today: she wrote that she had read 'an extremely interesting article written by Lloyd George for the paper *The Sunday Express*' on August 12, 1934: 'Why there will be no War for Ten Years'.[107] In these letters we seem to find the usual Etta. There is only one cautious but unmistakable hint of anti-fascism, found in a letter in which she indicated which passengers she would take on board to then scuttle the ship: 'Perhaps you may guess whom by the initials M. & H. [...] and just send it adrift toward the rocks'.[108]

However, it was not only the Italian political situation that cast a shadow over the De Viti de Marco family. There was also a sad private matter. Their first-born, James, after his glorious return from the front, showed signs of depression; they attempted to cure him by sending him to live in London for a while. Then, years later, he was diagnosed with a mental illness, and he was admitted to a clinic in 1931. It was a family tragedy with complex ramifications.[109] In June 1937, her daughter Lucia told friends that her mother was not well.[110] However, in February 1938, in a hand-written letter from Rome, Etta told Zanotti Bianco she had enjoyed an excursion with Lucia.[111] In 1939, when her sister-in-law Carolina went to visit her, she was shocked by the state of her health:

[106] Letter to Gaetano Mosca, April 25, 1925, Archive Gaetano Mosca, Rome, La Sapienza, folder 174.

[107] Letter to Gaetano Mosca, August 15, 1934, Archive Gaetano Mosca, Rome, La Sapienza, folder 174.

[108] We think that M. and H. refer to Mussolini and Hitler. Letter from Etta to Zanotti Bianco dated December 19, 1933. Archive of Associazione Nazionale per gli Interessi del Mezzogiorno d'Italia (ANIMI), folder Umberto Zanotti Bianco (1889–1963), Rome.

[109] The sad story of James's mental illness and the conflicts that followed are the subject of a research that the author currently has in progress.

[110] Letters from Lucia de Viti de Marco to Zanotti Bianco. Archive of Associazione Nazionale per gli Interessi del Mezzogiorno d'Italia (ANIMI), folder Umberto Zanotti Bianco (1889–1963), Rome.

[111] Letter from Etta to Zanotti Bianco dated February 27, 1938. Archive of Associazione Nazionale per gli Interessi del Mezzogiorno d'Italia (ANIMI), folder Umberto Zanotti Bianco (1889–1963), Rome.

most likely, Etta had lost her memory.[112] She died in Rome on August 28, 1939, and today she rests in the De Viti de Marco family chapel in Salento.

2.10 Conclusion

A recent study examines the story of three women who lived at the turn of the twentieth century, all three, like Etta, the wives of well-known economists, and whose reactions differed greatly from the social and political context (Gouverneur 2019). What can we say on this point about our protagonist? The ideas expressed by Etta in her articles cannot be called original with respect to Antonio's, but they certainly were original in the panorama of Italy in the liberal age, the period when the De Viti de Marcos together were a driving force in the efforts to form a radical, pro-free trade, liberal-democratic party. Some witnesses reported a rather submissive attitude on Etta's part (Chirilli 2016: 24). However, she actually exerted a strong influence over her husband: it was certainly thanks to her that Antonio took a position in favour of divorce and the women's vote in parliament.[113] And it was thanks to the direct contact with Anglo-Saxon culture that his democratic political orientation was reinforced, inspired by the English liberals, and later on by Wilson's vision (Martelloni and Mosca 2018). The rare public writings and many private papers of Etta de Viti de Marco demonstrate the importance of this rarely studied figure, who, with her reflections and her activism, was present in some of the most significant cultural and political movements of the liberal era: from practical feminism to modernism, from liberal radicalism through to interventionism.

However sympathetic our account may be, it is impossible to fully render the vivacity, the passion, the intense and at times impetuous tone found in Etta's correspondence when she describes the countryside of the South of Italy, her political ideals, her intellectual interests, her anthropological considerations and her democratic convictions. Liberal Italy,

[112] Eleonora Duse's daughter wrote: 'In 1950 I heard that Etta had lost her memory [...] (from Miss Hungton related to the Dunhams)'. Enrichetta Marchetti Bullough, *Note a margine* in Maria Ida Biggi (2010: 349).

[113] The proposal for a bill in favour of divorce was approved in the Chamber in 1903, but then it was withdrawn. A similar story happened with the female suffrage in 1920, as already mentioned.

pre-war Italy, was a world in ferment, full of faith in progress, where there was the firm belief that one's personal commitment could speed up and expand the development of humankind, contributing to civilising the population. Etta fully embraced this dream. She also shared in its twilight and its end, despite being a strong woman, a 'stoic'[114] capable of bearing adversity, a woman who said of herself: 'I do not really fear bad weather'.[115]

References

Anonymous. 1895. Marriage Announcements. *New York Times*, June 4.

Anonymous. 1896. Return from Abroad of Many Well-Known Persons. *The Evening Star*, August 5, 2.

Anonymous. 1897. *Social Register*, vol. 11(1). New York, November, 1896.

Anonymous. 1901. Obituary Notice. *New York Times*, May 1.

Anonymous. 1906. Il manifesto della Commissione italiana. *La Stampa sportiva* (1 April): 6.

Anonymous. 1907. Bollettino del Consiglio Nazionale delle Donne Italiane. *Vita Femminile Italiana* 1 (3): 280–293.

Anonymous. 1908. Notizie. *La nuova antologia*, 34.

Anonymous. 1910. Miss Helen Dunham Weds. *The New York Times*, September, 3.

Anonymous. 1915. Centomila persone acclamano per le vie di Roma la Patria, il Re, Salandra e la guerra. *Il Resto del carlino* (17 May): 2.

Anstruther-Thomson, John. 1904. *Eighty Years' Reminiscences*. New York: Longmans, Green and Co.

Augello, Massimo M., Marco E. L. Guidi, and Giovanni Pavanelli, eds. 2016. *Economia e opinione pubblica nell'Italia liberale. Gli economisti e la stampa quotidiana*. Milan: Angeli.

Bacile di Castiglione, Gennaro. 1927. *Castelli pugliesi*. Rome: Buona Stampa.

Biggi, Maria Ida, ed. 2010. *Ma Pupa, Henriette. Le lettere di Eleonora Duse alla figlia*. Venice: Marsilio.

[114] In her *Annales*, in describing a car accident that happened in 1936, her sister-in-law Carolina writes that Etta showed 'stoicism'; the word 'stoic' reappears in a letter from her son James to the princess Henriette Barberini of May 14, 1952. Archive Carolina de Viti de Marco and Giulia Starace, Le Costantine Foundation, Casamassella (Lecce).

[115] Letter from Etta to Zanotti Bianco, December 31, 1931. Archive of Associazione Nazionale per gli Interessi del Mezzogiorno d'Italia (ANIMI), folder Umberto Zanotti Bianco (1889–1963), Rome.

Cardini, Antonio. 1981. *Stato liberale e protezionismo in Italia (1890–1900).* Bologna: Il Mulino.

Cardini, Antonio. 1985. *Antonio de Viti de Marco. La democrazia incompiuta (1858–1943).* Rome-Bari: Laterza.

Cardini, Antonio. 1986. Gaetano Salvemini e Antonio De Viti de Marco. In *Gaetano Salvemini tra politica e storia*, ed. Gaetano Cingari, 248–276. Rome-Bari: Laterza.

Cardini, Antonio. 2009. *Storia del liberismo. Stato e mercato dal liberalismo alla democrazia.* Naples-Rome: Edizioni scientifiche italiane.

Castronovo, Valerio et al. 1979. *La stampa italiana nell'età liberale*. Rome-Bari: Laterza.

Chirilli, Emilia. 2016. Memories. In *Antonio de Viti de Marco, A Story Worth Remembering*, ed. Manuela Mosca, 15–35. New York: Palgrave Macmillan.

Creighton, Mandell. 1882–1894. *A History of the Papacy During the Period of the Reformation*. London: Longmans, Green.

Denitto, Anna Lucia. 2008. Introduzione. In *Mezzogiorno e democrazia liberale. Antologia degli scritti*, eds. Antonio de Viti de Marco, and Anna Lucia Denitto, 5–55. Bari: Palomar.

De Viti de Marco, Antonio. 1885. *Moneta e Prezzi*. Città di Castello: Lapi.

De Viti de Marco, Antonio. 1890/2001. The Telephone Industry and State Exercise of Said. In *Roots of the Italian School of Economics and Finance: From Ferrara (1857) to Einaudi (1944)*, vol. III, eds. Mario Baldassarri and Pierluigi Ciocca, 505–529. New York: Palgrave.

De Viti de Marco Antonio. 1914. Per la costituzione di una Lega Italo-Britannica. In *La guerra europea. Scritti e discorsi*, 32–34. Rome: Edizione dell'Unità.

De Viti de Marco, Antonio. 1928/1936. *First Principles of Public Finance*. London: Jonathan Cape, 1936.

De Viti de Marco, Antonio. 1930. *Un trentennio di lotte politiche, 1894–1922.* Rome: Collezione meridionale editrice.

De Viti de Marco, Antonio (E.d.V.). 1898a. La questione dei telefoni in Inghilterra. *Giornale Degli Economisti* 9 (17): 351–361.

De Viti de Marco, Antonio. 1898b. Rivalità internazionali in Cina. *Giornale Degli Economisti* 9 (17): 547–562.

De Viti de Marco, Etta (D.). 1903–04. Imperialismo, protezionismo e liberismo in Inghilterra. *Giornale Degli Economisti* 27 (1903), September: 249 ff.; November: 470 ff.; *Giornale Degli Economisti* 28 (1904), January: 48 ff.; February: 155 ff.

De Viti de Marco, Etta. 1908. Assistenza e previdenza. *Vita Femminile Italiana* 2 (6): 620–632.

De Viti de Marco, Etta (E.L.D.). 1915a. Giustizia militare o giustizia tedesca? Il caso Edith Cavell. *La Voce, Edizione Politica* 7 (13): 673–677.

De Viti de Marco, Etta. 1915b. America e Civiltà. *Il Resto del Carlino*, September 6.

Feez, Susan. 2013. *Montessori: The Australian Story*. Sydney: UNSW Press.

Felice, Flavio. 2006. Le libéralism radical des premières années du XXe siècle en Italie. Maffeo Pantaleoni—Antonio De Viti de Marco. In *Histoire du libéralisme en Europe*, eds. Philippe Nemo and Jean Petitot, 619–650. Paris: PUF.

Ganci, Salvatore Massimo. 1959. *Democrazia e socialismo in Italia*. Milan: Fondazione Feltrinelli.

Geraldini, Arnaldo. 1953. Il figlio del Prof. De Viti de Marco, interdetto, inabilitato o capace? *Il Messaggero* (17 September): 3.

Gouverneur, Virginie. 2019. Harriet Taylor Mill, Mary Paley Marshall and Beatrice Potter Webb. Women Economists and Economists' Wives. In *The Routledge Handbook of the History of Women's Economic Thought*, eds. Kirsten Madden and Robert W. Dimand, 73–89. London and New York: Routledge.

Hobhouse, Balme J. 2015. *Agent of Peace: Emily Hobhouse and Her Courageous Attempt to End the First World War*. Stroud: The History Press.

Kramer, Rita. 1976. *Maria Montessori: A Biography*. Chicago: The University of Chicago Press.

Martelloni, Francesco, and Manuela Mosca. 2018. De Viti de Marco, the "European war" and President Wilson. *Journal of Economic Thought* 40 (2): 179–199.

Mazzola, Ugo. 1895. *L'imposta progressiva in economia pura e sociale*. Naples: Marchese.

Mezzomonti, Elisa. 1934. Meysenbug, Malwida, Baronessa von. In *Enciclopedia Italiana Treccani*. Rome: Istituto dell'enciclopedia italiana.

Miller, Tom. 2018. The 1901 Theodore Luling House—118 East 70th Street. In *Daytonian in Manhattan*, 22 March, available at http://daytoninmanhattan.blogspot.com/2018/03/the-1901-theodore-luling-house-118-east.html.

Mosca, Manuela. 2008. De Viti de Marco e il Mezzogiorno: Nuova luce dai quotidiani. *Itinerari Di Ricerca Storica* 28 (1): 135–159.

Mosca, Manuela. 2016. *Antonio de Viti de Marco. A Story Worth Remembering*. New York: Palgrave Macmillan.

Page, Thomas N. 1915. The Earthquake in the Abruzzi. *Scribner's Magazine* 57: 419–430.

Pareto, Vilfredo. 1960. *Lettere a Pantaleoni*, ed. Gabriele De Rosa. Rome: Banca Nazionale del Lavoro.

Proust, Marcel. 1920–21/1925. *The Guermantes Way*. New York: Seltzer.

Richards, Laura E., and Elliott Maud Howe. 1915/2018. *Julia Ward Howe, 1819–1910*. Frankfurt am Main: Outlook.

Ross, Janet. 1889. *The Land of Manfred, Prince of Tarentum and King of Sicily*. London: Murray.

Ryan, Eilish. 1997. *Rosemary Haughton: Witness to Hope*. Kansas City: Sheed & Ward.

Salvemini, Gaetano. 1949. Ricordando Antonio De Viti De Marco. *La Controcorrente* (2 December).

Séché, Alphonse, and Romain Rolland. 1962. *Ces jours lointains. Lettres et autres écrits*. Paris: Michel.

Tea, Eva. 1932. *Giacomo Boni nella vita del suo tempo*. Milan: Ceschina.

Tedesco, Luca. 2002. *L'alternativa liberista in Italia. Crisi di fine secolo, antiprotezionismo e finanza democratica nei liberisti radicali (1898–1904)*. Soveria Mannelli: Rubbettino.

Tedesco, Luca. 2008. La Lega antiprotezionista e il suo primo convegno nazionale (Milano, 21 maggio 1914). In *Il canto del cigno del liberoscambismo: la Lega antiprotezionista e il suo primo convegno nazionale*, 5–48. Manduria: Lacaita.

Vivarelli, Roberto. 1981. *Il fallimento del liberalismo. Studi sulle origini del fascismo*. Bologna: Il Mulino.

Zanotti Bianco, Umberto. 1962/1964. Antonio de Viti de Marco (1858–1943). In *Meridione e meridionalisti*, 327–355. Rome: Collezione meridionale editrice.

CHAPTER 3

Alice Hallgarten Franchetti: A Woman Beyond Barriers

Maria Luciana Buseghin

3.1 Introduction

This chapter is devoted to Alice Hallgarten, an American Jew of German origin. Although she was linked to the social, economic and cultural milieu that characterised the elites of her time, she distinguished herself by demonstrating a depth of understanding which was way ahead of her time. In fact, Alice overcame the barriers imposed by the social and cultural structure of the society in which she lived. Thanks to a particular combination of personality traits and first-hand real-life experiences, Alice's cosmopolitan education, deep and unconventional spirituality, aspiration and commitment to the realisation of social justice, female emancipation and universal peace together formed the basis of her ideals and life goals.

M. L. Buseghin (✉)
Lecce, Italy

E. Laurenzi and M. Mosca (eds.), *A Female Activist Elite in Italy (1890–1920)*, https://doi.org/10.1007/978-3-030-87159-8_3

3.2 Family History

Alice was born in New York on June 23, 1874, to J. Adolph Hallgarten[1] and Julia Nordheimer[2]: both of whom were Ashkenazi Jews of German origin. She lived in the United States until 1883, when she moved to Frankfurt with her family due to the poor health of her father, who died of tuberculosis two years later. The disease of the century also claimed her brother Walter Nordheimer Hallgarten,[3] to whom she was very attached, in 1908, and her mother in 1909.[4]

Today, we remember the great commitment, professional success, cosmopolitanism and love for travel, patronage and generosity in philanthropic activities, addressed to both Jews and non-Jews, of all the Hallgartens who lived in the United States or Germany between the nineteenth and twentieth centuries. In this period, observant Jews—as well as secular ones who were often assimilated in the general process of nationalisation and secularisation of Western culture—acted, sometimes unwittingly, according to the traditional precept (*mitzvah*) of charity and justice (*zedakah*): since all that we have comes from the Lord, solidarity with the poor is a specific duty. Accordingly, a strong and compelling reason pushed the Jewish upper and middle bourgeoisie to 'generous use of means for purposes of sociality, education, popular culture' (Capuzzo 2019: 203). This behaviour was also significantly present in moderate nineteenth-century liberalism, whose aggregation was also linked to philanthropic societies dedicated to various forms of charity and socio-humanitarian assistance.

Alice's father, Adolph, gained a reputation as a benefactor thanks to his donations (including the co-financing of the Hebrew Deaf-Mute Institute), which were many and generous, as stated in his obituary (Stascheit 2003: 118–119). Having emigrated to the United States in 1850 (Scudder 1937: 317), he was a pharmaceutical wholesaler and majority shareholder of Lanman & Kemp; a member of the board of directors of Mount Sinai Hospital in New York from 1872 to 1883, and its youngest president from 1876 to 1879.

[1] Born in Mainz on November 6, 1835, died in Wiesbaden on February 13, 1885.

[2] Born in Toronto on December 28, 1846, died in Rome on June 1, 1909.

[3] Born in New York in 1868, died in Todtmoos in 1908.

[4] For the complex events of the Hallgarten family, see Buseghin (2002, 2013).

Her brother Walter, after inheriting a considerable fortune from his uncle Julius Hallgarten[5] and from his father Adolph, dedicated himself to banking for two years, living in Hamburg, London and New York. Walter abandoned this activity because he wanted to see the world: he travelled and wrote under the pseudonym Old Traveller *Notes of Travel on Five Continents* (189?). The book was very popular with tourists thanks to the large amount of useful and common-sense advice it offered about all the countries of the world, except South America. Travelling was just one of his passions: the others were music and painting, passions he had inherited from his mother Julia and his uncle Julius. He also followed the example of both in the philanthropic patronage that he exercised towards individual and institutional subjects from the world of painting, music, theatre and literature (most of which he did secretly, so much so that only a few close friends were aware of it). In the banking business, he limited his activities to looking after, also on Alice's behalf (Nordheimer 1908: 7–9), the Bank Hallgarten & Company founded by Lazarus Hallgarten,[6] who was recognised as a pioneer of international finance. In fact, Lazarus opened an exchange office for immigrants in 1850 and then, at the beginning of the following decade, he set up a real investment bank that became part of the Wall Street group known as Our Crowd. The bank, which also served an exclusive private clientele, had offices in Chicago, Paris, Geneva, Brussels, Rome and Berlin and maintained close relations with German, English and Dutch financial institutions.[7]

Among the majority shareholders (including Lazarus' sons and sons-in-law), Charles/Karl[8] stands out. He was one of the three children that

[5] Born in Mainz in 1842, died in Davos in 1884.

[6] Born in Mainz in 1806, died in New York in 1875.

[7] In 1974 Hallgarten & Co. merged with FS Moseley, a company founded in Boston in 1879: this resulted in the formation of Moseley Hallgarten & Estabrook, which closed the following year after various circumstances linked to the infamous 'Black Monday' of 1987. The company was re-founded in New York in 2003 as Hallgarten & Company LLC by former directors of Polyconomics, an economic think tank, and it follows the approach of the classical Austrian school of economics. Hallgarten & Company, which also has offices in London and Buenos Aires, is a company devoted exclusively to investment banks in the natural resources sector, especially mining, oil and gas. See *Encyclopaedia Judaica, ad vocem* 'Hallgarten'. The group 'Our Crowd' included, among others, Bache & Co., Lehman Brothers, Goldman Sachs, J. & W. Seligman & Co. e Kuhn Loeb & Co. See Birmingham (1967: 8–11).

[8] Born in Mainz in 1838, died in Frankfurt am Main in 1908.

Lazarus had with Eleonore Darmstaedter.[9] Alice had a special relationship with him, especially after her father's death, in 1885. Charles was her point of reference until 1908, the year he died in Frankfurt, where Alice often went to visit him. Therefore, we can consider Alice as the cultural daughter of Charles; the young woman spent her adolescence between Frankfurt and Hamburg and engaged in the activities that were associated with upper-class girls at the time. These included piano lessons, and it is said that she even had the honour of receiving lessons from Liszt; during this period, the family environment taught Alice a certain way of reacting and behaving in the face of life's demands and challenges. Charles, who returned to Germany from the United States, remained a partner of Hallgarten & Co. and a citizen of New York, which he would visit at least once a year. He opened an office to assist the dispossessed in Frankfurt, and he worked there on a daily basis even in his old age, assisted only by a secretary: he is still remembered in Germany each year for his philanthropic activity. Charles' activity was never charity, a practice that often maintains the problem without solving it, but real enlightened philanthropy. Its aim was to remove people from the situation of need so that they would no longer have to reach out, by creating conditions and structures designed to induce their economic and cultural growth and eliminate the relationship of rich-poor subjection. Charles held important positions in the Alliance Israélite Universelle, the Hilfsverein der Deutschen Juden and the Jewish Colonization Association, working hard for the salvation of the Jewish victims of the Russian pogroms. He helped these victims to emigrate, especially to Argentina. He even had time to devote his attention to the press denunciation of anti-Semitism, and wrote an essay about it at the end of the nineteenth century (Hallgarten 1897). He did all of this despite not being religious: his explanation was that by helping the Jews he was helping humanity. In line with this statement, he promoted and supported, in collaboration with many associations, both Jewish and non-Jewish, the most diverse socio-humanitarian initiatives. These included a shelter in Frankfurt for single mothers who were unemployed and who had been expelled by their families, where they were assisted in everything, including legal matters, at Charles' request. He also worked hard in the social housing sector: he donated land to those who wanted to build a house; he had new neighbourhoods designed and built

[9] Born in Mannheim in 1813, died in New York in 1870.

for the poor classes, in which each housing unit had to have a meeting room to encourage socialisation (debates, parties, birthdays) and a space dedicated to childcare. He also collaborated in the founding of an association for public education, and in 1912 he contributed to private funding for the foundation of the University of Frankfurt (Schembs and Lustiger 2003).

We will see how the many initiatives undertaken by Alice Hallgarten strongly echo those of her uncle Charles. Cordelia von den Steinen referred to their relationship in 2011, during the exhibition of her terracotta sculptures in honour of Alice, who was cousin of her grandmother Eleanor Rose, daughter of Ida Hallgarten,[10] Adolph's sister. In an interview, which is valuable in terms of how it reconstructs the history of the family, she stated:

> Alice's way of doing things is so similar to Uncle Charles's that I wondered what their relationships were: both of them took decisive actions with great organizational and managerial capacity, in the context of both conceptual and entrepreneurial modernity. (Buseghin 2011: 26)

3.3 Life with Leopoldo Franchetti

The philanthropic activity in which Alice had been educated from her youth found momentum and substance thanks to her union with Leopoldo Franchetti.[11] Leopoldo was a Sephardic Jew from Livorno, whose family of entrepreneurs and traders had arrived in Grand-ducal Tuscany (Italy) from North Africa in the eighteenth century. He was a deputy of the Kingdom of Italy from 1882 to 1909, the year he was appointed senator; he was a politician of conservative-reformist orientation, and dedicated twenty-five years of parliamentary activity to the defence of the rural masses that he believed had been neglected by the liberal political class and ignored by the democratic and socialist ones. Among Leopoldo's parliamentary battles, his campaign against malaria is worth remembering: in 1898, he founded the Society for Malaria Studies,[12] and from 1900 to 1904 he collaborated on the extension and debate on the bills to regulate the state's exercise of quinine antimalarial

[10] Born in 1837, died in 1899.

[11] Born in Livorno on May 31, 1847, died in Rome on November 4, 1917.

[12] With Angelo Celli and Giustino Fortunato.

therapy.[13] He was also heavily involved in several research projects, in the struggle for the development of the Southern Italian regions, which were poorer than the rest of the country, and in the debate on emigration and colonialism. In 1910—with other protagonists of political and cultural Italy of the time[14]—he founded ANIMEMI, later known simply as ANIMI (Associazione Nazionale per gli Interessi del Mezzogiorno d'Italia, National Association for the Interests of Southern Italy), and was its president until his death. Among the parliamentary investigations, the one on the Navy conducted from 1904 to 1908 was particularly demanding and painful for him, and he devoted a lot of energy to it and this resulted in an abysmal chronic fatigue, which was perhaps more moral than physical given the disappointment caused by his findings.[15] This investigation is frequently referred to by Alice in the letters she wrote from 1901 to 1911 to Maria Pasqui Marchetti, one of Alice's closest and most important collaborators, and to whom we will come back later. Writing on June 30, 1904, from Les Veldes in Austrian Carniola, where she spent long periods of rest to recover her strength from a still unclear illness, Alice said:

> I had the great joy of the surprise of a visit from my good husband. He had to travel 48 hours to be 16 with me!! I found him well, but very tired, and I can't wait to reunite with him in Spezia, where he will still have months to work. (Buseghin 2002: 178)

But let us go back to the period when Alice and Leopoldo first met, and about which Sofia Cammarota Adorno[16] provides us with some valuable information. The daughter of Enrichetta Caldani and Giuseppe Cornero, a Piedmontese politician of Mazzinian inspiration, in 1882, Sofia married Gaetano Cammarota Adorno,[17] an exponent from the

[13] See Zanotti Bianco (1950), Buseghin (2002: 472–490), and Pezzino and Tacchini (2002).

[14] Including names like Pasquale Villari, Antonio Fogazzaro, Giustino Fortunato, Gaetano Salvemini and Tommaso Gallarati Scotti.

[15] See Zanotti Bianco (1950), Buseghin (2002: 472–490), Pezzino and Tacchini (2002), Breschi (2014), and Rogari (2019).

[16] Born in Rocca d'Arazzo in 1853, died on May 29, 1939.

[17] Born in Naples in 1828, died in 1909.

Neapolitan upper-middle class with a commitment to the liberal movements. She was also a member of ANIMI, first as a promoter and supporter of welfare activities, from 1918 as a member of the Board of Directors, and later a board member of the Religious Charity Regina Margherita, universal heir of Baron Leopoldo Franchetti. Sofia tells us about Alice and Leopoldo's engagement in a letter dated August 8 (with no indication of the year, but certainly in the 1920s), sent from Villa Montesca to Umberto Zanotti Bianco,[18] who was looking for materials for his biographical book on Franchetti:

> the engagement [...] took place after they intimately worked together with the agricultural colony [...] I hear the voice again; I see the excited face of my sweet Franchetti when she approached me at a meeting in the Taverna House of the Council of Italian Women. She whispered to me: I got engaged! ... They loved each other, tortured each other, rose up and ended up in a union of good that is still expressed in works. (Musci 2018: 9)

Therefore, the engagement dates back to 1899, since the group referred to by Sofia Cammarota met in Rome for the first time on May 4, 1899. Alice and Leopoldo got married in a civil ceremony in Rome on July 9, 1900, according to the registry office certificate, although oral tradition has it that the marriage took place in March or May in Città di Castello.[19] They led an intense life for eleven years, constantly moving between their Roman residence and Villa Montesca in Città di Castello. Their first Roman residence was a small villa in Via Boncompagni 19, which has changed its use over time, becoming a delightful hotel named after roses.[20] The second residence was the Villa Wolkonsky,[21] also in Rome, formerly the nineteenth-century residence of important personalities and a favourite among writers and men of letters; during the Second World War, it became the seat of the German command, and therefore, passed to the United Kingdom by law of war, was restored and became

[18] In the previous chapter, we have already come across the name of Umberto Zanotti Bianco, archaeologist, politician and anti-fascist.

[19] Città di Castello is a town in the Umbria region, in central Italy.

[20] This is a curious name considering that the owners did not know whether the Franchettis had lived there, and that Alice loved this flower so much.

[21] The address was via del Conte Rosso 38.

the first residence of the English Embassy in 1947, and then the personal home of the Ambassador.

Villa Montesca was built by Leopoldo on the slopes of Mount Arnato[22] between 1885 and 1889, on a project by the Florentine architect Giuseppe Boccini and decorated by well-known artists and artisans, from Tuscany and Perugia. Even from a distance, the eye is still struck by the majestic structure of the villa with a double loggia from which you can enjoy 'a heavenly view [...] in a heavenly air', as Wolfram von den Steinen, son of Eleanor Hallgarten, wrote in her travel diary; the young seventeen-year-old man would remember his aunt Alice throughout his life for the 'perfect impression' she had made on him and the days spent at Villa Montesca which he defined as 'among the most beautiful of my life, because they were fulfilled in inner peace and in the enjoyment of the ever increasing inner happiness. [...] And so, we lived silently, quietly, happily'.[23] Certainly, the enjoyment of the vast park that Leopoldo wanted to surround the villa with was not unrelated to this profound and luminous impression; the park was created by reclaiming the landside hill covered with scrub and by planting woods and rare plants.[24]

Alice and Leopoldo's life was full of travel linked to their socio-humanitarian, pedagogical and political initiatives and their multiple international relations. The trips were sometimes motivated only by a search for art and leisure, which seemed to be a therapy for the emotional instability and depressive states that Leopoldo suffered. Alice rarely confided her husband's difficulties, except for a few references in some letters to Paul Sabatier[25] and Maria Pasqui Marchetti. In the first of December 3, 1902, she wrote: 'My husband's nerves are tired; but this is still a secret so please do not tell anyone about it' (Fossati, 1987–88: 308); in the second, of August 8, 1903, for example, Alice writes from Oakhurst Oxted, Surrey in England:

[22] Monte Arnato is a summit in Città di Castello.

[23] Von den Steinen Private Archive.

[24] For further information on Villa Montesca see Buseghin (2002: 557–559).

[25] Paul Sabatier was born in Saint-Michel-de-Chabrillanoux, Cevennie August 3, 1858 and died in Paris on March 5, 1928. For Sabatier's bio-bibliography and his relationship with the Franchettis see Buseghin (2002: 503–506, 2013: 22–26). We have already met this person in the previous chapter.

> I have only good news to give you about me, through an ideally calm and happy period, because I have never seen my husband more serene and happier than in this beautiful country where nature, friends and art come together to make us enjoy true peace of mind. I enjoy everything with the consciousness of a person who knows storms. (Buseghin, 2002: 144)
>
> What was once alluded to with the words 'weakness of nerves' or state of melancholy or some other similar expression was a condition shared by several members of the Franchetti family; the case of Leopoldo is mentioned in the text of Massimo Ludovico De Giampietro of Zurich,[26] a descendant of the Franchettis on the part of his mother Ludovica Valeria Franchetti of Munich and in the biography of Franchetti written by Umberto Zanotti Bianco. (1950: 80)

The emotional harmony and complete operational consonance with her husband in the initiatives they carried out together were fundamental for Alice, as she herself declares in several letters to Maria Pasqui Marchetti: on May 8, 1903, she writes: 'a new lesson for me is not to try, not even the good, if I am not in unison with that one, to whom I have dedicated my life' (Buseghin 2002: 53, 134). And Leopoldo corresponded deeply to this loving dedication, also by changing his behaviour. Particularly significant is a letter dated February 15, 1905, written by Alice to a friend:

> Love wins everything and the feeling that animates me and Poldo [Leopoldo] is strong and big enough to consider every difficulty of our character only as a stumbling block from which we climb higher up to the door that closes the path to harmony.[27]

From many of the letters from Alice to Marchetti, it is clear that she followed her husband's political and parliamentary activity, perhaps more out of concern that the intense work would exhaust his strength than by participating in the thematic discussions in some way. She sometimes mentions this kind of commitment, also in some letters to Paul Sabatier, but always does so when asked and without ever going into the merits of the issues. The direct relationship with Leopoldo's colleagues was also

[26] Massimo De Giampietro, son of Valeria Lodovica Franchetti, Leopoldo's cousin, gave a speech in Villa Montesca to present Bistoni (1997), 29 November 1998.

[27] See Musci (2018) and Buseghin (2019: 241). Unless stated otherwise, the translations of the quoted texts are our own.

rare: the few exceptions included Antonio Fogazzaro, a writer engaged in local administration and social welfare, and educational battles more than national politics, despite being a senator and partner of ANIMI. Alice also maintained an epistolary relationship with him, in which, among other things, the common acquaintance of Felicitas Buchner emerges.

Felicitas[28] (or Felicita as she preferred to be called) came from a Bavarian Jewish family and was a pedagogist of Catholic activism and a publicist, and she was director of the Vocational School for women that the Franchettis founded in Città di Castello in 1909.[29] Alice only adds her greetings to some of the many extant letters of the correspondence between Leopoldo Franchetti and Pasquale Villari,[30] despite the fact that Villari had been among the very few people present at their wedding, and it is clear from said correspondence that the Franchettis attended as a couple. Leopoldo always recognised the Neapolitan historian and politician as his main teacher and wanted him to be honorary president of ANIMI from 1910 until his death, which took place just over a month after Leopoldo's own death. We can see, even from these details, that Alice was not all that interested in politics in the traditional sense, parliamentary or otherwise, but rather in politics in the sense and value attributed to it in the second half of the twentieth century[31]: in the many social welfare and economic support initiatives that Alice undertook, alone or with her husband, first in Rome, and then in Città di Castello, there are clearly many characteristics identified as political, as functional to the care of the common world and its social networks. In this regard, it should be emphasised that in many of these initiatives there are instances of the practical and theoretical feminism of the time, which we can now look upon as a moral and political revolution.[32]

[28] Born in Ebermannsstadt on November 13, 1856, died in Munich (?) after April 25, 1944.

[29] See below, § 3.7.

[30] Pasquale Villari (Naples October 3, 1827–Florence December 7, 1917) was a senator from 1884 and Minister of Public Education between 1891 and 1892.

[31] These meanings and values are clearly expressed, in their history and in their transformations, in the essays by Forcina and by Birules and Fuster in this same volume (see Chapters 8 and 9).

[32] For more details on practical feminism see Chapter 1 and Part II below. The term is also referred to by Sofia Bisi Albini (1856–1919), philanthropist, writer and columnist,

3.4 Social Welfare Activities

Alice's protector and guide was Malwida Rivalier von Meysenbug,[33] a German philosopher and writer, and this was down to a series of characteristics: wisdom, anticipation of feminist themes and experiences, a dedication to children's education, and above all, the personal itinerary of interior research, self-formation and spiritual growth which led to the choice of liberation and self-determination of one's own destiny. Immediately after Malwida's death, Alice financed the translation and publication of her most important work: *Memoiren einer Idealistin*, a three-volume work published by Auerbach in Stuttgart in 1875–1876 (Meysenbug 1904; Barbetta 2006).

We should remember that Alice and Leopoldo met thanks to their common engagement in philanthropic initiatives, according to Francesco Stagnitta, who, as their doctor, was very close to the Franchettis (Buseghin 2002: 498–501, 2013: 17–19). This encounter took place in the Pharmacy of the San Lorenzo district in Rome, founded in 1897 as a pharmacy of the Union for Good, whose founding members include Alice and Don Brizio Casciola,[34] a modernist priest, originally from Umbria (Aronica 1998: 29–34, 243).[35] This association was founded in 1894 to aid the homeless in the poorest neighbourhood of Rome: its members were Stagnitta himself, Leopoldo and Alice, and other prominent figures in the Roman social, cultural and political life of the time.[36] The pharmacy served as a reference point for various other charitable works, including the San Lorenzo Health Care, a work founded on the proposal of Don Brizio and managed by the Union of San Lorenzo. The latter was founded in 1896 from the aforementioned Union for the Good; Alice was one of its partners and she was also part of the group of visitors who regularly went to visit the eighty families located by the Union of San Lorenzo in the buildings owned by the Bank of Italy; their task was to watch over the 'morality and hygiene, teaching and friendly exhorting,

who founded and directed the previously mentioned magazine *Vita femminile italiana* (1907–1913) and of which Alice was an active supporter.

[33] Born in Kassel on October 28, 1816, died in Rome on April 26, 1903. We have already introduced this figure in the previous chapter.

[34] Born in Montefalco on July 31, 1871, died in Naples on December 12, 1957.

[35] Umbria is a region of central Italy.

[36] Including Giuseppina Le Maire and Giulio Salvadori.

providing wisely where necessary, looking for work for the unemployed', 'accustoming to providence' and 'collecting the small amount of rent weekly'.[37]

However, the Roman enterprise that the Franchettis cared for most was an agricultural colony, a project which unfortunately ended badly. Ernesto Nathan,[38] a long-time friend of Leopoldo, had assigned a large area in Rome in 1898[39] to the social and educational philanthropy of the Franchettis. With the financial help of Julia Nordheimer Hallgarten and the collaboration of Don Brizio Casciola, they reactivated an abandoned popular dormitory, called Sonzogno. Thus, at the end of November 1898, the structure became a Tolstoian agricultural colony for destitute and often abandoned children. The experiment ended in 1904, the year that the 'new clerical-moderate Roman administration, out of hatred for Nathan and Franchetti, took the large area away from us' writes Don Brizio.[40] Leopoldo, who had been its president from the beginning, in 1901, perhaps foreseeing this ominous outcome, had tried unsuccessfully to consolidate its position, proposing its transfer to the Ministry of Agriculture, Industry and Commerce and the Municipality of Rome itself (Musci 2018: 10). Don Brizio, disliked by ecclesiastical authority, was forced to leave, while some of the boys found refuge in a new colony (Buonricovero), always Tolstoian and always financially supported and managed by the Franchettis. The enterprise soon proved a failure, which Alice herself admitted to her great regret, as expressed in the

[37] From the diary that Antonietta Giacomelli (co-founder of the association, polemicist and well-known writer at the time) wrote in Trieste in 1932 (quoted in Fossati 1997: 95–98, fn. 36). See also Fossati (2007).

[38] Ernesto Nathan (London October 5, 1845–Rome April 9, 1921), politician, republican of Mazzini and Freemason training, lay and anti-clerical, was elected councilor of the Municipality of Rome in April 1898, and later was appointed councilor for the bursar and cultural heritage, an administrative post of great importance in a period in which Rome, the capital of Italy only from 1871, had to face a tumultuous building and demographic growth; he was mayor from 1907 to December 1913.

[39] Between Via Flaminia, the Tiber and the Parioli.

[40] Casciola, after 1950, wrote an autobiographical memoir (preserved in the Casciola Archives, 'San Tommaso' Theological Institute of Messina) in which he highlighted his educational activity; this memoir was later published in Aronica (1998: 239–256); for the history of the Franchetti colony, see Aronica (1998: 34–44, 246).

letters sent to Maria Pasqui Marchetti[41] and Paul Sabatier.[42] The latter is another important figure in terms of understanding Alice's philanthropic commitment and spiritual life; they probably met in the Union for Good. Sabatier, a Calvinist pastor, theologian and man of letters, was particularly interested in the figure of St. Francis, about whom he wrote some major works of historical and religious criticism, inaugurating modern Franciscan historiography with the use of medieval sources, especially those of the Franciscan Order (Sabatier 1894/1931). But a passion for St. Francis and a sharing of modernist ideas was not the only thing that united the Franchettis and Sabatier, although it was perhaps the most significant for Alice; indeed, both spouses had an intense relationship of friendship and solidarity with the pastor in projects and works, as evidenced by their close correspondence from 1902 to 1911.[43]

3.5 Traditional Female Works Between Weaving, Embroidery and Emancipation

Alice Hallgarten was part of the Ladies' Committee of the Roman Federation of Women's Works: this organisation mostly consisted of works for charity (at the time there were thirty-six in all), and of individual members who were not linked to any specific work. Alice was one of the patronesses, and the Marquise De Viti de Marco was one of the councillors.[44] The Federation was set up in 1899 following a proposal that had

[41] Letter from Alice to Maria Pasqui Marchetti dated January 9, 1902, in Buseghin (2002: 101).

[42] Letter dated December 26, 1903, signed by Alice Hallgarten and December 25, 1904, signed by both spouses, published in Fossati (1987–88).

[43] The Sabatier-Franchetti correspondence consists for the most part of letters, but also of business cards and postcards, written by Alice and/or Leopoldo from 1902 to 1911, as well as many of Sabatier's answers in copies made, as usual, by his collaborator Marguerite Stoltz; the correspondence is kept in the Sabatier Archive (personal archive of Paul Sabatier which includes correspondence from 1890 to 1928, some manuscripts, magazine clippings and personal files) and was donated to the Study Center for the History of Modernism (Foundation Romolo Murri, University of Urbino) in 1979 by Louise Juston-Sabatier, daughter of the Protestant pastor in gratitude to Lorenzo Bedeschi, a great scholar of religious reform and the modernist movement, who had founded the Center in 1964; Bedeschi died in 2006, the correspondence merged into the Murri Foundation of the University of Urbino also founded by Bedeschi, in 1989, together with Carlo Bo.

[44] See Anonymous (1902: 3, 6). On the Marquise de Viti de Marco, see Chapters 2 and 5 of this book.

emerged the previous year during a meeting of the Roman group interested in women's issues with Mrs. Sandford, the Canadian delegate of the International Council of Women. Mrs. Sanford proposed that the Roman ladies participate in the London Congress, which was attended by a representative of the Roman Committee with a project drawn up by the group. Subsequently, thanks to the insistence of Lavinia Taverna, the National Council of Italian Women (CNDI) was founded, which, as Countess Taverna wrote in 1902, 'It also returns within the order of philanthropy and an intensely feminist love of the motherland (1902: 131–132, 139–140). Maria Pasolini Ponti was part of the Roman Federation and the CNDI (Taricone 2000–01) and a very close friend of Leopoldo at least from the 1880s, and she was also a founding member of Italian Female Industries (Industrie Femminili Italiane, IFI).[45]

It was probably from these experiences that the idea of a weaving workshop was instilled in Alice. In 1908, she founded her company, which is still in operation today under the name 'Tela Umbra. Lini tessuti a mano dal 1908' (Hand-woven linen since 1908) with mixed public–private participation: the Region of Umbria, the Municipality of Città di Castello and its working members.[46] As early as August 21, 1903, Alice wrote to Maria Pasqui Marchetti from London: 'I have found here the loom model which, I believe, will be an advance for our peasant women' (Buseghin 2002: 146). Her idea was to transform female skills transmitted from generation to generation, mostly thanks to the practice of 'learning with the eyes', into professional work activities,[47] convinced that 'a job suitable for the person and justly paid' was the main instrument of emancipation, in the spirit of Malwida von Meysenbug.[48] Alice wrote to Paul

[45] See chapter 1 above.

[46] See Bistoni (1997: 190–267) and Buseghin (1998a: 19–24, b: 123–136, 2013: 63–92).

[47] Roberta Fossati (2002: 160) defines Franchetti's philanthropic activity as 'cultural work', to emphasise that it was 'a precise, constant, directed, planned activity that Alice had consciously chosen for herself. […] In this regard, it was a work, but one strongly characterized and nourished by affections, relationships, in which several cultural worlds will converge and interact'.

[48] Letters from Alice to Maria Pasqui Marchetti dated May 14, 1909: 154, and April 23, 1903, in Buseghin (2002: 131). Alice was 'a spiritual daughter of Malwida of Meysenbug'. Umberto Zanotti Bianco, a friend and close collaborator of Leopoldo's, writes that Franchetti 'judged lacking in common sense, so strong was the attraction of

Sabatier on June 7, 1908, from Villa Montesca about the first steps of the laboratory:

> Dear friend, Thank you so much for your good letter. I am working here with a lot of love, but in great solitude of soul, and I need a person like you, capable of understanding and also of propagating. Soon, I will have a not indifferent loom plant, and I need some large orders of hemp fabrics for sheets etc. You will not be able to clearly understand all these things without coming here. Do this for the good of Umbria!

And on July 25, 1908:

> My business is booming. I would never have believed that an industry – and it is really taking on the importance of one – could be so nice. It is manual work, but it is good for the soul and forms a bond of good understanding between everyone. (Fossati 1987–88: 335, 337)

Alice followed in the smallest details, as a true entrepreneur, the weaving activity, informing herself in detail of the type of looms in operation, the quality of the yarns, the type of fabrics made and the finishing of personal and home accessories with fringes or lace. She was not only interested in the profitability of production, accounting and administration, but also in the quality of life in the laboratory, which was of primary importance to her. The letters to Maria Pasqui Marchetti are littered with almost daily requests, but also with words of praise and gratitude, as, for example, in that of May 14, 1909:

> Dearest, I don't need to tell you with what intimate sense of satisfaction I read about your triumph in Perugia. This result is exclusively due to the intelligent love and constant fidelity of each day that you have also dedicated to this branch of female activity. [...] Will Mrs Buchner or you

that dream of human redemption, which united all those willing, but to which his intelligence denied any possibility of implementation' (Zanotti Bianco 1950: 80). Unfortunately, we do not have any letters from Alice to Malwida. We know instead that Alice signed herself 'your Mamina' in letters addressed to Maria Pasqui Marchetti. Ultimately, we can say that we also find in the importance attributed by Alice to a cultural, not purely biological mother-daughter relationship – precisely from her who never had children – the enveloping presence of the 'female genealogy [...] protector, source of inexhaustible wisdom and tenderness, but also a warning of a task to be fulfilled', which Marisa Forcina discusses in Chapter 8.

> speak to the women of the Laboratory of the good they must provide for the future, carrying out this order in a way not only to satisfy it, but in a way that deserves the trust shown and establishes a true reputation for the goodness of Umbrian work?[49]

In 1913, Aurelia Josz, a dear friend and the author of Alice's most beautiful obituary, wrote that:

> The canvases have progressively improved and have found an ever-increasing number of buyers, by chance, the industry, passive in the early years due to huge expenses, is now starting to be self-sufficient. (1913: 10)

Thousands of metres of hemp and cotton fabrics were produced by the laboratory as they came out of the looms or were transformed into clothes, underwear or household linen in a laboratory in Pisa: they were donated by the Franchettis to the victims of the earthquake that struck Sicily and Calabria in 1908, and of course this was done at their expense: the same happened in all those cases in which they also supplied various institutions with various materials and money, as for example in 1909 when they donated linen to the hospital of Città di Castello (Bistoni 1997: 65).

Alice's conception of work, both relating to daily and subsistence activities and to education, was deeply religious. This characteristic could not fail to derive from the traditional Jewish vision of the world and of life that can be found in her correspondence: the frequency with which she resorted to the practice of blessing, and the fact that she considered reflection and study a prayer, are also clues pointing to this conclusion. Moreover, in her letters we can read numerous innovative formulas of prayer and numerous invitations to pray addressed to teachers and pupils. Etta De Viti de Marco also pointed out that for the women of Abruzzo, for whom she had revived 'embroidery in viarella [...], the work in itself [was] a form of prayer'.[50]

[49] See Buseghin (2002: 350). Felicita Buchner supported Maria Marchetti in the direction of the laboratory at that time.

[50] See her letter to Bates-Batcheller, whom she met in the Rome office of IFI (Bates-Batcheller 1906/2013: 315–318). The 'viarella embroidery' is actually a bobbin lace made both with and without a design. For the schools of Pescocostanzo and Gessopalena, see Tomei Finamore (1906).

The Tela Umbra's cloth company presented some absolutely innovative characteristics that emerge in Alice's letters to Maria Pasqui Marchetti, as well as in some papers written in her hand and in the organic Statute of the Religious Charity. In this sense, we read that the laboratory was

> established for the conservation, in the applications still appreciated, of the ancient Umbrian art of weaving with hand looms and to allow mothers of families to attend to a paid job without concern for their children, who, in the meantime, are kept and fed in the kindergarten attached to the Laboratory.[51]

The *Internal Regulations* of the laboratory (a copy of which had to be signed by all the workers) clarified its purpose (help 'needy mothers' through the offer of work) and the management conditions: free premises, equipment, raw materials and organisation for the sale of the product, terms of employment, categories of workers, different methods of remuneration, paid holidays.[52] The workers had to comply with the workshop hours, withdrawing an 'attendance medal' placed in a medal table at the entrance and returning it at the exit. However, as stated in Article 2:

> To facilitate the workers' fulfilment of their duties towards the family, the Laboratory has annexed, by the will of the testators, a kindergarten

[51] Articles 5, 9, 10 and 11 of the *Statute* relate to the Tela Umbra company: see Archive of the Religious Charity Regina Margherita—Franchetti Foundation (hereinafter: AOPRMFF), Villa Montesca, Città di Castello, General Administration of the Franchetti Foundation, Administrative correspondence 1917–1982, Administration, b. 14, f. 48: *Organic Statute of the Religious Charity Regina Margherita Approved by Royal Decree of 22 August 1925*, typed; Anonymous (1955: b. 1, f. 1). The registration in the Register of Companies of the Chamber of Commerce of Umbria is also from 1925: it appears that the Tela Umbra Laboratory—with the starting date in the year 1908, category: hand weaving, as an industrial plant for hand weaving, with 40 workers (while in 1908 there were 15 founding workers and 2 loom masters, with only 14 looms)—it is based both in the Villa Montesca, former residence of the Franchettis, and in via S. Antonio (Palazzo Tomassini) which is owned by Religious Charity Regina Margherita and whose director is Maria Marchetti (Historical Archive of the Perugia Chamber of Commerce, R.D. n. 4653).

[52] The weaving workers had to be paid in proportion to the work done, which had to be continuous, while teachers were on a fixed daily wage.

for their children, and the timetable, compatible with the needs of the Laboratory, is adapted to the needs of these worker-mothers.[53]

It should also be emphasised that, by Alice's will, preference was given to single mothers when hiring, and weavers could keep their children in a cradle next to the loom; a company kindergarten functioned for children aged three to eight. Another extraordinary innovation for the time was the flexible hours: the workers left work at noon to take care of family duties. In addition, a weekly afternoon home economics school was held at the company headquarters every Thursday for girls who, among other things, also learnt to knit for family needs; there was also an evening carpentry school for young people who had to learn how to build furniture for their future marital home. Also, a course was held on Thursdays for the care of infants, a matter that Alice had also addressed by establishing Maternal Aid, a service established in collaboration with Dr. Betti of Città di Castello's Hospital: mothers were taught to weigh and look after new-borns, a practice that was part of the health and hygiene education of the time. The Franchetti family's care for children also extended to founding the Citerna kindergarten in 1910, named after Alice (Buseghin 2013: 34–36).

3.6 Promotion of Canvases and Laces

Another important element of Alice's entrepreneurship was her ability to promote the products of the laboratory which she advertised with samples of canvases and laces that she, or some of her intellectual friends, presented at conferences, mostly on issues related to female emancipation. Others she sold to her Roman friends or those residing in Rome with their husbands who were deputies and senators, including several who belonged to the old and new nobility.[54] Tela Umbra cloths were also sold to the patronesses of the Italian Female Industries for embroidery work since the fabrics of the laboratory were famous for their perfect framing, an indispensable feature for many types of counted-thread embroidery

[53] See Buseghin (2013: 66). AOPRMFF, General Administration of the Franchetti Foundation, *Statutes and Regulations 1924–1959*: Religious Charity Regina Margherita (1957, b. 1, f. 2).

[54] We should not forget that it was she who introduced Maria Montessori to Queen Margherita (Bisi Albini 1910), and we will return later to this point.

(and this remained so at least until the end of the 1960s, with orders ranging from Switzerland to Australia) (Buseghin 2005: 150, 2013: 73–74, 91–92).

In the corporate archive of Tela Umbra,[55] it has been possible to trace the names of some of the ladies who bought embroidery cloths during the twentieth century; these included the aforementioned Etta de Viti de Marco.[56] The garments woven and embroidered in the workshops founded by the latter,[57] including some tablecloths, were made with the typical fabric from the workshop of Tela Umbra, called '*quadruccio*', embroidered or with needle lace applications. These textile objects are specific proof that there was a relationship between the De Viti and Franchetti, at least in relation to their school-workshops, and the purchases of canvases at the Città di Castello's company. We must remember that both Etta and Alice had been founding partners of Italian Female Industries in 1903 (Anonymous 1914); furthermore, they were members of the Roman Federation of the CNDI; finally, both Alice and Etta participated in the First National Conference of Italian Women held from April 23 to April 30, 1908, which recalled 'in Rome how many women work in Italy for women's education, for the economic improvement of female workers' (Bisi Albini 1908) and about which Alice wrote to Marietta on April 30, 1908 (Buseghin 2002: 311).

Among the purchasers of Tela Umbra fabrics we also find: Countess Edith Bronson Rucellai of Florence of the Tuscan IFI Committee, linked to Carolina Amari[58] and the Trespiano school near Florence; Cora Slocomb by Brazzà Fagagna, founder of the famous lace school[59]; Baroness Vittoria Luce Danzetta, who partnered of Marquise Romeyne Robert Ranieri di Sorbello in the foundation of Italian Decorative Arts, a Perugian cooperative for the marketing of Italian fabrics, embroideries and lace, in the early 1920s.

[55] The archive contains the correspondence relating to the management and production of the Laboratory: correspondence, accounting documents, documents relating to the movement of the canvas warehouse and those relating to purchases.

[56] Chapters 2 and 5 of this book are devoted to Etta de Viti de Marco.

[57] Regarding this point, see the second part of this volume.

[58] Carolina Amari was an Italian philanthropist. In 1905, she founded the School of Italian Industries in New York, where embroidery and lace were produced, made by young emigrant women.

[59] See below Chapter 4.

Alice had a friendly relationship with Romeyne, who had already founded a school of embroidery in 1904[60] and who was a shareholder of the Italian Female Industries; they would meet up frequently at least between 1907 and 1910, and their relationship also involved their families, and naturally included exchange visits to their respective textile workshops (Buseghin 2020b: 118–122). The Marquise Romeyne di Sorbello continued visiting the Tela Umbra workshop even after Alice's death and also buying canvases, demonstrating fidelity in friendship and a spirit of collaboration also with Maria Pasqui Marchetti, who ran the laboratory until 1952.[61] Romeyne, who was also originally from the United States, was, like Alice, was dedicated to the social and cultural emancipation of women. Between 1902 and 1903, with her American friend Nathalie Dana, who had come to visit her from the United States, she conducted a field survey in the estates of her husband, Marquis Ruggero Ranieri, in search of traditional local work. She consequently decided to found an embroidery school-workshop to provide employment for peasant women. She gave them a job that would emancipate them from work in the fields and from total subjection to their fathers and husbands and passed on their savings and welfare criteria by opening a bank or post office book. The school also gave instruction on personal care and hygiene, and also in relation to cleaning needs in the embroidery work that had to be performed with skill, precision and industriousness: these qualities were attested by a booklet with the history of each worker and her job. The artistic direction of the school was entrusted to the aforementioned Carolina Amari, who revived traditional techniques and decorative motifs, sometimes reworked by Amari herself or by Romeyne. The designs were embroidered on canvases, mostly purchased from the workshop of her friend Alice, with Sorbello stitch (a complex of stitches), or with some other traditional stitches, mostly simple and effective, also because of the yarn and colours used. Romeyne had considerable entrepreneurial skills and ran the laboratory as a modern enterprise from 1904 to 1934, also taking on the duties of Amari when she had to

[60] The Ranieri di Sorbello at Villa Pischiello School of Embroidery. Villa Pischiello is a building from 1720, near Perugia, in the Italian region of Umbria.

[61] The daughter of 'Marietta', Malwida Marchetti Montemaggi (Città di Castello September 6, 1907 to October 5, 2000) told us this detail (personal interview by author, December 7, 1991) at the Tela Umbra laboratory in Città di Castello.

replace her after a few years. She put into practice an American philosophy of production and life that provided, for example, the keeping of accounts with the 'modern American system' also practiced in the shop of the Italian Decorative Arts opened in the centre of Perugia[62] (Buseghin 2005: 155–158).

Tryphosa B. Bates-Batcheller, an enterprising American lady, lived in Rome for a few months in 1905, visiting the Roman aristocracy and frequenting the headquarters of Italian Female Industries on via Marco Minghetti, which had become a sort of living room for Italian and American ladies who were passionate about textiles. In a long letter dated March 31, 1905, she writes:

> Here are three of the most energetic workers in this society (the Countess Brazzà, the Marquise di [sic] Viti de Marco, the Marquise di Sorbello) all bearing long and noble Italian names; but we are proud to claim them as American women, who have gone into the Old World, and are not only a credit to the title that they bear, but an honour to the name of womanhood, for the energy and ability they have shown in advancing the conditions of the country which they have adopted as their own. (Bates-Batcheller 1906/2013: 319–320)

3.7 The Franchetti Vocational School for Women

Home economics in all its specific subjects, including those relating to the care of children, the elderly, the sick and the injured, was the fulcrum of the Women's Vocational School that the Franchettis established in Città di Castello in 1909, with director Felicita Buchner (Buseghin 2002: 525–535, 2013: 58–63). The purpose of the school was

> 1st To prepare good family mothers and good housewives; 2nd To train teachers of home economics for vocational schools, orphanages and other women's boarding schools and also for itinerant chairs and home education schools similar to those existing with beneficial effects [in other European countries]. (Buchner 1909: 1)

[62] Perugia is the capital city of the region of Umbria in central Italy.

The school, aimed at young people of all classes, also provided single paid courses, while

> several [...] special short-term courses for girls just out of elementary school, for workers; for peasant women, for young mothers and every two years during the summer holidays, for primary and secondary school teachers [...] will be free. (Anonymous 1909: 1)

The courses in elementary sociology and the methodology of scientific pedagogy (with a detailed description of the subjects) planned to be taught by Maria Montessori, took place in August 1909 under the name of Scientific Pedagogy. From all Alice's letters sent to Maria Pasqui Marchetti, Sabatier, Montessori and other correspondents, it emerges that for her the most important work was that dedicated to education: in this regard, we must point out the importance of the education and instruction of women, both self-training and scholastic, in the Jewish cultural and religious tradition in Italy from at least the eighteenth century (Buseghin 2008: 126–127).

In the schools founded by Alice in the Villa Montesca, they taught the teachers who had been carefully selected by her, and they had to clearly understand that their work was a mission, as Alice wrote to Maria Pasqui Marchetti on July 26, 1902 (Buseghin 2002: 111). Therefore, they had to be conscientious and good but also 'morally and physically strong', Alice recommended on January 9, 1909 (Buseghin 2002: 331); the teachers had to be attentive to their health and not frail and delicate, because it was exhausting work (Buseghin 2002: 26). Alice considered the school the most important job of all, so much so that she was very keen to ensure that everything in her beloved company was successful, and also because she wanted Maria Pasqui Marchetti, who also directed the schools in addition to the laboratory, to take care of the school. In addition, Alice always inquired about the 'exact moral and material status of each family' to study together with Maria Pasqui Marchetti 'the best methods to make the work of general education ever more effective', as she wrote on June 25, 1904 (Buseghin 2002: 177).

3.8 The Franchetti Schools

The rural schools of Villa Montesca and Rovigliano[63] were founded by Leopoldo and Alice between 1901 and 1902. Franchetti Schools were a hotbed of ideas and methodological experiments thanks to Alice and Leopoldo's network of relationships with international scholars and their many trips in search of innovative teaching tools (including geographical, naturalistic and human anatomy maps). Well-known and respected European and American pedagogists collaborated in the planning and implementation of innovative experimental courses in their schools, and they mostly met during their travels.[64]

The already mentioned Maria Pasqui Marchetti[65] directed these education centres until 1951. She was their first teacher and was employed by Alice through the direct interest of Leopoldo; Alice was immediately impressed with her when they were introduced in the summer of 1901. Leopoldo's close friend and collaborator on his trip to Eritrea was the brother of 'Pasqui', as they called her, and it was he who recommended his sister to Leopoldo (Bistoni 1997: 78, 142). Maria Pasqui Marchetti, also known as Marietta, was considered by Alice as her 'acting spirit at Montesca'.[66] In Alice's letters to her, we can read numerous declarations of affection and appreciation for her educational work, and more generally for that carried out in favour of the spiritual, moral and material growth of peasant families. Particularly significant to assess the depth of the spiritual relationship between the two women is a letter that Alice wrote to Marietta on January 21, 1907:

> Yes, our communion on Mount Cedrone—the 'Agape' of many years of true community by now—has given me too new peace, new strength. I came back with something more in me, an increased faith, a certainty that our work will cease only with our life, and not even then, because it will continue in consequences beyond what our brain can ever understand.

[63] Rovigliano is part of the municipality of Città di Castello in the province of Perugia in the Umbria region.

[64] From Lucy Latter (England 1870 – Mysore 1907), to Berta La Mothe, to Vida Scudder (Madura December 15, 1861 to Wellesley October 9, 1954), to Florence Converse (New Orleans 1871 to 1951), to Felicitas Buchner, to Maria Montessori (Chiaravalle August 31, 1870 to Noordwijk am See May 6, 1952).

[65] Born in Città di Castello December 24, 1880, died on June 25, 1955.

[66] See Buseghin (2002: 490–493) and Fabiani and Tomassini (2009: 39–50).

Blessed are we who feel it like this, we accept with joy and humility all its pains, all its pure and holy satisfactions. (Buseghin 2002: 248)

As mentioned above, there are numerous blessing affirmations for 'that life of work in common for which it is worth making every sacrifice', she wrote from Bern on August 24, 1905 (Buseghin 2002: 203). On October 16, 1906, the blessing also involved Marietta: 'God bless you and bless the work that unites us forever' (Buseghin 2002: 228).

Affection and blessings also involved other collaborators, including in particular Mary Douglas-Hamilton, whom Alice called Tonia and who she loved greatly; on December 2, 1909, she wrote to Marietta and Tonia: 'Work quietly and happily, as the stars move, without fury, but never standing still, continuing their way in accordance with the Great Law. And God bless you!' (Buseghin 2002: 363). Mary Douglas-Hamilton[67] was the daughter of an English Protestant canon and the maternal niece of a Montreal pharmacist called Joseph Bowles; she married Kit Ingoldby, a physician in the English army with whom she lived in colonial India, becoming a widow in 1928 after having two children: Tonia and Christopher. She was an active and generous person up into old age, according to her niece Rosamund Hamilton Ingoldby Bance.[68] Mary arrived at Villa Montesca from England in March 1907 with Lucy Latter, an English educator and pedagogist whom Leopoldo and Alice had met in London in 1906. Latter, a great admirer of the theories of Pestalozzi and Fröbel,[69] invented an innovative teaching method linked to the study of plant life (Buseghin 2002: 514–517). The two pedagogists designed courses based on the model of those of the Nature Study Union, which Alice herself had attended in London in 1906 (Buseghin 2002: 365, 515). In addition, they developed six lessons with the new experiential teaching methods: one of these methods involved the use of a school garden so that the children could observe nature directly and develop their knowledge.

[67] Born in Winslow Buckinghamshire on May 1, 1885, died in St. Albans Hertfordshire on December 26, 1977.

[68] She kindly provided us with the diary and some autobiographical notes of Mary written between April 1907 and August 1910: these documents have allowed us to reconstruct the events narrated here.

[69] Johann Heinrich Pestalozzi was a Swiss pedagogue, and Friedrich Wilhelm Fröbel was a German student of Pestalozzi.

In early April 1907, Maria Montessori also arrived at Villa Montesca and she later treasured the methodology that Latter had codified in her manual for teaching gardening in schools and kindergartens: *School Gardenery for Little Children*, published in London in 1906 (Latter 1906). The volume was translated by Bice Ravà on behalf of Alice Franchetti, who had it published at her expense in 1908 under the title *Il giardinaggio insegnato ai bambini* (Latter 1908). Montessori, in the *Manuale di pedagogia scientifica* (Manual of Scientific Pedagogy), published in 1921, wrote: 'The ideal of the children's home, in this regard, is to imitate what is best done in those schools that owe their inspiration most to Mrs. Latter' (Montessori 1921: 28), but in subsequent editions the name of Latter disappeared, as the pedagogist, among the many merits, had the defect of tending not to recognise the contribution of others.

Mary Douglas-Hamilton was also a friend and companion of Alice's (as ever very much in tune with her in Franciscan spirituality): she was proficient in languages speaking French, German and Italian and together with her first-class honours degree in Botany and Science, she was a well-qualified and useful addition to Alice's team, especially when accompanying Alice on her European travels. She lived with Alice and Leopoldo between Rome and Città di Castello until 1910. In this period, she collaborated on various school activities, including experimental beekeeping and the cultivation of vegetable gardens and experimental fields, conceived by Leopoldo together with Eugenio Faina[70] The two men were united by their passion and agrarian skills as well as by politics and their commitment to the development of the Southern Italian regions. The significant contribution made by Leopoldo to the setting up of the rural schools of Villa Montesca and Rovigliano was later widely recognised and disseminated

[70] Eugenio Faina (San Venanzo April 2, 1846, to San Venanzo February 2, 1926) was elected as deputy in the elections of 1880, in which he was Franchetti's running mate, and remained so until 1892, the year he was appointed senator; he was chairman of the 1906 parliamentary commission of inquiry into the conditions of peasants in the southern provinces and in Sicily. In 1887, Faina established in Perugia the Agricultural Foundation and in 1896, he set up the Experimental Agricultural Institute, thanks to which he introduced innovative methodologies in agricultural cultivation; starting from 1912, he experimented with a post-elementary rural school for the professional training of agricultural workers, known as Scuola Faina, which soon spread to other municipalities in Umbria as well as to other regions, determining the establishment of a National Rural School (Travaglini 1994).

by Giuseppe Lombardo Radice[71] a philosopher and pedagogist who, from 1915 and for about twenty years, followed the experience of the Franchetti Schools, becoming their major promoter (Lombardo Radice 1925/1931: 36–37). Moreover, this commitment of Franchetti's was consistent with his activity as the owner of the Autonomous Farm of the Royal House Franchetti in Città di Castello: in fact, he devoted attention and energy to the agricultural management of his estates, modernising techniques and cultivation and harvesting processes, planting new crops or developing them, as in the case of tobacco (Biagioli 2002). The cultivation practices of fields and vegetable gardens were later supervised by Alice herself,[72] and they constituted one of the most successful elements of the Franchetti schools, together with those of the botanical calendar and the experimental meteorological station.

Alice had a special relationship with Maria Montessori, as evidenced by some of her letters to the pedagogist preserved in Holland, and in which we can see a profound harmony on a spiritual and ideal level. Alice, who already in the first letter, attributed to 1908, addressed Maria as 'Dear friend, soul sister', thanks to her in the last letter of February 1911 for having understood

> the endless and limitless devotion I have for you and for the work, and for loving myself personally, apart from the ideals that unite us. [...] I hold you to my heart, blessing you a thousand times.[73]

There are many passages in the letters sent to Maria Pasqui Marchetti in which Alice speaks of Maria Montessori with respect and admiration, recommending the care of the preparations to host the latter in every detail. Maria Montessori felt comfortable enough at the Villa Montesca to write, in the spring of 1909 and apparently in just twenty days, her first important work *Il metodo della pedagogia scientifica applicato all'educazione infantile nelle case dei bambini* (The method of scientific

[71] Born in Catania in 1879, died in Cortina in 1938.

[72] With the collaboration of Mary, Marietta and Bertha La Mothe.

[73] Association Montessori International Archive, Amsterdam. The author would like to thank Carolina Montessori who sent her a photographic copy of all the Montessori-Franchetti correspondence and allowed her to publish it in its entirety in the section dedicated to the relations between the Franchettis and Montessori, in Buseghin (2021), where the correspondence between Leopoldo and Maria Montessori, preserved in the ANIMI Historical Archive in Rome, is also published.

pedagogy applied to infant education in children's homes), which was published and paid for by the Franchettis (Montessori 1909).[74]

In the same period, Alice and Leopoldo organised the first course in scientific pedagogy held at the Villa Montesca from August 1 to August 31. The course was attended by teachers and school directors from all over Italy (Montessori 1909: 67–68), and it promoted and propagated the Montessori method in kindergartens and primary schools. Mary Douglas-Hamilton also attended the course and received her certificate of achievement from Montessori.[75] From her diary we also know that 'The Baron [Leopoldo Franchetti] arranged for Queen Margherita to visit the Children's House in the San Lorenzo neighbourhood in Rome to see how the Montessori learning system worked'.[76] Leopoldo himself must surely have been deeply impressed by the visit he made to the Children's House in autumn 1908, and he was persuaded to go there by Alice who, for this very reason, had gone to welcome her husband in Brindisi on his return from one of his trips to Africa. It was this visit that prompted Leopoldo to suggest and then almost to force Montessori to write her first book on the method. The pedagogist accepted hospitality at the Villa Wolkonsky, where she stayed with Elisabetta Ballerini, her pupil and close collaborator, as well as Anna Fedeli and Anna Maria Maccheroni[77] who tells us the story (Maccheroni 1947). In her own biography, Mary Douglas-Hamilton states that she took and provided the photographs of the children in the Children's houses in Rome for this first book of Montessori's.

The first Children's House opened in Rome on January 6, 1907, based on the idea of the engineer Edoardo Talamo[78]; towards the end of 1906, he invited Montessori to take care of organising schools for the children of the tenants of the tenements, including over four hundred buildings, in the San Lorenzo district (Buseghin 2020a: 162). A Children's House was also functioning in Villa Montesca at least as early as 1909, according to

[74] See Buseghin (2009, 2020a).

[75] Rosamund Bance, her granddaughter, keeps this certificate, along with many other documents.

[76] Mary Douglas-Hamilton's diary, 1909, manuscript.

[77] Born in 1876, died in 1965, she was a pianist from Livorno (Tuscany).

[78] Born in Cava de' Tirreni on November 16, 1858, died in Rome February 3, 1916, he was an engineer and architect, general director of the Roman Institute of Beni Stabili.

what Hamilton writes,[79] while Alice speaks of it explicitly only in a letter dated September 20, 1911, as a House built on the model of those established with the Montessori method in Rome and Milan. The Montessori method was probably applied to the kindergarten that already existed in the villa from at least 1904, with the help of Mary (Buseghin 2002: 445, 179).

According to Franchetti's correspondence, Douglas-Hamilton's diary and the memoirs of Nathalie Dana, Romeyne's dear friend since her youth (Dana 1963: 180), it was Alice who introduced Montessori to Ranieri di Sorbello. This is most likely as the Montessori method was introduced into the multi-class rural elementary school set up at Villa Pischiello on December 19, 1903, by the marquise and Alice followed its progress with interest.[80] In May 1907, Alice, Romeyne and Mary visited the Exhibition of Ancient Umbrian Art in Perugia which included a rich section dedicated to Fabrics and Embroideries consisting of three hundred works.[81] Mary reports this in her diary, which also mentions that Alice accompanied her to the Children's House in Rome in 1910 with Romeyne (but she does not specify which of the two houses established in the San Lorenzo district between January and March 1907 it was). It should also be emphasised that the children of Romeyne and Marquis Ruggero Ranieri di Sorbello attended the Montesca School from 1909, following an individual path, especially in the presence of Montessori, who used them as testers of new teaching materials (Pazzini 2019: 47).

Finally, it should not be forgotten that Montessori also owed a great deal to Alice in relation to the promotion of the international courses on her method: Alice was the person who suggested that she wrote the first article on the Children's House of San Lorenzo in Rome for the English magazine *The Journal of Education* (May 1909), and precisely, a lively debate arose from the publication of the article in the American

[79] Mary Douglas-Hamilton's diary, 1909, manuscript.

[80] See footnote 65.

[81] Mary Douglas-Hamilton's diary, 1909, manuscript; for the details of Alice, Romeyne and Maria's frequentation, see Buseghin (2019). The exhibition, inaugurated on April 29, 1907, is a milestone in the history of museography and museology because it opened up new interesting perspectives for research and the study of Umbrian art from the Middle Ages to the Renaissance: see the catalogue edited by Giulio Urbini (1907); in 1908, a rich volume with 251 illustrations was published: *L'arte umbra alla mostra di Perugia* (Umbrian art at the Perugia Exhibition), see Umberto Gnoli (1908).

magazine *Kindergarten Primary Magazine*, which dedicated three articles to the School of San Lorenzo. Of these, the first two (December 1909 and March 1910) were by Jenny Merril (O'Donnel 2014: 82), 'a kindergarten inspector who knew Italy well and who was a close friend of Alice Hallgarten Franchetti' (Babini and Lama 2000: 27). Valeria Babini and Luisa Lama regard Alice as 'the influential sponsor who worked in the shadows to support the genius of the Montessori method in the United States', also underlining that Montessori wanted to dedicate the American edition of the volume to her memory.

Sixty-five Americans took part in the first international course held at the pedagogist's house in Rome from January 16 to May 15, 1913, making up the majority of the listeners of 17 nationalities[82]; in 1913, when Montessori made her first visit to the United States[83] and the National Montessori Association was founded in Washington, and over sixty teachers were working in private schools in Los Angeles, Boston and New York (O'Donnel 2014: 83); a second International Course was held by Montessori in 1914, from February 23 to June 30 at Castel Sant'Angelo.[84]

As a closing remark, it should not be overlooked that there was a deep spiritual understanding between Alice Hallgarten and Maria Montessori on the basis of a common sensitivity and their common belonging to the Theosophical Society (for Alice perhaps only a loose connection to the society, but for Maria a documented affiliation). It seems that it was the pedagogist who introduced the Theosophical Society to Italy, the first section of which was founded in Rome in 1902. Alice and Maria were promoters of peace and harmony in a vision of the interconnected universe in which education and instruction, school and family derive from cosmic laws which, if respected, bring harmony, evolution and universal liberation.

[82] In the previous chapter, we have seen that Etta De Viti de Marco hosted the first of the three lessons of the course held by Montessori in her living room in 1913.

[83] On this first trip to the United States, Montessori kept a diary, which was published for the first time in English in 2013 by Carolina Montessori (Montessori 2013).

[84] Castel Sant'Angelo is a famous monument in Rome commissioned by Hadrian, Roman Emperor from 117 to 138.

3.9 Conclusion

In these years, the sisterhood of soul, the state of joy and a grateful trust of the universe characterised the thoughts, feelings and actions of many, more or less openly feminist, women including Alice. They created a network and multiple opportunities to meet: for example, Alice organised several meetings at Villa Montesca to disseminate Montessori thought, and we know that in May 1908 Alice convinced Maria and other friends, all guests at Villa Montesca, to go to visit Paul Sabatier in Assisi (Fossati 1987–88: 327–328, 332). What united all of them, however, was love and the promotion of 'true education' aimed at arousing feelings of independence, a critical sense and individual responsibility, a love of freedom and the fulfilment of good and the realisation of a material and spiritual life in an ethical and supportive perspective.

References

Anonymous. 1902. *Resoconto della federazione romana delle opere di attività femminile*. Rome: Tipografia cooperativa sociale.

Anonymous. 1909. Istituto Franchetti in Città di Castello. *Gioventù nova 87* 5 (5).

Anonymous. 1914. *Industrie Femminili Italiane 'Italicum Decus'*. Rome: Tipografia dell'Unione Editrice.

Anonymous. 1955. *Statuto organico Opera Pia 'Regina Margherita'*. Rome: Garzanti.

Aronica, Ferdinando. 1998. *Don Brizio Casciola*. Soveria Mannelli: Rubbettino.

Babini, Valeria P., and Luisa Lama. 2000. *Una 'donna nuova': Il femminismo scientifico di Maria Montessori*. Milan: Angeli.

Barbetta, Maria Cecilia. 2006. *Malwida von Meysenbug, una idealista nel suo tempo. Da Kassel all'esilio londinese (1816–1852)*. Verona: QuiEdit.

Bates-Batcheller, Tryphosa B. 1906/2013. *Glimpses of Italian Court Life. Happy Days in Italia Adorata*. Delhi: Hard Press.

Biagioli, Giuliana. 2002. Leopoldo Franchetti e la sua opera di proprietario terriero. In *Alice e Leopoldo Franchetti e il loro tempo*, eds. Paolo Pezzino and Alvaro Tacchini, 115–156. Città di Castello: Petruzzi.

Birmingham, Stephen. 1967. *Our Crowd: The Great Jewish Family of New York*. New York: Harper & Row.

Bisi Albini, Sofia. 1908. Il femminismo in Italia e il Primo Congresso nazionale delle donne italiane. *Vita Femminile Italiana* 2 (4): 363–368.

Bisi Albini, Sofia. 1910. Il trionfo di una donna Maria Montessori. *Vita Femminile Italiana* 4 (5): 482–485.

Bistoni, Vittor Ugo. 1997. *Grandezza e decadenza delle Istituzioni Franchetti*. Città di Castello: Edimond.

Breschi, Danilo. 2014. Franchetti Leopoldo (Livorno, 1847—Roma, 1917). In *Dizionario del liberalismo italiano*, vol. II, 510–515. Soveria Mannelli: Rubbettino.

Buchner, Felicitas. 1909. Corsi d'istruzione per la vita pratica nella istituenda scuola Franchetti in Città di Castello (provincia di Perugia). *Vita Femminile Italiana* 3 (3): 282–284.

Buseghin, Maria Luciana. 1998a. *Alice and the Wonder Wave*. Città di Castello: Tela Umbra.

Buseghin, Maria Luciana. 1998b. La "Tela umbra" di Città di Castello: Una storia di donne. *Rivista dell'Associazione dell'Alta Valle Del Tevere* 2 (6): 123–136.

Buseghin, Maria Luciana. 2002. *Cara Marietta... Lettere di Alice Hallgarten Franchetti (1901–1911)*. Città di Castello: Tela Umbra.

Buseghin, Maria Luciana. 2005. I volti diversi del lavoro femminile: modelli di comportamento e pratica imprenditoriale nelle opere tessili in Umbria tra Ottocento e Novecento. In *Donne imprenditrici nella storia dell'Umbria. Ipotesi e percorsi di ricerca*, ed. Barbara Curli, 111–166. Milan: Angeli.

Buseghin, Maria Luciana. 2008. L'epistolario di Alice Hallgarten Franchetti: memorie femminili dell'Italia ebraica. In *Gisa Giani. La memoria al femminile*, eds. Marilena Rossi Caponeri and Elisabetta David, 125–137. Terni: Archivio di Stato di Terni.

Buseghin, Maria Luciana. 2009. Maria Montessori, Alice Hallgarten e Leopoldo Franchetti: un incontro determinante per la storia della pedagogia. In *Oggi non sono andata a parare le pecore... La memoria delle scuole rurali di Montesca e Rovigliano di Città di Castello*, eds. Anna Angelica Fabiani and Francesca Tomassini, 51–64. Perugia: Soprintendenza Archivistica per l'Umbria.

Buseghin, Maria Luciana. 2011. Le opere di Alice e Cordelia: sulle tracce di un sogno e alla scoperta di un segno. Promozione umana e sapienza del linguaggio dalla tessitura alla terracotta. In *Omaggio ad Alice. Sculture di Cordelia von den Steinen per Alice Hallgarten*, AA. VV, 23–27. Città di Castello: Edizioni Tela Umbra.

Buseghin, Maria Luciana. 2013. *Alice Hallgarten Franchetti un modello di imprenditrice nell'Italia tra '800 e '900*. Selci Lama: Pliniana.

Buseghin, Maria Luciana. 2019. Leopoldo Franchetti e Alice Hallgarten. Opere socio-pedagogiche tra Roma e Città di Castello. In *Leopoldo Franchetti, la nuova destra e il modello toscano*, ed. Sandro Rogari, 241–259. Soveria Mannelli: Rubbettino,

Buseghin, Maria Luciana. 2020a. Leopoldo Franchetti, Alice Hallgarten e Maria Montessori: un sogno comune di educazione innovativa. In *Maria Montessori e il suo tempo*, ed. Fabio Fabbri, 154–171. Rome: Castelvecchi.

Buseghin, Maria Luciana. 2020b. La rete sociopedagogica di Alice Hallgarten Franchetti tra femminismo, istitutrici e maestre: Malwida von Meysenbug, Felicitas Buchner e Mary Douglas-Hamilton. In *Governanti e istitutrici tra Ottocento e Novecento. Ruolo sociale e immagini letterarie*, eds. Isabella Nardi and Antonella Valoroso, 107–138. Quaderni della Fondazione Ranieri di Sorbello 7. Bologna: Pendragon.

Buseghin, Maria Luciana. 2021. *Sulle tracce di un sogno. Vicende e passioni di Leopoldo Franchetti (1847–1917)*. mimeo.

Capuzzo, Ester. 2019. Franchetti e l'ebraismo. In *Leopoldo Franchetti, la nuova Destra e il modello Toscano*, ed. Sandro Rogari, 199–207. Soveria Mannelli: Rubbettino.

Dana, Nathalie. 1963. *Young in New York. A Memoir of a Victorian Girlhood*. New York: Garden City/Doubleday.

Fabiani, Anna Angelica, and Francesca Tomassini. 2009. L'attività di Maria Pasqui Marchetti dalle carte d'archivio della Fondazione Franchetti di Città di Castello. In *Oggi non sono andata a parare le pecore... La memoria delle scuole rurali di Montesca e Rovigliano di Città di Castello*, eds. Anna Angelica Fabiani and Francesca Tomassini, 39–50. Perugia: Soprintendenza Archivistica per l'Umbria.

Fossati, Roberta. 1987–88. Alice Hallgarten Franchetti e le sue iniziative alla Montesca. *Fonti e documenti. Rivista annuale* 16–17: 269–347.

Fossati, Roberta. 1997. *Élites Femminili e nuovi modelli religiosi nell'Italia tra Otto e Novecento*. Urbino: Fondazione Romolo Murri/Quattro Venti.

Fossati, Roberta. 2002. Il lavoro culturale e la vita affettiva di Alice Hallgarten Franchetti. In *Alice e Leopoldo Franchetti e il loro tempo*, eds. Paolo Pezzino and Alvaro Tacchini, 157–194. Città di Castello: Petruzzi.

Fossati, Roberta. 2007. L'impegno sociale dell'Unione per il bene. In *Per le strade del mondo. Laiche e religiose fra Otto e Novecento*, ed. Stefania Bartoloni, 313–336. Bologna: Il Mulino.

Gnoli, Umberto. 1908. *L'arte umbra alla Mostra di Perugia*. Bergamo: Istituto italiano d'arti grafiche.

Hallgarten, Charles. 1897. *Neues über den Antisemitismus: Vortrag gehalten in einer Versammlung am 14 Februar 1897*. Frankfurt am Main: Golde.

Josz, Aurelia. 1913. Fiammella francescana. *Nuova Antologia, V* 164 (90): 278–285.

Latter, Lucy R. 1906. *School Gardenery for Little Children*. London: Swan, Sonnenschein.

Latter, Lucy R. 1908. *Il giardinaggio insegnato ai bambini*. Rome-Milan: Dante Alighieri.

Lombardo Radice, Giuseppe. 1925/1931. *Athena fanciulla. Scienza e poesia della scuola serena*. Florence: Bemporad.

Maccheroni, Anna Maria. 1947. *A True Romance: Doctor Maria Montessori as I Knew Her*. Edinburgh: The Darien Press.

May, Maude G. 1909. A New Method in Infant Education. *The Journal of Education* 41: 645–647.

von Meysenbug, Malwida. 1904. *Memoiren einer Idealistin*. Stuttgart: Auerbach.

Montessori, Maria. 1909. *Corso di pedagogia scientifica. Appunti e note sulle lezioni della dottoressa Maria Montessori, docente dell'Università di Roma*. Città di Castello: Soc. Tipografica Editrice Cooperativa.

Montessori, Maria. 1913/2013. *Maria Montessori Sails to America: A Private Diary*, ed. Carolina Montessori. Amsterdam: Pierson.

Montessori, Maria. 1921. *Manuale di pedagogia scientifica*. Naples: Alberto Morano.

Musci Leonardo, ed. 2018. *Inventario carte di e su Leopoldo Franchetti conservate dall'Associazione nazionale per gli interessi del Mezzogiorno d'Italia (ANIMI)*. mimeo.

Nordheimer, William. 1908. *Walter Nordheimer Hallgarten*. London: The Chiswick Press.

O'Donnel, Marion. 2014. *Maria Montessori*. London: Bloomsbury.

Old Traveller (Walter Hallgarten). 189?. *Notes of Travel on Five Continents*. New York: Knickerbocker Press

Pazzini, Claudia. 2019. *Coltivare l'immaginario. Letture e albi illustrati dei bambini di Palazzo Sorbello*. Perugia: Fondazione Ranieri di Sorbello.

Pezzino, Paolo, and Alvaro Tacchini, eds. 2002. *Alice e Leopoldo Franchetti e il loro tempo*. Città di Castello: Petruzzi.

Religious Charity Regina Margherita. 1925. *Statuto organico, approvato con decreto reale del 22 agosto 1925*. mimeo.

Rogari, Sandro, ed. 2019. *Leopoldo Franchetti, la nuova destra e il modello toscano*. Soveria Mannelli: Rubbettino.

Sabatier, Paul. 1894/1931. *Vie de Saint François d'Assise*. Paris: Libraire Fischbacher.

Schembs, Hans-Otto., and Arno Lustiger. 2003. *Charles Hallgarten. Leben und Wirken des Frankfurter Sozialreformers und Philantropen*. Frankfurt am Main: Societäts-Verlag.

Scudder, Vida. 1937. *On Journey*. New York: Dutton.

Stascheit, Ulrich. 2003. Charles Hallgartens Jahre in New York. Drei Brueder, drei Wohltaeter. In *Charles Hallgarten. Leben und Wirken des Frankfurter Sozialreformers und Philantropen*, eds. Hans-Otto Schembs and Arno Lustiger, 118–120. Frankfurt am Main: Societäts-Verlag.

Taricone, Fiorenza. 2000–01. Il Consiglio nazionale delle donne italiane. In *La questione femminile dall'Unità d'Italia a Giolitti*, ed. Giuseppina Accardo. Rome: Università di Roma 3, available at http://www.donneconoscenzastorica.it/vecchio/testi/accardidonne/actutconsiglio.htm.

Taverna, Lavinia. 1902. Federazione romana delle opere di attività femminile. In *Esposizione di arte e di lavori femminili. Primavera 1902. Operosità femminile italiana*, Federazione Romana delle Opere Femminili, ed. Sezione Lavoro, 11–140. Rome: Rosy Amadori.

Tomei Finamore, Rosmunda. 1906. Le industrie femminili d'Abruzzo. In *Le industrie femminili Italiane. Cooperativa nazionale sede centrale via Marco Minghetti*, 209–220. Rome-Milan: Pilade Rocco.

Travaglini, Carlo. 1994. *Faina, Eugenio, in Dizionario biografico degli italiani, 212–217*, vol. 44. Rome: Treccani.

Urbini, Giulio. 1907. *Mostra d'arte antica umbra.* Perugia: Bartelli.

Zanotti Bianco, Umberto. 1950. *Saggio storico sulla vita e attività politica di Leopoldo Franchetti.* Rome: Associazione Nazionale per gli Interessi del Mezzogiorno d'Italia.

CHAPTER 4

Cora Slocomb Savorgnan di Brazzà: An Artisan of Peace and Social Justice

Idanna Pucci

> I would snatch the tallest pine from the mountains and, dipping it in the crater of Etna, would write the name of my beloved laborious, patient peasant women upon the skies, that it might compel the gaze of the whole world.
>
> Cora Slocomb di Brazzà.[1]

4.1 Introduction

Very often, when I think of Cora Slocomb Savorgnan di Brazzà (New Orleans 1862 - Rome 1944), I forget that she was my maternal great-grandmother, and this naturally pleases me because it means I am able to perceive her objectively, just as she deserves. It has not always been like

[1] Much of the information contained in this chapter comes from the Idanna Pucci Archive, focused on the life of Cora Slocomb, her American family as well as her adopted Italian family, Savorgnan di Brazzà. Unless stated otherwise, the translations of the quoted texts are our own.

I. Pucci (✉)
Lecce, Italy

E. Laurenzi and M. Mosca (eds.), *A Female Activist Elite in Italy (1890–1920)*, https://doi.org/10.1007/978-3-030-87159-8_4

that. Not so very long ago, Cora was for me simply my American great-grandmother of Friulian[2] adoption and none of the family ever mentioned her name. Since I did not grow up with my mother, I did not have many opportunities to ask about her. My memory of her was shrouded in fog. Only much later in life did I realise that the silence was due to the taboo that existed until recently about any illness involving the mind.

But then, by a strange coincidence, I found myself one day wanting to know more, and it was not easy. So, in 1985 I began a 'pilgrimage to the sources' between one continent and another, a kind of treasure hunt that continues today. The more I went ahead and discovered something about Cora, the more I felt pushed to break the spell of tragic silence surrounding her person. And the more I continued, the more she came to life in all her dynamic personality: a woman ahead of the times, moved by a great idealism, capable of genuinely changing the daily life of many people less fortunate than herself. And the more she emerged from that isolation imposed by her illness—of which she proved to be aware—the more importance she acquired in my eyes, regaining the human face that had been lost in the labyrinth of her suffering. I also saw how tangible the rights that had been taken away from her were, but which she had fought so hard for others to have, until her physical collapse at the age of forty-four.

The seed for her redemption was planted with the publication of my book *The Lady of Sing Sing*, which was the result of my pilgrimage to the sources (Pucci 2020). From that moment, Cora began to make itself known, triggering other research studies until she found her rightful place not only in the history of Friuli, but also on the international scene. I am certain that if Cora could come back to her adopted land today, she would find the support she so deserved when, practically singlehanded, she oversaw the Lace Schools she had established and that she ran as cooperatives in a way that, over a century later, is still ahead of time.[3]

[2] Friuli Venezia Giulia (often called just Friuli) is a northeastern region of Italy.

[3] The Brazzà School Cooperatives were situated in the municipalities of Brazzacco, Fagagna, Martignacco, and San Vito di Fagagna, in the region of Friuli. The nearest to Brazzà was in the hamlet of Santa Margherita (Brazzacco) in a building completely restored by Cora near the church (Toppazzini Tondello 2002).

4.2 The Lace Schools

During her early years in Louisiana, Cora had learned to make lace, following designs handed down through her mother's Quaker family. Soon after marrying my great-grandfather Detalmo Savorgnan di Brazzà, from a noble family dating back to the Middle Ages and settling on the Brazzà estate, near Udine,[4] Cora introduced this art into the Friuli region, integrating it with the local decorative motifs and making it a means to improve the conditions of peasant women. She created a lace-making cooperative, which was not only the first of its kind in Italy, but which also became one of the most active centres of lace production in the country (Pucci 2020).

The cooperative provided the women with a means of sustenance without keeping them from their domestic or farm work, employing them during the long winter months when it was impossible to labour in the wheat and corn fields. By 1891 the industry was in full swing. On a wave of enthusiasm, and also thanks to Cora's business acumen, orders arrived from the United States, France, England, Hungary and even Chile.

Cora personally wrote a short history of the origin and progress of her Cooperative Lace Schools that she printed in small pamphlets in four languages—Italian, French, German and English – to distribute to all the clients and friends (Slocomb 1900).[5]

> In Italy, on the 8th of September 1891, the first Local Agricultural Show for peasants took place. What most interested the humble crowd was a group of six little girls, each with a pillow on their knees and bobbins in hand, working slowly but accurately at the production of lace.
>
> A fortnight before the show, the Countess Detalmo di Brazzà Savorgnan, formerly Miss Cora Slocomb of New Orleans, United States of America, had gathered these children together and, within this short time, taught them how to handle the bobbins and make the first points, followed by lace ten centimeters wide woven with sixty threads in the style known as *torchon*.
>
> The experiment succeeded. These embryonic lacemakers proved to their friends and schoolmates that the pretty industry could be acquired without great difficulty, and the latter applied to join the class. The Countess

[4] Udine is a city in Friuli Venezia Giulia.

[5] The book was printed for the Paris Exposition of 1900 where the Brazzà Lace was awarded two gold and two silver medals.

accepted all she could instruct for no other teacher was to be found in the neighborhood, and that autumn her pupils numbered forty.

She shared the views of the Italian philanthropist Ruggiero Bonghi,[6] and she said: 'The needy classes must be encompassed by the love of those who are prosperous; these should not wait for assistance to be asked, but should offer it freely, almost force it upon them; and this assistance must not consist in alms giving, but in the creation of institutions. Alms humiliate and the bitterness of accepting them affects the character; an institution once created, however, becomes the possession of him for whom it has been created'. The Countess, therefore, as the soil seemed congenial, sought to cultivate the industry of lace making.

Assisted then by Signorina Dorina Bearzi she taught the pupils of Brazzà and rapidly trained the best to become teachers in those places where branch schools were desired. Thus, were founded the school of Fagagna (with the assistance of the Pecile family) and seven others.

The teaching in these schools aims at furnishing a remunerative occupation to the peasants and daughters of laborers and artisans for the hours when their household duties and gardens, or the cultivation of the fields, do not require their attention, time which would otherwise be wasted, for home spinning and weaving have ceased because of the cheap and attractive factory-made goods to be found everywhere. Neither are all physically adapted to work in the fields and factories. Manual labor cannot always be exacted from women and growing girls. For the delicate, the weak, and the deformed, for the hands otherwise condemned to idleness, the schools offer, not only occupation, but diversion, encouragement and the opportunity to earn a living.

With the increase of pupils arose the difficulty in selling their work for which there was no demand in Friuli. The founder was assisted in overcoming this difficulty by friends in Rome and, thanks to this, despite their imperfections, the products of the infant industry were disposed of in 1892 and part of 1893.

These same friends assisted the Countess by lending her samples of antique lace that, united with the collection belonging to her mother, Mrs. Slocomb, have given to the lace since produced by the schools an antique

[6] Ruggiero Bonghi (1826–1895) was an Italian writer and politician of liberal orientation.

and original style. Of further assistance was the collection of samples illustrative of the story of antique and modern lace and the studies made for the preparation of a book.[7]

The latter collection, after serving in the Italian Women's Exhibition at the Chicago Exposition, was acquired by the Philadelphia Museum of Art.

The production of lace in the schools had grown more rapidly than the demand, and together with examples from the lace workshops of Burano, Umbria, and other parts of Italy, it led the way to the Exposition of Chicago by the Committee of Ladies belonging to every Italian province, which was organized and presided over by the Countess di Brazzà.

Thanks to the medals and diplomas received wherever the Cooperative Lace Schools of Brazzà have exhibited and the consequent increase in sales, their struggle for existence is still successful. And, although these schools owe their foundation to private generosity, they are forced to struggle ceaselessly as ordinary manufacturers, as they have no subsidy whatsoever to assist in supporting them.

The girls are not only trained to seek for the greatest perfection in the lace making but are taught to use the greatest variety in the combination of threads (called points), and the exact reproduction the antique, using only materials of the best quality which can be found. These are furnished with the most varied designs in which the antique character is carefully maintained. These designs are studied from original books, prints, pictures and documents belonging to Museums and private collections of lace.

The administration of the schools receives with gratitude the loan of designs, and is glad of orders to complete antique trimmings, its object being ever to perfect and increase the assortment of laces.

The expenses of the administration, of instruction and of the opening of new schools are met by voluntary contributions and a percentage of the sales. The lacemakers are paid by the job and receive an increase of pay in proportion to the demand for their work and the price at which it is sold.

The ages at which pupils are admitted vary from 7 to 15 years, excepting children who have learned the first points at home and the defective and deformed. Pupils who have not satisfied the public-school requirements are not allowed to attend the lace school during public school hours.

In each school there is a collection box for the sick. Every year, the schools offer prizes as follows.

A First prize for kindness to companions, amiability to superiors and obedience to the rules.

[7] Cora was not only a master lacemaker, but also an expert on the history of lace. On the occasion of the Chicago World Fair, she wrote and illustrated a classic on Italian lace in Slocomb (1893).

A Second prize for teaching with the greatest industry to less quick-to-learn companions.

A Third prize for the most perfect work.

These prizes are thus distributed because kindness to an equal and amiability to a superior are more important in the development of a human being than manual dexterity. The ultimate aim of the Cooperative Lace Schools of Brazzà, while providing work and an honest means of self-support, focuses on developing in the pupils the noblest sentiments as well as training them for the highest usefulness in life.

4.3 Business and Marketing

Cora was indeed an unusual person: extremely gifted as a painter and writer, a voracious reader and an environmentalist at heart. Yet, she was also endowed with a down-to-earth business acumen and had a natural flair for marketing that was crucial for any commercial endeavour. She was truly ahead of her time with her spontaneous talents.

The American market was the largest, but it was protected. Promoter, pedagogue and now trade reformer, Cora struggled for the abolition of American tariffs on foreign lace. She wrote a ten-page booklet, *The Human and Urgent Side of the Tariff Question* (Slocomb 1897a) which she sent to every member of the US Congress. In the end, she managed to get them to reduce the import duty on lace and other handicrafts from sixty to fifteen per cent by advancing the argument that this would diminish the influx of immigrants. On the cover, she quoted Alfred Tennyson's words: 'Because right is right, to follow right were wisdom' (Tennyson 1829).

Cora would often hold entertaining seminars for the lacemakers on how to conquer the American market. 'You must make exotic and original designs' she would tell them. 'Americans worship the new. They fear being caught with old styles'. The lacemakers of Brazzà soon acquired fame as the Queen's lacemakers, thanks to the regular orders which came from Queen Margherita of Italy, who had a great regard for Cora. At the 1893 International Exposition in Chicago, Brazzà lace was chosen as a prime example of Italian craftsmanship. Standing next to the samples she was so proud of, Cora spoke on the life of Italian peasant women. Addressing a large audience was not new to her, and she liked to improvise.

I want to include her speech here in its entirety so that the reader can listen to her voice, her sensitive observations and love for her adopted land and its people, however simple. Cora was a born storyteller, and her observations conceal her inner aspirations. Her speech, which was subsequently published that year, was mostly extemporaneous (Slocomb 1894: 697–703)[8]:

> The peasant women of Italy. Who of you on hearing these words does not think of the opera chorus gesticulating as gracefully as jointed dolls expressing emotion by clock work, or the swarthy fruit seller at a busy street corner or of some weary family of immigrants who probably more than once have crossed your path?
>
> And yet the peasant women of Italy among their native fields, olive groves and vineyards resemble none of these, and I trust when we part you will be truly acquainted with our humble sisters across the seas and carry away in your heart one grain of the rich harvest of love I bear them.
>
> I will introduce you to those I have known intimately in Friuli, for it is better to have a clear impression of a group than a confused memory of a mass, the more so as the peasants in the north of Italy live in isolated homes, and each household forms a complete miniature government, composed of many generations and ramifications of relatives of many families, submitting to a regularly patriarchal administration of their interests.
>
> Some of these peasant-homesteads, with their courtyards, barns and out-houses, shelter no less than fifty human beings, scores of quadrupeds and hundreds of feathered bipeds. The father of the oldest branch directs the others, or if he feels the conglomerated existences. No individual feels entitled to sign a contract or undertake any enterprise without consent of his chief or else formally cutting loose from the guidance of his relatives who will show him no pity if once he breaks from the old traditions of co-operative duty among the members of peasant clans.
>
> Should the hereditary chief prove incapable of guiding the household, he is formally deposed by his relatives, and another member of his family, endowed with the necessary ability, is elected by vote to take his place. The women as well as the men are consulted. Among the peasants, the ancient Biblical appreciation of a numerous offspring flourishes. To remain

[8] In Chicago, Cora was accompanied by Countess Maria Pasolini dell'Onda, who was also very active in the social advancement of women in Italy. Among the contributors to the Exhibition of Italian lace was Countess Andreana Marcello whose lace production in Burano, Venice was also well known at the time.

childless or be forced to replace the willing toilsome hands of sons and daughters by hired help is felt to be a disgrace.

Much is to be learned by visiting this unfrequented province, which lies directly north of Venice, and so I trust you will permit me to lead your imagination through some of the pleasant experiences that await you there.

The fast-express leaves Venice at 2 o'clock every afternoon and is due to arrive in Udine, the capital of Friuli,[9] at 4:20. It first crosses the massive viaduct, rising above the blue lagoon, which is ever dotted with orange and red lateen sails. The salt marshes and sluggish waterways extend sleepily on our right like a worn-out combatant as well as the sacred fortress of Marghera, so gloriously defended in 1849 by a few brave men in the Italian rebellion against foreign rule, when the Austrians hemmed the volunteers in on every side except the city. There another more dreaded foe, the 'cholera', wielded the scepter. All had surrendered except this handful of staunch hearts who still fought on single-handed – until in the baptism of their own blood and misery the dross engendered by the ease of centuries was washed from their characters and every Venetian was born again a hero.

The train crosses the rich Venetian plains; then it turns to the East and seems to lose itself on the verdant plain of Friuli, the great *Patria* or fatherland, from which the Venetians fled a thousand years ago before the devastating hordes of bloody Attila, known as 'the plague of God'. Now all is pretty, prosperous, and peaceful. Waving fields of grain and rippling watercourses sparkle in the sunshine. The neat roads, leading to well-filled barns, are planted with great shade trees. The peasant houses are large, the meadows rich, and the gray cattle fat and sleepy. All seems to speak of contentment.

One is aroused with a kind of moral shock at sight of the old Villa Manin[10] with its memories of turbulence and war. For, by an irony of fate, this beautiful home of the last Doge of the Venetian Republic was chosen as a resting place by the modern Cæsar, Napoleon 1st, when he was studying the peace of Campoformio,[11] which forged the chain of Venetian slavery to Austria. Here on this very spot, it was welded with gold rung from her children upon the neck of the once proud Venetian Republic by purchasing Austria to furnish the conqueror – alas Italian by birth – with the sinews able to carry onto fresh fields of misery his conquering banners and their attendant train of woes.

[9] The capital of Friuli is actually Trieste, but Udine is considered its historical capital.

[10] Villa Manin, a Venetian villa located in the province of Udine, is a monumental architectural complex built in the sixteenth century.

[11] The Treaty of Campo Formio (1797) was a peace treaty between France and Austria, signed after the defeat of Austria by Napoleon Bonaparte.

The train whistles twice. The modern suburbs of a prosperous little city come in sight. The past is lost in the present. The thirty thousand inhabitants of Udine greet you with the clatter of iron foundries, cotton and flourmills and hundreds of other enterprises. United Italy has arisen, strengthened by its long period of suffering. We pass through the turreted city gate and you gaze in wonder upon gushing fountains, electric lights, gas burners, tramways, and telephone wires interlaced curiously among the ancient palaces.

A miniature parliament existed on the citadel of Udine centuries before the proud barons of England compelled King John in 1215 to sign the Magna Charta, assuring to their descendants liberty and representation. This little *Patria* can, therefore, boast of having been one of the oldest countries in Europe to possess a representative assemblage by election and by inheritance, divided into two bodies, the Peers and the Commons. They met yearly in Udine to decide on the well being of the country. This parliament only ceased to exist when Napoleon conquered Italy.

We cannot linger. Time is flying, and we must hasten so that you may become acquainted with the people up in the hills around the castle and learn to love them a little before we part.

The carriage spins out of the gate at the other end of the town and drives between the Indian cornfields, called here Turkish grain, and the vineyards. The road is macadamized and very white. It is flanked on either side by deep ditches and mulberry trees that have been cropped to acquire a chubby and rotund personality. There are millions of them, stretching row upon row, as far as the eye can see. Their leaves serve to feed the silkworms. Italy produces one-fourth of the silk consumed in the world, and Friuli is one of the two provinces that yields the most silk in the country.

The peasant men who pass salute respectfully The women instead are very proud, reserved and dignified, and never bow unless they are acquainted. The strong soft homespun in which these people are clothed is made from the left-over silk which is washed, carded, spun, dyed and woven at home by the women and then turned by the village tailors into most comfortable and durable costumes. These fabrics are sadly being replaced with cheap factory materials, also sown by the village tailors. The peasant women consider that none but men can fashion garments worthy of admiration.

The horses climb up and up through picturesque villages, past flowering walls and verdant vineyards, orchards and copses. On every side, bits of charming landscape, studded with villages, attract the eye. You are in Friuli, the third most populous country in the world, with only China and Belgium having more inhabitants to the square mile.

The carriage drives along a rough causeway flanked by old acacia trees. At the end stands between massive stone columns an open iron gate draped in wisteria and roses, forming a graceful frame to a medieval ruined castle that closes the vista. From its highest tower float the Stars and Stripes and the Tricolor of United Italy, sanctified by the White Cross of Savoy.

We have reached home. A hubbub of sweet feminine voices caresses the ear. Down the old terrace steps swarm half a hundred girls led by a grey-haired old hunchback. They scramble to kiss our hands, and murmur 'Servito suo' [At your service]. They are very neat, with their white aprons and sleeves and bonny kerchiefs. They are the children of the Home Lace School, who learn the new patterns and then teach them in turn to their one hundred and fifty companions in the neighboring villages. Many of the little ones have been to the public school all morning, and the older ones come from the fields or the stables. As soon as they can get away, they hasten to their lace cushions as if to an entertainment, fresh and merry as chattering magpies.

We do not wish them to forget what they have learned at school, and so each girl is compelled to write her own name and address on the piece of lace she has made as well as its price and the date when she finished it. While working, they sing street litanies and lovely part songs, as well as the stirring war choruses of young Italy. A chaplain visits them twice a week as well as a teacher who recounts anecdotes about the helpful lives that members of their class have led, and tell them of the great charitable organizations and institutions founded through self-abnegation.

Each morning the girls begin the day by uniting in prayer. If the priest is not expected, then one of his stories is repeated for the amusement of everyone. If you asked Italia,[12] our most lovable and industrious lace-maker, she would repeat the following story in her soft and modest accent: 'One day, not so many years ago – I forget the date, but I think it was about 1830 – a priest in Sicily entered one of the most squalid houses of his parish just at the hour when the family was about to partake of its midday meal. He was politely invited to join, and what was his surprise? After the blessing he was asked to see each cut off the most delicate part of his portion and place it on a plate in the center of the table. He asked for an explanation of this strange action. The father answered: 'You see we have no money to spare with which to help our neighbors, but we find that if each of us gives away a big mouthful of food, it costs nothing and will suffice to remind us of those who have nothing to eat. The united bits are more than enough to feed an old man who comes daily to get what we have saved for him'.

[12] Italia in this case is a Christian name.

The priest marveled at the example of true Christian charity set by this simple household and went away with the thought that what can be done by just one family could be done by many other families. And at present, owing to his teachings, each day that the sun rises on Sicily, six thousand poor people are fed with the mouthfuls of the poor.

Oh, my compatriots, you and I grew up with tales of Mafia and bloodshed poisoning our hearts against the Sicilians, while their poorest were developing this noblest brotherhood which teaches to take the bread from one's own hungry mouth to feed a poorer neighbor. You and I were reading of the Sicilian vespers reeking with blood, while from the scanty dinners of the poor ascended to the Lord a sweeter savor than from our rich and dainty boards.

The lacemakers know scores of such stories. Learning thus daily about the great influence for good which even the lowliest can exert, let us also learn from them never to neglect the smallest opportunities, for they are the stepping-stones set by Providence to bridge the deep chasm existing between egotistical selfishness and our frail humanity.

These seven-year-old lacemakers will join the older ones in showing with pride their lace pillows. Each one is the absolute owner of what she makes and can even sell it on her own. In that case, she must charge a small percentage above the price paid to her and hand it in to the cashier to assist in defraying the expenses incurred for electricity, heating, and the administration of the lace school by which she has profited to learn her art.

The simple tools used are loaned to them, but any wanton loss or destruction of these objects is deducted from their earnings. The accounts are settled monthly, and the price paid for the lace increases above the regular percentage in proportion to its quality in relation to the sample, and a percentage is deducted if this falls below or is needlessly spoiled.

The scale of payment is governed by the price we can obtain for the lace. Hence, we seek to originate new designs and have objects made which will attract the wealthy. Could we command enough work, there are thousands of women in Friuli alone waiting to join our schools or organize themselves into cooperatives.

The race that inhabits Friuli and speaks its languages is robust, handsome, intelligent and patient.

The women do not work as regularly as the men in the fields, but assist them there whenever necessary, and as they have the usual feminine fear of storms, one often sees when the thunder growls a posse of the weaker sex huddled together beneath a projecting bank, praying in abject fear. The women in the high-perched village are the first to spy the thundercaps scudding along toward the quarter of the heavens that arches their homes, and they hurry to the church-tower and ring the bells to call the laborers from the fields and the old to their orisons. They ring with a will, for they believe that by establishing an aerial commotion through the swinging, reverberating bells the devastator can be warded off. As the storm approaches, the prayer of the bells is heard ringing clear and strong between the gusts of wind. It increases to a wild entreaty in the on-rush of the tempest, and the wild clamor breaks in a frenzy of despair when the storm bursts.

Then begins the deep tolling of the great passing bell as the battered flowers and lacerated branches are carried along, tossed and torn by the blast and bruised by the cutting sheets of ice, fit emblems of the dying hopes of the hard-working peasants and the anguish of crushed nature.

The voices of the village bells die away in a quivering sob, which seems wrung from their metal hearts in pity for the devastation around them. At the vesper hour, they will rise again clear, despite the past, to praise God. Fit reminders of the Eternal Spring, the sunshine and the fresh budding and blossoming that lie beyond.

Since peasant and proprietor suffer alike from these terrific rain and hail storms, the gentlefolk of Friuli are seeking in every way to render their tenants familiar with all the means for rapidly substituting fresh crops for those destroyed. They also seek to supply them with other means of earning a livelihood in inclement weather so that they may maintain their families and meet their financial obligations with the proceeds of their manual industry.

About twenty-five years ago a gentleman farmer named Gabriele Luigi Pecile died in Fagagna, a village with about two thousand inhabitants. He left an income that consists of five hundred dollars, to be spent yearly on agricultural instruction for the peasants, and assisting any enterprise or industry started in the place that promised to add to their physical or moral development.

Despite its modest proportions, this small sum has not only provided for the villagers admirable lectures on agricultural and economic topics and competitive prizes for the best crop of grain, etc., to the acre; it has also established an agricultural intelligence office for the peasants, to which is due a great improvement in the productiveness of the neighborhood; and by means of discreetly placed loans for importing foreign stock in the aim of obtaining a much finer race of cattle and pigs.

It has also donated to the village a model vineyard, tended by the peasants, where experiments are made with every kind of grape vine to discover the one best adapted to the exigencies of the climate. Many cooperative establishments flourish under its guiding influence. All of these were founded by emitting small bonds worth two dollars each, mostly subscribed for by the peasantry.

One of these supplies the province with the seed or eggs for the silk-worm culture, prepared according to the system introduced by the great Pasteur when he lived in the province and studied the disease that was destroying the silk industry of Southern Europe. This establishment, with the exception of the director, is run entirely by sixty peasant women, who perform the minute microscopic work, as well as all the other delicate branches of the culture, with such exactitude that the eggs from this co-operative establishment have reached the highest standard.

The Pecile fund has also assisted the peasants to build the cooperative ice-houses which are filled with snow and ice by the people gratuitously every winter, and from which each has a right to free ice in time of necessity. It instituted the cooperative dairy, to which the villagers bring the surplus milk from their cattle, which is churned by women into butter and cheese according to the most approved Swiss systems or retailed to other members of the society. By its judicious initiative, it rendered possible the opening of a splendidly appointed cooperative slaughterhouse. It also provides lessons in mechanical drawing, and it has founded a school of basket-making attended by fifty or sixty peasants and children, which is now self-supporting.

See what a colossal work can be accomplished in twenty-five years by a paltry five hundred dollars well administered!

The gentlemen in the province have followed its example, and award prizes to their tenants for the greatest percentage of grapes or grain produced per acre under their cultivation, and for the greatest number of pounds of silk returned for the eggs distributed. But we all found that a greater stimulant and more extended competition were needed.

Many, yes too many, exhibitions for mechanics had been held in the cities of Italy. We knew all that could be known about their work but we were ignorant of our neighbors in the country. They lived apart, and were reticent, modest, and clung to old worn out customs. They were doing little that was practical in their leisure hours – in the winter evenings – and while listening to legend and story, or joining in tender or merry part songs called '*villotte*', of which they were themselves the authors.

We decided to copy the English Cottage Garden shows in a broad sense. Instead of one village and a few cottages, seven great municipalities with a score of villages clubbed together. Each poor village can have a cottage garden show each year. Every inhabitant can bring a knit stocking, a neatly made frock, a pumpkin, a basket of peaches, a sheaf of wheat, a boot, a shoe, or a basket. The point is showing to each what others have done with no better means than their own.

We had our machinery hall full of spades, plows, thrashers and simple agricultural implements and furniture made by the peasants. We had our manufacturer building full of coarse stuffs and garments woven and fashioned by the peasant women; full of spoons and utensils and ornaments made by the men. We had our horticultural and agricultural display, and going out into the fields we judged the houses and the farms themselves as well as their produce that was brought to the fair.

We had our stock pavilion full of small animals. Besides this we had a gallery containing the best foreign models for simple objects and a book in which all could inscribe their names and the number of the object they wished to copy.

We had a band, a speech from the senator of the district, a distribution of prizes, when each worthy peasant, man or woman, was called by name and the class of his production and reason of his choice announced. He answered and mounted the old stone steps of the castle terrace with a proud heart to receive his two-or-three dollars award; or the prizes were graded according to the importance of the exhibit, and the man whose farm was in the best agricultural and economic condition received decidedly more than the man who had grown an exceptionally fine cabbage.

Last evening, I received a letter announcing that my lace schools had just been awarded the gold medal at the National Italian Exhibition of agricultural industries at Cesena.[13]

And what were the reasons for this progress? First, because seeing what others could do inspired a healthy incentive and a desire to outstrip those of the neighboring villages in the percentage of prizes carried off by the home community. Secondly, we had judiciously used it to acquaint the peasants with fresh means of income. Among others, we had taught six girls in a fortnight how to make a simple bobbin lace; and as they worked merrily before their astonished neighbors who stood densely packed before them, they inspired all the girls with a desire to learn the dainty lace art and the children asked us to open schools.

When the fathers saw that the girls were wisely directed and never kept from doing their work in the fields as well as from caring for and leading the cattle to pasture, or from helping their mothers with the washing at the brook, they willingly sent them to the school.

When they saw that their little maids became neat, respectful, contented, and brought home pretty stories to enliven the evenings in the stable, and the bright silver coins to swell the family hoard, then the whole countryside was converted. For the cheapness of the cotton goods

[13] Cesena is a city in the Emilia-Romagna region in the north of Italy.

has discouraged the women from weaving and they waste their leisure hours in crocheting and tatting and gossip.

The priests and the heads of the households begin to appreciate that, while in no way it interferes with their usual laborious tasks, it adds to the financial resources of the family.

Among our lacemakers we have hunched-backs and lame and deformed bodies of every kind, and some that have spent thirty years on rude beds of pain. The lace children, like the sunbeams, have penetrated everywhere and taught them the easy twists and delicate turns by which their unlovely fingers could evolve the soft white lace.

Think of the ignorant mind, as dark, as squalid, as miserable as the roof chamber to which this useless member of a busy household was banished, left alone in solitude, filled suddenly with the inspiring thought that in its decrepitude it could earn as much and be as useful to the family as the blooming maidens out in the fields.

Think of the room now filled with the pleasant clatter of the bobbins, the pleasant chatter of the children who have come to work beside their aunty and tell her what their dear *maestra* [teacher] said of their work when they carried it in on last payday.

Watch the women and children trudging through ice and snow for many a weary mile to learn the new art. See them yielding to the education of the heart and spending their modest earnings to help their mothers or some dear invalid to a simple comfort they would not have dreamed of getting for them a few months before. Hearken to the terrific roar of the vast ocean of thirty million Italian voices behind them, asking if I have fulfilled the mission for which I came.

In the silent watches of the night, it awakens me to wonder if I am doing my best; to search for what means remains as yet untried to touch your hearts.

Above the roar in machinery hall, above the sharp crack of the fireworks, above the music of the bands, above the applause of the multitude, above the thunder of the storms in this White City, I hear it.

Like Heine,[14] I would snatch the tallest pine from the mountains, and dipping it in the crater of Etna, would write the name of my beloved (the laborious, patient peasant women) upon the skies, that it might compel the gaze of the whole world.

Can you wonder, with this great opportunity, the Congress of all nations, drawing to its close, each nerve is stretched to snapping, the flesh is forgotten, each heartstring is vibrating in the agonizing desire to make all these voices reach your ears through my one frail organ? They are crying to

[14] The reference is to the German poet Johann Heinrich Heine (1797–1856).

you for your friendship, for your patronage. It means to them their homes, their children, their all. They are not begging; they offer you their work, the product of honest manual toil that is being driven from the market by machines which can never be weary or hungry or ill, which can never die, but also have no souls to lose through the temptations of misery.

The frail fingers of these women and children are competing with iron rods and steam power, and yet have courage; for the lace, the home-spuns into which are entwined their dreams, their prayers, their songs and their tears, are unsurpassed. What I am striving for I can never accomplish. But you can do it if you only will.

The storekeepers tell me that if there was a demand for Italian goods, they would place them in stock. They say to me: 'Create the demand, we will do the rest'.

I entreat you to ask in the shops for Italian lace, Italian silks, Italian home-spuns. Fashion will follow your summons, such is your power. I can speak, but yours is the nobler part, you can act. Act, only act; the modest Italian women of the people in their far-off country homes will feel the benefit. Their loving prayers have sustained me in my hours of trial; their dear, blotted letters come to me across the waters full of confiding faith and longing to know what I am doing for them in my fatherland. Poor, darlings, because they love me, they think me omnipotent. To you I confide their future. It is safe if you grant my prayer, though it hangs upon a frail shred of lace.

God grant that you may never again set eyes upon a piece of lace, however modest, without being reminded of what you can do for the hardworking women of the people in Italy.

The implications of Cora's presence at the Chicago World Fair are well described by fashion historian Manuela Soldi (2017: 27) in her work 'Before Italian Fashion: Textile Craftsmanship in Italy (1861–1911)':

Of even greater significance today is the influence of the event organized in 1893 by Cora di Brazzà and her companions, which occupied the entire Italian wing of the Women's Building at the Chicago Exhibition. This was the first major exhibition of Italian women's work abroad, and presented their work as of recognized excellence, fit to be used for the benefit of the national image in an international context. An increasingly tight knot was being tied, meanwhile, between the struggle for the emancipation and promotion of handicrafts, in both manufacturing and domestic contexts, to allow less well-off women to support themselves.

4.4 Multiple Groundbreaking Activities

Cora's imaginative entrepreneurial talent was not limited to the founding of the Lace Cooperatives. From the very first moment of her life in Italy, she envisioned Friuli as a base for multiple groundbreaking activities that could benefit the people. In 1891, just four years after her marriage, she started a Toy Workshop in the town of Fagagna, not far from Brazzà. She had returned from Germany and a visit to the towns of Sonneberg and Nuremberg. There, she had found a wide array toys which inspired her to design and produce dolls dressed in Friulan traditional costumes, and animals: white doves to hang in cradles—never before seen in Italy—donkeys, chicken, camels, and of course bears, all in *lenci* cloth.[15]

The same year, 1891, Cora walked into a small shop selling coffee, tea and spices in Martignacco, a few miles from Brazzà. The owner, Angela Corder Denser, was a widow with six children. One of her children, Giuseppe, a passionate cook, had just baked a few biscuits—his own recipe—for his younger brother who was weak and sick. Cora tasted a biscuit. It was delicious. The boy smiled and said it was 're-energizing' and would give strength to his brother. So, Cora invited Angela and her son to sell their biscuits at the Craft Fair she organised every year in Brazzà. The biscuits became instantly popular, so much so that the shop expanded into a small factory. The first biscuits had the word 'Brazzà' impressed. The factory is still alive and well after over 120 years. It is no longer a small business. Indeed, it is so big that it has changed its name to Food Group Delser, exporting their delicious delicacies all over the world. But the original recipe of the biscuits is still a well-kept secret (Sestito 2008).

At the same time, she decided to also focus her marketing talent on the unique hybrid violet created by her botanist brother-in-law Filippo di Brazzà. Within weeks, orders started to pour in from her network across Europe. The violet was the offspring from a white violet Filippo had found growing wild on the Tuscan coast, and the well-known violet

[15] Even in this, Cora was ahead of time. The Lenci cloth is non-woven and therefore does not have any warp and weft. It is obtained by felting wool fibres, usually from cadet sheep or mohair goat hair. It is not a fabric, and so it does not fray when cut and does not need finishing seams. Officially, it was invented in Turin much later, in 1919, by a company called Lenci, but Cora used it twenty years earlier to create the beautifully crafted dolls and animals that became very popular in the whole region and beyond. Two of Cora's close friends became her collaborators in the toy venture: the American Lilih Ascoli Nathan, and Countess Antonia Ponti Suardi, a great lace collector (Sestito 2008).

of Parma, the colour of sapphire. The result was a snow-white violet that exuded a delicate spring-like fragrance that enamoured even Sissi, the last Empress of the Austrian-Hungarian Empire, who received regular deliveries at her palace in Vienna. In England, it was known as 'Pure White Count di Brazzà', and in 1883 it was awarded the first prize by the Royal Horticultural Society. I must point out that during the years from 1891 to the 1920s, the main source of income for the women of the region surrounding Udine came from Cora's lace cooperatives as well the trade of the white violet of Brazzà with its enchanted scent (Saccavini 2014: 124–129).

It is not surprising then that, in 1903, her adopted land elected the American Countess Cora di Brazzà first president of the Italian Female Industries. By then, Brazzà lace had found its way into exclusive shops in all the main cities of North America: from Toronto to New York and even New Orleans. The Italian Female Industries was an important organisation at the time and completely groundbreaking. It was a totally innovative initiative—cultural, social, economic and political. As we have seen, the economic-commercial structure of this first female industrial association had all the characteristics needed to support competitive business ventures of Italian products crafted by women internationally.[16]

As president, Cora became a national voice on behalf of the 'working woman', rejecting all those who believed that any type of work would drive women away from their true role in life: caring for the family and educating the children. In Milan, the first exhibition on women's crafts was curated by Cora herself in 1906. The catalogue published with her introduction included these words:

> In carrying out this program, we are comforted by the fact that our female workers' struggle to survive is relieved by the refreshing balm of art. We are confident that in future, if zeal and patience do not fail us, there will come a day when the remotest corners of Italy will gratefully acknowledge the name of the Italian Female Industries. (Slocomb 1906)

4.5 Seven Rules of Harmony

Cora's personal philosophy was summed up in her *Seven Rules of Harmony*, which were part of the regulations of the lacemaking School

[16] See Chapter 1 above.

Cooperatives. A flier with the seven rules was given to all buyers and visitors. No one could ignore her philosophy because her inspiring words were on display for all to see at the entrance of each of the cooperatives and school buildings, attended by an average of 150 students.

1. May the sacred spirit of peace be a living power in your life so that you may contribute time, thought, and money to its cause.
2. Never listen without protest to unjust accusations against the members of your family or your community.
3. Try to understand the spirit of national laws and obey them; but try also to take interest in the modification of those laws that, in your view, oppress any given class of society.
4. May your thoughts and active efforts serve to develop a national and patriotic spirit, and do not criticize without prior knowledge the administration of the family and the nation.
5. Treat the birds and animals, and all living creatures in the world of flora and fauna with kindness and justice. Do not destroy, unless it is for your survival or for the protection of the weak. Make it your duty and purpose to plant, nourish, and propagate all that might lead to the moral and physical improvement of your family, home, and nation.
6. Teach your children and employees the spirit of justice and peace, trying to develop around your sentiments of harmony.
7. Let not a single day pass without a word or one action that may help transmit the cause of peace, whether at home or outside.

Cora chose the three-leafed clover as her symbol because, she said, if one already possesses a four leafed clover, the hope of finding the lucky one was nil. That symbol became such a source of inspiration to her that she redesigned the immense lawn at the heart of the wonderful park of Brazzà in the shape of a three-leafed clover. This romantic green oasis, filled in the summer with wild daisies, red poppies and tiny purple flowers, was surrounded on all sides by a dense forest of Himalayan *deodaras*, cedars of Lebanon, tropical palms, weeping willows and countless other varieties of trees and plants.

The best time to visit this magnificent park was on the day of celebration of the lacemaking schools, when prizes were given out for the year's best samples. The day usually began with a mass in the private chapel devoted to Saint Leonard. A Unitarian, Cora felt at ease in all sanctuaries and always sat in the first pew along with the younger lacemakers, who wore their traditional costume. Inevitably, she wore a lace blouse, the finest example of their work.

In 1903, Cora's only child, Idanna, whom she had named after her adored paternal Aunt Ida Ann, was fifteen years old. Having to leave for a trip around Europe to raise funds for the victims of the disastrous earthquake that had struck the Italian southern region of Calabria, Cora gave precise instructions to the governess, Inetta Stangher, whom she had hired to reside in Brazzà and follow her daughter's education. Cora's commitments often required her to be absent, and of course she was constantly torn between her calling on behalf of social justice and her daily presence next to her beloved daughter and husband.

Her educational manifesto was closely linked to the *Seven Rules of Harmony*. Clearly, whether it was in her private, intimate life or in the broader public sphere, she aspired to the same ideals:

> Idanna shall be woken by the maid half an hour before the time she is to arise. The time will be set according to the season, her health and the circumstances. The maid shall light the fire before opening the window. Fifteen minutes later, she shall return to close the window and attend to the fire.
>
> During this half hour, Idanna shall devote her thoughts to God, beginning with the words: 'Glory to God in the Highest and on Earth, Peace, and Good Will. We praise thee, we worship thee, we glorify thee'.
>
> Her thoughts will then go to her duty towards the community, towards her parents, her governess, Miss Stangher, towards the servants and all the neighbors, even those who are most unpleasant, stupid and boring.
>
> She must then remember each morning, even when it is raining, the beauty and generosity of the sun and all the love and wellbeing that God has given her day by day since her birth.
>
> She shall thank God from the depths of her heart for any sorrows and disappointments, thinking that in this way God gives her the chance to perceive the suffering of millions of human beings on Earth, her brothers and sisters, less fortunate than herself. Idanna shall also thank God for the great example set by the martyrs and saints, by our ancestors and parents.
>
> She must never give up this half hour of dialog with God to attend to any pleasure, commitment or duty, except when there is an emergency, or someone needs help. This morning meditation is the source of physical, moral and intellectual wellbeing and is the most important moment of the day.

Idanna shall then have a bath, if possible cold. Afterwards, before dressing and attending to her hair, she will hear from the tutor the lessons planned for the day.

Idanna has a very delicate head of hair and I cannot entrust the maid with this task. It will therefore be Miss Stangher who will comb her hair. Naturally I would happily do it myself, but when I am absent or simply have no time, the governess must stand in for the mother.

After breakfast, time shall be devoted to household matters, with a precise record kept. The servants shall be given their orders for the day and then Miss Stangher and Idanna shall go out to do any indispensable errands. In rainy weather they shall stay at home to mend the linen and tidy up the closets. All this shall last no more than an hour and a half.

Then reciting and lessons until lunchtime.

After lunch the time should be spent with the family, chatting and also if possible, playing music. This will be followed by an hour's rest or an hour's walk, weather permitting. Afterwards there shall be three hours of lessons.

Altogether there are 8 hours of lessons and household matters, 8 hours' sleep, and 8 hours of dressing, walks, parties and enjoyment. While Idanna is getting ready with the help of the maid, Miss Stangher shall help me and these two hours a day will be included in the total of the 16 hours indicated above.

If Miss Stangher should also wish to devote time to the lace school it will only be as a volunteer, for she will never be asked to do so.

On holidays, the lessons shall be on the catechism and the holy Gospel, and also on history, but the program for this has not yet been drafted.

Her studies are designed to prepare Idanna for two great roles in life, that of mother and protector of the home and the community, and that of educator in shaping the new generation. These are the woman's roles.

People of all backgrounds and origins are moved and inspired by music. For this reason, music is more important than exercise and perfection of the body.

Equally important is domestic economy which I will teach her along with her tutor, and that is, economy as the secret of leading a refined life without waste, while helping as many people as possible with the surplus from the table, of clothing, and of our daily comforts.

The four modern languages: I can take care of Italian and English, while French and German need to be learnt as a way of understanding the character of the predominant modern nations. Latin must be studied for access to the sources of Western civilization, and it is the language of the prayers and liturgy in the Catholic religion.

Writing and spelling in the four main languages must be correct and this is achieved by dictating the nations' geography and history.

The history of France must not be studied in Italian just as the history of Germany must not be studied in French. This would only cause confusion. If a country's history cannot be studied through its language, then the easier rule is to read its best authors in translation.

I would like next year to be devoted to the study of ancient and modern geography and the history of the populations along with perfecting languages. This will be followed by historical deductions and the fostering of a humanitarian spirit.

When one encounters an event or scientific fact whose meaning is unknown, the lesson shall be interrupted in order to look it up in the encyclopaedia and briefly examine the question.

I want the study of book-keeping – which is necessary – to replace the study of mathematics. If dear Miss Stangher or myself are not able to do the teaching, then we shall call in teachers or Idanna will attend courses in Rome.

Technical drawing must also be a subject of study. Afterwards, at the age of 18, when she has completed all the subjects, Idanna will be able to spend more time on the fine arts of music and painting.

But first of all, she must aim at becoming a useful woman, and only after that amusing and decorative.

I shall teach both Idanna and Miss Stangher to type, an essential skill in modern education.

And next winter in Rome, all three of us together shall take lessons in shorthand, equally necessary for the modern woman.

The history schedule and the program for this summer is to be drafted by Professor Cinguini, while the music program will be decided by the music teacher, Miss Gui. The rest of the schedule will depend on Miss Stangher.

When Cora was closely supervising her daughter's unusual education so that my grandmother would become a useful member of society as well as a citizen of the world, ten long years had passed since the dramatic events in New York City that had led Cora to play a pivotal role in a battle for justice against the American establishment.

4.6 Against the Death Penalty

In 1895, a young immigrant from Southern Italy, Maria Barbella, was tried and convicted in New York of murdering the man who promised eternal love, but then drugged and raped her. Maria would have been the first woman to die in America in the newly invented electric chair if Cora had not sailed from Europe to come to her rescue after reading about the case in *The New York Times*, which arrived regularly in Brazzà. Cora was an activist at heart and could not sit back in the face of grave social injustice. This trial of a defenceless, illiterate twenty-two-year-old Italian woman convicted by a court completely governed by men was deeply troubling for her. Yes, in those days, the entire court from the jury to the lawyers and judges, were all men.

The question of capital punishment had never before been publicly debated in the United States, where owning a gun was—and still is—seen as a divine right. However, Cora was inherently a forward-thinking, non-violent progressive, with a mind of her own even regarding the death penalty. She quickly managed to find the only two lawyers in New York who agreed with her stance against legalised state executions. She hired them, and courageously launched the first national campaign against capital punishment.

With her great marketing and public relations skills, Cora mobilised Manhattan's tabloid press and high society on behalf of Maria's cause. She was not alone in her efforts. One woman, Mrs. Rebecca Foster, became Cora's close ally. She was known as the 'Angel of the Tombs' because of her regular visits to the infamous city prison of New York, where men and women awaited trial (Devins 1902).

Famous suffragettes such as Elisabeth Cady Stanton and Susan B. Anthony spoke at rallies organised across the country, joined by such gentlemen as the noted public intellectual Robert Ingersoll and the magnate Austin Corbin who voiced their support for Maria Barbella.[17]

However, Cora had no idea that the powerful inventor Thomas Edison had aligned his forces against the young woman, and Cora herself. As the electric chair could be powered only with the AC current of his rival

[17] Elisabeth Cady Stanton (1815–1902) was a leader of the women's rights movement in the U.S. Susan B. Anthony (1820–1906) was an American women's rights activist. Robert Green Ingersoll (1833–1899) was an American lawyer and writer. Austin Corbin (1827–1896) was an American banking and railroad entrepreneur.

Westinghouse, the future of Edison's DC direct current in America would benefit from Maria's execution. By using the more powerful current to electrocute the young Italian woman, Edison hoped to provoke fear and terror in the public and secure for the Edison Electric Light Company, the national monopoly on electricity.

This dramatic story which was on the front pages of the major American newspapers in 1895–1896 had been completely buried by the passing of time or perhaps even deliberately. I came across it by chance in a small booklet, printed on recycled paper, written by Cora's husband Detalmo, my great-grandfather. And this discovery, as I mentioned before, led to my book *The Lady of Sing Sing*. More importantly, it led to Cora's emergence from the tragic silence and anonymity that had been imposed by her terrible illness, which struck suddenly in 1906 when she was only 'halfway through the journey of her life'.[18]

4.7 The Flag of Peace

When I think of Cora's contribution to the first international peace movement, when I think of her creativity as a businesswoman, not to mention her artistic and literary bent—they seemed to exist to serve others, to 'educate' the new generations in peace, love of craftsmanship and in respect for nature and every living thing.

In her novel, *Ampharita: An American Idyll* (Slocomb 1897b), Cora introduces us to the world of the indigenous Pima people of the Sierra Madre. She was convinced that their wisdom and profound knowledge of nature was endangered by the unchecked advance of modernity. With perfect insight, Cora describes culture as an extraordinary treasure and conveys its importance for the future.

And it was the image of Cora, in the isolation in which she was forced to live for thirty-seven years until her death, that accompanied me to Geneva when I entered the League of Nations building. I was there to look up some documents from the first international movement for peace

[18] Her illness was diagnosed as Morbo of Paget—an osteoporosis of the bones—which, in her case, apparently had affected her cranium. We will never know for sure, but she did suffer from excruciating headaches that no painkiller could alleviate and which came and went frequently. When this happened, she would completely lose her mind and sense of being, time and place. So, she had to live under constant supervision in special clinics, far from home.

and disarmament (The Union for Universal Peace) of which I knew Cora had been a constant, active member.

After all, the Quaker principles of non-violence and peace were deeply embedded in her heart and mind. Cora had been raised by her Quakeress mother, Abigail Day Slocomb, with those foundational beliefs that were later manifested in her numerous social activities.

I could now physically lay my hands on the files that bear her name. It was this movement that gave birth to the League of Nations. The historical archive contains Cora's correspondence with Elie Ducommun, the Swiss founder of the first peace movement, from 1897 until his death in 1905. Of this apostle of peace, Giovanni Bovio wrote:

> He is a, shining mirage for humanity that brings together all those who would like to see the fearsome political organizations – namely, those organizations that can only survive by invading, conquering and killing – replaced by human unity, benevolent peace, public law that can be broken by neither the anarchic's dagger, nor the executioner's blade, nor the soldier's musket.[19]

It seemed as if Cora, along with the first champions of peace, had already had the foreboding of the two future world wars with their millions of dead.

In 1897, shortly after a visit to the Red Cross headquarters in Geneva, Cora felt compelled to design a flag of peace. She knew well the power of visual symbols and strongly believed that peace workers needed a single image to represent their work. Cora wrote:

> The Longing for Universal Peace and the desire that disagreements be settled by arbitration instead of fighting grows daily.
>
> Many societies have been organized to propagate the principles of peace, which are at the foundations of religion as well as of progress and national prosperity.
>
> At Berne, Switzerland, is situated an International Peace Bureau, which has branches and secretaries in the chief cities of the world. An International Congress for Peace and Arbitration is held yearly in one or another of the capital cities where peace associations flourish.

[19] Idanna Pucci Archive.

In consequence, arbitration has achieved good work and many arbitration treaties exist.

Peace societies uniformly teach the universal brotherhood of man; as yet, however, no universal banner has been created to rally all races and creeds, no universal badge has been selected to identify the members of a militia for peace.

The necessity for such a banner and badge, and the impetus which they must give to the universal peace movement and international organization, cannot be overestimated. Individual, distinctive, unsectarian, both in color and design, to avoid arousing religious and political prejudices, it must contain the symbols of all for which it stands and be adopted without delay by all peace associations and peace seekers.[20]

Cora was aware of an earlier idea for a peace flag proposed in 1891 by Henri Pettit, a member of the peace movement. Pettit suggested placing a white border around each nation's flag, and then adding the word 'Peace'. But Cora was not convinced.

In her view, this would result in as many peace flags as national flags—and bind each citizen to their state, not the peace movement. Instead, she envisaged a single, universal symbol of peace, one that could transcend national identity and communicate the cosmopolitan values intrinsic in peace work.

She imagined the flag fluttering in the wind above the words: *Pro Concordia Labor* (I Work for Peace) with three colours: yellow, purple and white. Her design would be unique and impossible to be confused with any national flag. Cora described her flag's symbolism with these words:

The tricolor, like the triangle, is emblematic of liberty, unity and fraternity, as the THREE throughout all time has stood in religion for Divine Love, Absolute Wisdom, Universal Harmony, and in nature for Air, Earth and Water.

[20] Cora's words were published as a flier with the following footnote at the bottom. 'All interested will kindly address 'The Peace Flag', care of Le Bureau Internationale de la Paix, Berne, Suisse; 'The Peace Flag', care of American Secretary of International Peace Bureau, 619 F Street, Northwest, Washington D.C.; 'The Peace Flag', care of L. Prang & Co., Publishers, 286 Roxbury Street, Boston, Mass. From whom and all booksellers these cards can be obtained for five cents each and postage'. Cora's description of the Peace Flag's symbolism was on the back of the flier.

The flag, therefore, which symbolizes all these must be a tricolor, composed of yellow, purple, and white.

YELLOW, because this is the color of active love, of energy, and of creative paternal force, attributes of the sunlight, ripeness and plenty.

PURPLE, because this is the color of triumph achieved through constancy, self-sacrifice and perseverance, which are feminine or maternal attributes.

WHITE, because this is the color of innocence and purity, attributes of the young and inexperienced.

These emblematic colors are placed to illustrate the development of humanity. The child spirit (white) first appears sustained by the mother spirit (purple), for the innocent must learn through patient teaching that self-sacrificing spirit which mediates between the weak and the strong, creating endurance, the source of aspiration, the crest of Universal Peace; while the paternal element (yellow), with its power and will, holds humanity to the blue staff of promise and fidelity of purpose.

The Star of Destiny caps the flagstaff and occupies the exalted position in the crest upon the central field of the flag. The soaring wings of a dove sustain the hands of a man and a woman, clasped above the shield, destined for the national arms or the devices of each society. The crest is emblematic of that friendly cooperation in labor and aspiration which raises humanity from individualism and self-seeking brutishness to mutual benevolence and universal equity.

The motto *Pro Concordia Labor* (I work for Peace) may be placed upon the flag beneath the shield, or on one of the white streamers from the flagstaff, with the motto of a nation or society on the other.

These were visionary thoughts in an age governed by mutually hostile colonial empires, when populations were divided and subjected to a policy inspired by social Darwinism—that is, the survival of the strongest and most powerful.

In spring 1897, Cora wrote to Elie Ducommun in a rough type-written copy some thoughts prior to the first peace convention to be held in Mystic, Connecticut the following August:

All the world's young at school learn far too many stories of war and massacres and too little about the arts and sciences or the inventions that have benefited humanity, but above all they learn little or nothing about the triumph of humanitarian principles. We must try – individually and collectively – to convince the mothers, the teachers and the citizens of the world to train the young in the rules of harmony and the practice

> of justice and also to love and defend the Peace Flag to strengthen the bond of fraternity and universal solidarity towards every creed, nationality or color, as the symbol of what is noblest in life.[21]

Then a few months later, on July 28, in another letter to Decommun, Cora said,

> To manage to achieve peace externally, one must have peace in the soul and goodness in the heart. That is why we composed the *seven rules of harmony* which are accessible to all those who can read, and which should be translated into different languages.[22]

The Peace Flag designed by Cora was first unfurled on August 27, 1897, at the 31st International Universal Peace Union convention in Mystic, Connecticut. The gathering took place in a grove situated on a hill over Mystic, where a Peace Temple had been erected that could hold one thousand people. Leading pacifists of the world came together and drafted the first Manifesto of Human Rights.[23]

Ironically, just five miles away from Mystic, in Stonington, Cora had spent many holidays as a child, as it was the ancestral home of her maternal family. Cora's beloved grandfather, James Ingersoll Day, had passed away just before the Mystic peace meeting, and her mother had returned there to live after selling her home in New Orleans.

Two months later, on October 27, the Peace flag was adopted by the U.S. chapter of the International Council of Women which appointed Cora to be the Chair of the Committee on Peace and Arbitration.[24] When the great women's rights leader, Susan B. Anthony, first saw the flag, she was moved and spoke of its connection to the profound relationship between one's inner world and peace work. She laid her hand on

[21] Idanna Pucci Archive.

[22] Idanna Pucci Archive.

[23] The text of this Manifesto is hauntingly similar to Cora's philosophy, and she surely had a hand in its drafting. Half a century later, in 1948, the message and words may well have served as the foundation of the *Universal Declaration of Human Rights,* which is the landmark document of the United Nations.

[24] In 1899, the flag was also adopted by The International Peace Bureau in Bern, Switzerland.

her breast and said 'the first person to begin this work of peace is right here'.[25]

During this time, Cora developed a strong bond with the Austro-Bohemian pacifist and author, Baroness Bertha von Suttner, who affectionately called her *friedensschwester* or 'peace sister'. Bertha dedicated her life to promoting peace and she often spoke publicly about the evolution of the human species.

'Humanity develops upward' she would say. 'We are called to hasten the development of a higher and more fortunate type of human being'. Cora's flag mirrored Bertha's sentiments.

During a financially difficult moment in her life, Bertha worked briefly as a secretary in Paris for the Swedish inventor, Alfred Nobel. She quickly realised that all of Nobel's vast wealth came from his manufacturing of dynamite and other deadly weapons. This she could not bear. Bertha spoke her mind and told Mr. Nobel that she could no longer work for him and left. However, she kept an ongoing correspondence with him until his death in 1896. Bertha certainly awoke Nobel's conscience. It may well be that she inspired Nobel to include a peace prize in his philanthropic legacy.

Bertha later became famous, not only for her extraordinary peace work, but also for her career as a writer and particularly for her book *Die Waffen Nieder!* (Lay Down Your Arms) (von Suttner 1889/1892), which was translated into 12 languages. In 1905, she was awarded the Nobel Peace Prize, the second recipient after Marie Curie.

Cora tried to take part every year in the meeting at Mystic. She became a strong presence on the American democratic scene in her role as President of the Committee on Peace and Arbitration of the International Council of Women, also for the issue of the fight against the death penalty and the campaign she started in 1895. The numerous other campaigns that followed over the years—also after Cora's withdrawal from public life—were crucial in the United Nations' stance against capital punishment which then resulted in the UN resolution for a global moratorium in 2007, to which many countries gave their support.

Finally, again in 2007, the United Nations issued the resolution on the *Declaration on the Rights of Indigenous Peoples*. Four countries voted against it: United States, Canada, Australia and New Zealand, that is,

[25] Idanna Pucci Archive.

the very countries that have committed crimes against indigenous populations. But the seed sowed by Cora has borne fruit after no less than 112 years.

From Rome, on December 19th 1906, shortly after Elie Ducommun's death, Cora wrote in French to his widow:

> Allow me in the name of my family and of the many women and children who in the future will benefit from the pacifist education that would never have come about if your beloved husband had not opened the way .... That God may console you and that each tear you shed may be a rose to embody your husband's work, so that it may survive, grow and become ever stronger.[26]

The letter, bearing Cora's tired signature, was not hand-written by her, but by the person to whom she was forced to dictate. The letter ends with these words:

> These foundation stones of humanity can be buried and even forgotten, but the strength they give the building and its resistance against the storm will continue all the same.[27]

Without realising it, Cora had put all of herself into those words. In fact, a few months later, she too bid the world adieu, forever.

Her tragic fate not only turned her life upside down but perhaps had even more serious consequences than those caused for instance by a deadly road accident—because she remained alive but was no longer 'herself'. And as a result, many families in Friuli fell back into poverty or ended up emigrating to Argentina or the United States because their life depended on Cora's social commitment and her untiring, dynamic spirit. And with her absence, all the things to which she had worked so hard, not only in Italy but also in America, little by little ceased to exist. Perhaps, that is why I always try to keep in mind the terrible solitude in which Cora had to live from 1906 until she died in 1944. In this way I feel that I am giving meaning to her life as a whole, respecting her also for that part of her destiny that was so unjust, bringing out her ideas and somehow conjuring her back to life.

[26] Idanna Pucci Archive.

[27] Idanna Pucci Archive.

That day, in the spring of 2007, while I was immersed in the discovery of Cora's correspondence with Elie Decommun and her role in the first peace movement, how could I have known that the Flag of Peace, which she conceived and designed, would eventually bring Cora back to life in the most meaningful and permanent way?

The *Pro Concordia Labor* Peace flag, so actively connected to the Peace Movement before WWI, was dormant for decades. But on August 27, 2013, it was suddenly awakened in the Netherlands. The flag was unfurled in a ceremony to celebrate Cora's 'peace sister' Bertha von Suttner that coincided with the centenary of the Peace Palace in The Hague. Bertha's legacy in women's rights, peace and international law had links with the Peace Palace. In 2014, one hundred years after Bertha's death, Cora's flag was put on display at the permanent Bertha von Suttner exhibition at her former castle in Harmannsdorf, Austria.

But there is more. Cora's peace flag is now intimately connected with Central Michigan University in America because of its eminent former President E. C. Warriner, who was very active in the peace movement throughout his life (1866–1945). Beginning in 2015, each year in May, the flag is raised on Peace Day in front of Warriner Hall.

In 2017, it served to commemorate the U.S. entry into World War I—which was supposed to end all wars. In 2017, it also marked the 23rd anniversary of the Rwandan genocide, a watershed moment that contributed to the birth of the International Criminal Court in The Hague. In April 2018, the flag was unfurled on the 50th anniversary of the assassination of Martin Luther King; and the following year, to celebrate the anniversary of Gandhi's birth as the champion of *satyagraha* or 'Truth Force' which inspired Dr. King.

4.8 Conclusion

I want to close this ode to Cora by sharing the wonderful news of the Cora di Brazzà Foundation. In 2019, Dr. Hope Elizabeth May, an American philosopher and lawyer whose work is centred on peace and education, established the foundation which grew organically from the Bertha von Suttner Project in connection with the 100th anniversary of the Peace Palace in the Hague, Netherlands.

Cora's flag has become the symbol of education about peace activism, serving to celebrate and remember historic activists of the global peace movement. Every time her 'Pro Concordia Labor' flag is raised somewhere in today's world, she is remembered and her name lives on.

Appendix: Timeline of the life of Cora Slocomb Savorgnan di Brazzà

1862
Born in New Orleans on January 7th at the height of the Civil War. Only daughter of the Confederate Captain, Cuthbert Harrison Slocomb and Abigail Day, a quakeress from a wealthy Connecticut family.

1873
Her father dies on January 1st at only 42 years of age during rescue operations in one of the many New Orleans floods. He was a prominent personality and esteemed philanthropist.

1881
Crowned New Orleans Queen of Carnival.

1883
Cora is admitted to the prestigious Munich Academy of Art where she studies under Frank Duvenek, the well-known American painter from Ohio.

1887
In Rome she meets Detalmo, one of the fifteen children of Ascanio Savorgnan di Brazzà and Giacinta Simonetti.

Marries Detalmo in New York on October 18th. Cora lives between Rome and the Castle of Brazzà in Friuli.

1888
Birth on December 18th of Idanna, Cora and Detalmo's only child.

1891
She sets up the first lace school at the Castle of Brazzacco. Six more schools follow in surrounding towns.

Opening of the first toy workshop, supported by the Queen Mother (which will continue until 1918).

First local agricultural show, involving seven municipalities. First toy display. This would be repeated for fifteen years.

Elie Decommun from Switzerland founds the first movement for peace and disarmament (*The Union of Universal Peace*) with which Cora collaborated all her life.

1892
The Fagagna lace school becomes public, thanks to the support of Senator Gabriele Luigi Pecile.

Maria Barbella a young woman from Lucania disembarks in New York (one of the 247 Italians emigrating abroad that year). The girl would later become the first woman sentenced to death on the electric chair.

1893
The lace cooperatives are attended by 150 pupils (60 at Fagagna; 25 at Brazzacco; 25 at Martignacco and 20 at San Vito di Fagagna).

At the International Exposition of Chicago, the Brazzà lace is awarded the gold medal.

Publication of Cora's book, *A Guide to Old and New Lace in Italy* (Slocomb 1893).

1895
Cora travels to New York to start the first campaign against the death penalty in an attempt to save young Maria Barbella, a victim of rape, domestic abuse and abandonment, from the electric chair. Cora provides defense lawyers for Maria who appeal against the death sentence. Cora launches the first campaign against capital punishment to raise awareness among the American public for the cause of the poor immigrant, a victim of domestic abuse who was seduced and abandoned.

1896
Maria Barbella is granted the right to appeal.

Publication of Cora's play, *A Literary Farce* (Slocomb 1896)

1897
Publication of *Ampharita: An American Idyll* (Slocomb 1897b).

Draws up, for her daughter's tutor Inetta Stangher, *Program for the education of Idanna*, a true work of the art of pedagogy.

August: Cora is a delegate for the American Council of Women at the first peace convention at Mystic, Connecticut.

She designs the first peace flag.

The flag becomes the symbol of the International Universal Peace Union.

1899
The Peace Flag is adopted by The International Peace Bureau in Berne, Switzerland.

1900
The lace cooperatives win two gold medals at the Great Universal Exposition in Paris.

1903
Creation of the Italian Female Industries (IFI). Cora is elected President.

At the International Exposition in Udine, the work of the Friulian lacemakers is awarded two gold medals.

Points of sale for the lace open in America: in New York, St. Louis, Baltimore, Philadelphia, Washington and New Orleans.

1904
Wins an award at the International Exposition in London.

She travels to Germany with Idanna and Inetta Stangher to visit toy factories at Nuremberg and Sonnenberg.

1905
Calabria earthquake: she brings aid to the affected population.

At Montenapoleone Calabro she establishes the first cooperative in the south.

International Exposition of in Liege, Belgium.

Exposition in Udine of the toys created in the workshops founded by Cora.

Elie Decommun dies in Berne.

1906
Exposition of IFI products in Milan. The pavilion is destroyed by fire, and only the catalogue (Anonymous 1906) is saved. On that occasion, the toys were exhibited as well.

In Bologna, on her return journey from Calabria, Cora falls seriously ill. She becomes a patient of the avantgarde psychiatrist, Dr. Cesare Ferrari, with whom Detalmo forms a close friendship which will later continue with Idanna and family. From Bologna, Cora is taken first to Imola, then Forlì and finally to Villa Giuseppina in Rome, her final residence.

1907
Death of Giacinta Savorgnan di Brazzà, Cora's mather-in-law.

1908
International Exposition in Copenhagen and Vicenza.

Closure of the lace schools. The schools become independent under the guidance of Angelica Marcuzzi, who continues them in Cora's memory.

1914
August: Marriage of Idanna Savorgnan di Brazzà to the cavalry officer, Giuseppe Pirzio Biroli at the Castle of Brazzà.

1916
In Udine the first exhibition of Italian toys is held.

Zurich, 6 December: death of Cora's mother, Abby Day Slocomb.

1917
In Venice, 75 toys manufactured at Fagagna are exhibited.

A fire destroys the villa in Brazzà, along with all the furnishings from the New Orleans house where Cora grew up. Also lost is the huge library, her diaries and her correspondence.

1920
December 13th, Detalmo dies at Brazzà.

1921
The Brazzà school, located at Santa Margherita del Gruagno, closes down after thirty years and all the materials and equipment are donated to Naomi Nigris, the head of the School of Fagagna, where she continues to teach until 1960.

1923
The Brazzà villa—inherited by Idanna—is rebuilt on a plan by Provino Valle, a well-known architect from Udine.

1927
Cora appears to have improved so it is decided that she can come back to Brazzà. She is well for six months but then worsens and she is brought back to Villa Giuseppina in Rome.

1940
January 31st: Cora's daughter, Idanna, dies of myocarditis and is buried in the little cemetery of Santa Margherita near Brazzà.

1944
August 24th: Cora dies in Rome, and is buried in the family tomb in the Verano cemetery.

2017
Publication in Italy of the new edition of *La Signora di Sing Sing* written by Cora's great-granddaughter, Idanna Pucci, with a preface by Edgar Morin (Pucci 2017).

2019
Creation of the Fondazione Cora di Brazzà under the auspices of the Central Michigan University and the Peace Palace Library in The Hague, Netherlands, thanks to Prof. Hope Elizabeth May.

2020
Publication in America of the new edition of *The Lady of Sing Sing: An American Countess, an Italian Immigrant and their Epic Battle for Justice* (Pucci 2020).

References

Devins, John B. 1902. The Angel of the Tombs. A Tribute to Mrs. Rebecca Salome Foster. *New York Observer*, 28 August, 283–286.

Pucci, Idanna. 2017. *La Signora di Sing Sing*. Florence: Libreria Editrice Fiorentina.

Pucci, Idanna. 2020. *The Lady of Sing Sing: An American Countess, and Italian Immigrant, and Their Epic Battle for Justice in New York's Gilded Age*. New York: Simon & Schuster.

Saccavini, Chiara. 2014. *Storie di viole: come un piccolo fiore può influenzare il mondo*. Tricase: Youcanprint.

Sestito, Maria. 2008. Cora Slocomb: cose utili e arti gentili In *Friuli Venezia Giulia: artisti & artigiani nella terra dell'oro*, ed. Luigi Vitale, 73–79. Pavarolo: Coffee Table Books.

Slocomb, Cora. 1893. *A Guide to Old and New Lace in Italy*. Chicago: Conkey.

Slocomb, Cora. 1894. *A Celebration of Women Writers. 'The Italian Woman', by Countess Cora Ann Slocomb di Brazzà Savorgnan (1862–)*. In *The Congress of Women: Held in the Woman's Building, World's Columbian Exposition, Chicago, U.S.A.*, ed. Mary Kavanaigh Oldham Eagle, 697–703. Chicago: Monarch Book Company.

Slocomb, Cora. 1896. *A Literary Farce*. Boston: Arena.

Slocomb, Cora. 1897a. *The Human and Urgent Side of the Tariff Question*. New York: Andrew Kellogg Press.

Slocomb, Cora. 1897b. *Ampharita: An American Idyll*. New York: Peace Bureau.

Slocomb, Cora. 1900. *Notes on the Origin and Progress of the Cooperative Lace Schools of Brazzà*. S. Daniele: Pellarini.

Slocomb, Cora. 1906. Introduzione in *Ricordo dell'esposizione di Milano: 1906*. Milan: Rocca.

Soldi, Manuela. 2017. Before Italian Fashion: Textile Craftsmanship in Italy (1861–1911). In *Fashion Through History: Costumes, Symbols, Communication*, ed. Giovanna Motta and Antonello Biagini, vol. II, 21–30. New Castle upon Tyne: Cambridge Scholars Publishing.

Tennyson, Alfred. 1829/1842. Oeone In *Poems*, vol. I. London: Moxon.

Toppazzini Tondello, Mariangela, ed. 2002. *Cora Slocomb di Brazzà Savorgnan*. Moruzzo: Auser.

von Suttner, Bertha. 1889/1892. *Lay Down Your Arms*. London: Longmans, Greed.

PART II

From Generation to Generation: A Case Study

CHAPTER 5

Harriet Luthrop Dunham and Carolina de Viti de Marco: Emancipation Through Lacemaking

Elena Laurenzi

5.1 Introduction

This chapter is based almost exclusively on primary sources. It reconstructs the history of a political and social project created by two sisters-in-law belonging to the enlightened, progressive aristocracy and united by the philanthropic vision of early twentieth-century feminism: Harriet Lathrop Dunham and Carolina de Viti de Marco. In 1901, they set up a lacemaking school affiliated to the Italian Female Industries (IFI) in Casamassella, a small town in the Italian deep south. Its objective was to promote women's economic emancipation and political citizenship through the practice and development of traditional crafts.

E. Laurenzi (✉)
University of Salento, Lecce, Italy

E. Laurenzi and M. Mosca (eds.), *A Female Activist Elite in Italy (1890–1920)*, https://doi.org/10.1007/978-3-030-87159-8_5

5.2 The Political Philanthropy of Etta de Viti de Marco

The Marchioness Etta de Viti de Marco, in addition to being known for her economic and political writings and her joint work with her husband Antonio de Viti de Marco (see Chapter 2), was also a noted activist in the early twentieth-century Italian women's movement. She was one of the first signatories of the petition for women's suffrage presented to the Italian Parliament in 1906; even though this was rejected, it provoked widespread debate in both the political institutions and in civil society. She was also among the founders of the National Council of Italian Women (CNDI), an important body affiliated to the International Council of Women (Greetings 2000; Gubin et al. 2005), which brought together the main national feminist associations (Taricone 1996; Buttafuoco 1997). In this context, she mainly devoted herself to philanthropic initiatives aimed at improving women's economic, social and cultural conditions. Her most outstanding and original contribution to feminism was in the field of political philanthropy, which she helped expand both through her practical projects and her theoretical contributions. This link between feminism and pro-women economic initiatives was the common feature of a wide circle of American and English wives of Italian aristocrats, among whom we find such memorable figures as Romeyne Robert del Sorbello, Alice Hallgarten Franchetti (see Chapter 3) and Cora Slocomb di Brazzà (see Chapter 4). In fact, this group was largely responsible for shifting Catholic charity and female compassionate work models still prevailing in Italy towards the modern welfare state and benefits policies aimed at developing the potential of aid recipients (Fossati 2010). Etta de Viti de Marco was thus a key figure, not only because her initiatives transcended the private sphere to become institutional or semi-institutional (as in the office for coordinating aid projects in Rome, discussed below), but also because her keen intelligence led her to research and take an in-depth look at the theoretical and political foundations of the social security system.

In 1904, she set up the Information Office and Guide to Charity, which she saw as a sort of modern 'help desk', that is, as 'the centre for provision of support and the fulcrum firstly for orientation and then for coordination of all the various forms of charity' (Anonymous 1907a: 291).[1] The aims of the Office were clearly stated: for the benefactors,

[1] Unless stated otherwise, the translations of quoted texts are our own.

it was to inform and orient, suggesting the most suitable form of help, and if necessary, to offer mediation for a more effective and secure allocation of donations; for the beneficiaries, in addition to distributing the sums and goods collected, the Office was to direct the needy towards the appropriate institutions, implementing the processes necessary to satisfy appeals and requests for financial support, work, etc. (280). To complete the task, Etta saw to the compiling of a 'Guida romana della beneficienza, assistenza, istruzione, previdenza, mutualità' (Guide to charity, support, education, social security, and mutuality in Rome), which was published in the *Bulletin of the National Council of Italian Women* as 'a first, firm step towards the rational coordination of the thousand charity works proliferating in our city' (293). Once the early scepticism was overcome, her initiative found wholehearted support[2] and even international resonance, with the *New York Times* of July 24, 1910, devoting an article to it, highlighting the activity that today we call microcredit (Anonymous 1910a); it was also reported in the *Oakland Tribune* (Anonymous 1910b) and *Le Figaro* (Anonymous 1912).

She explained her ideas in the report she presented to the first congress of the National Council of Italian Women in Rome in 1908, where she was President of the Assistance and Prevention section (Frattini 2008). Speaking to an audience of feminist activists and interested male politicians, she had the opportunity to put forward her innovative vision of social assistance, distancing herself from both the Christian charity model and state paternalism (De Viti de Marco 1908). Her approach, in contrast, was derived from the Anglo-Saxon notion of self-help, while at the same time she stripped the 'hard' American version of its individualism, pursuit of the myth of success and faith in indefinite growth: individual freedom was an essential and non-negotiable part of her thinking. She was not prepared to sacrifice or downplay this principle, as was partially the case in some contemporary social assistance bodies (for example, those of the powerful Italian Women's Union), always on the verge of becoming *apparati* for social discipline (Pieroni Bortolotti 1975; Buttafuoco 1986, 1988; Imprenti 2012). This faith in individual liberty and the uniqueness of every person inclined her towards forms of self-organisation of society that were rooted in individual effort and the

[2] See E. W. Wakefield (1907); Anonymous (1907b: 657); see also Gori (2003).

cultivation of personal relationships, running counter to the depersonalisation of bureaucratic state intervention. In her presentation, Etta de Viti de Marco distinguished between the 'real poor' who were unable to earn enough to improve their position and those only temporarily in need. In the former case, she argued that private initiative should not be sacrificed to the state's interventions, since individual endeavour, sustained by feeling, was for her 'the specific condition ensuring that the functions of social assistance attributed to the state do not become fossilised in the formalities of an indifferent bureaucracy' (1908: 630). She also contended that the social assistance system degenerated when it was not kept in the public eye, either because employers tended to reduce wages to recover what they had paid in taxes, or because 'it is difficult to find a method of aiding the poor which in some way or to some extent does not have the effect of preserving their poverty' (631). She was aware of the rising unemployment in the context of the rapid economic and industrial development of the times and insisted on the need for initiatives promoting autonomy and reemployment, particularly advocating more craft and trade schools providing 'a general toolkit of manual skills and intellectual knowledge that [...] would ease the transition from one trade to another' (626). As far as minors and the elderly were concerned, she rejected refuges that imposed 'painful limitations on liberty' and recommended social prevention since, in contrast to assistance, it would ensure the maintenance of 'individuality' and 'personal independence' among the elderly (629).

5.3 The Italian Female Industries

Etta de Viti de Marco was an expert collector of lace and worked with the Italian Female Industries (IFI) in various areas: researching old techniques and patterns, training workers and commercialising the finished products. Her contribution was essential to the internationalisation of the enterprise since, thanks to her, the Italian experience spread to America and, as we will see in the next chapter, to South Africa. She worked particularly hard to promote IFI products in her native USA where she still enjoyed an extensive network of contacts. To this end, she collaborated actively with another important figure in the history of Italian political philanthropy, Carolina Amari (1866–1942). Daughter of the Sicilian historian and patriot Michele Amari, public education minister in Italy after unification, Carolina Amari was particularly skilled in technical design and lacework and she was also a bold organiser and entrepreneur. She also initiated the renovation and reorganisation of the Ginori Conti Professional School in Florence,[3] and set up her own lacemaking school in the rural hamlet of Trespiano, in Tuscany (see Palomba 2009). In 1906, with the support of De Viti de Marco and Florence Colgate, daughter of the founder of the Colgate Company, she opened a lacemaking school in New York for young Italian women immigrants with the aim of helping them free themselves from the underpaid and humiliating jobs they were normally destined for. Etta worked with her in studying and selecting patterns and promoting and selling the products.

Etta de Viti de Marco's commitment to philanthropic lacemaking projects had in fact both preceded and inspired the founding of the IFI. At the beginning of the century she had already been involved in recovering and promoting lacemaking in disadvantaged areas of Italy. Working with another American woman, Minnie Luck, who would also later become an IFI patroness, she studied and subsequently relaunched on the market the traditional lacework of Pescocostanzo, a small village in the Abruzzo, a remote and underdeveloped region in Southern central Italy. Her 'inspiring work' was praised in an article by Romualdo Pantini for *Emporium*, one of the most prominent magazines in the sector. Pantini (1905) highlighted the economic, social and cultural value of Etta de Viti de Marco's endeavours to rescue once prestigious and profitable craft techniques from oblivion. He wrote:

> The lace industry is traditional in Abruzzo. There was a time, also in that happy period, the 15th century, when L'Aquila[4] lace rivalled that of Venice and Genoa. Now, it is once again being honoured by all thanks to the inspiring work of the Marchioness Etta de Viti de Marco, and the support and encouragement of our queens has crowned their achievement with recognition. (Pantini 1905: 391)

The article went on to explain that the lacemaking tradition was currently being preserved by women working at home, left on their own

[3] The Ginori are an ancient noble family from Florence. In 1891, the Marquis Carlo Ginori, at the head of a city committee, established a female school in Florence for the free teaching of manual professions which, in 1905, with the support and wishes of Queen Elena, became the Royal Female Professional School of Florence.

[4] L'Aquila is the capital city of Abruzzo.

'to maintain the work of both the hoe and the needle' as a consequence of the emigration of their menfolk. In this context, techniques were often passed on orally: 'Some women create lace without designs or guides, simply from memory, and for this reason this lace is called *loose* lace' (392).

Etta de Viti de Marco and Minnie Luck recorded and fixed the patterns and techniques used, ensuring their authenticity and facilitating their transmission. But their work also tended to bring the symbolic and cultural value of embroidery to the fore and to enhance its value. Etta de Viti de Marco's social skills and anthropological curiosity enabled her to obtain an in-depth understanding of the many facets and potentials of this ancient feminine art, especially through her personal contact with the lacemakers themselves, observing and studying their intimate relationship with their craft. Patini wrote:

> One countrywoman told the Marchioness de Viti, in her rough dialect, that a piece of lace or weaving was useless without the affection woven into it, and whoever has the vaguest memory of Ruskin's healthy ideas on the beauty of manual work cannot but be surprised by this amazing coincidence of thought at such a great distance. (400)

In an article published in the *Giornale d'Italia*, Etta de Viti de Marco herself spoke of her work, describing the poor peasant houses she visited to learn techniques and organise production. In the following passage she shows her keen understanding of the complexity of lacemaking in which the craftswomen invested a quality of care that surpassed mere mechanical execution, bringing together dreams, imagination, religious feeling and reverence for their forebears.

> Inside these houses where the cold of the long winter lends life the feeling of a sort of confinement, which it does not lose even in the short summer, we still find industrious, humble women who, rarely going out, live in a world apart, composed entirely of their work and its technical problems. They study these to try out new stitches, they work out how to retrace, from scraps of paper stored in some old chest, designs drawn by hands many years dead, where often an idea is scarcely signalled, and to fathom it, they need a deep affinity with the artistic feeling with which the figures were first created. For these women, wrapped in a medieval silence, lacemaking provides almost the sole outlet for their imagination and religious feeling. How many dreams are recorded in these pieces of embroidery!

> Here they study truth and beauty, and in their work for the church, they fashion the adored symbols with devoted hearts, they study them, they enter into them, bringing them to life with a mystical passion. (de Viti de Marco, cited in Patini 1905: 401)

5.4 Carolina de Viti de Marco: Freedom Gained

The philanthropic work of Etta de Viti de Marco was steadfastly supported by her sister-in-law Carolina. Carolina de Viti de Marco was the youngest of the four children of Raffaele de Viti de Marco and Lucia Troysi. Both her parents belonged to important families of the *haute bourgeoisie* and southern aristocracy. Raffaele de Viti de Marco (1832–1885) was the son of the unhappy marriage of Carolina Carluccio and Antonio de Viti Anguissola; his mother was a religious, straitlaced member of a rich landowning family, while his father was a man of revolutionary spirit and enlightened, liberal ideas, active among the Freemasons and Carbonari, and always in flight from persecution by the Bourbon monarchs, who governed the South before Italy was unified under the House of Savoy. From his earliest childhood, Raffaele's father had entrusted him to the care of his lover the Marchioness Costanza Palmieri de Marco di Lecce, who legally adopted him when he came of age, naming him heir to her titles and fortune. As part of this inheritance, Raffaele acquired the family seat in Casamassella, a small town near the sea at Otranto, where he set up a house after his marriage in 1854. His wife, Lucia Troysi (1832–1875), came from a family of prominent jurists. Her father, also named Antonio, had held important political posts, while her mother, Caroline Sutton of Molesey, was English, the daughter of an admiral. Lucia was of delicate health and died prematurely at the age of 43; yet, despite her physical fragility, she had a strong, energetic personality which left a deep mark on the family. A lover of books, reserved and not at all inclined towards the social world of the elite, she was, instead, 'open to all that was new and innately sensitive towards social issues', and gifted with a 'lively sensitivity towards the needs of her time and a deep interest in the sufferings of the people' (Chirilli 2010: 58). She was also a republican, an admirer of Mazzini and Garibaldi. She took on herself the education of her children, choosing their readings and bringing them up according to her own ideals. The letters written to her from school by the adolescent Antonio de Viti de Marco show to what extent she had influenced the political development of the future economist and parliamentary deputy.

He shared every book he read with her, vented his innate rebelliousness against privilege and authority, commented vividly on the political fortunes and misfortunes of the day, and discussed with her the principles that later informed his mature work.

Caroline, for her part, received the typical education reserved for the daughters of well-off families (Soldani 1989: xi). Unlike their brothers, neither she nor her elder sister Costanza attended high school or university but were taught by private tutors. Their education was just as rigorous as that of their male counterparts. Apart from music and French, core subjects in the education of upper-class girls, Lucia wished her daughters to learn English, her mother tongue, and ensured that their cultural education was broad and rich. During the long periods that her illness forced her to spend away from home, she sent them musical scores and books of literature, poetry and history (Chirilli 2016). The sisters took piano lessons and classes in calligraphy and read the classics in their original languages. After their mother's death, they were entrusted to the care of the Countess Amalia Gubiani Gallo, a noblewoman director of a Music School for young women.

Carolina de Viti de Marco had a lively, curious mind and was a voracious reader throughout her life. Among the documents preserved in her archive[5] there are diaries and notebooks where she took notes on her reading and copied verses, aphorisms and maxims, transcribing long passages and sharing them with her family and friends, with whom she kept up an intense correspondence. Among her letters, also kept in the family archive, there are particularly interesting exchanges with Adele Rossi, wife of the philosopher Benedetto Croce,[6] with whom Carolina shared a deep and lasting friendship built around books and intimate confessions. Another important correspondence was with her nephew Girolamo Comi, a poet and thinker, promoter of ambitious cultural enterprises such as the journal *L'Albero* and a publishing house, which marked the intellectual life of his region in the first half of the twentieth century, opening it up to a wider international landscape (Giannone et al. 2019). The poet found a willing listener in his 'Aunt Pitty' (the family nickname

[5] Archive Carolina de Viti de Marco and Giulia Starace, Le Costantine Foundation, Casamassella (Lecce).

[6] Benedetto Croce (1866–1952) is considered one of the most important figures in Italian cultural history. He was a philosopher, historian, politician, literary critic, and writer.

for Carolina), fascinated by history and full of curiosity for the cultural and literary scene. He regularly sent her news of his poetic and publishing activities and faithfully carried out the research in libraries and archives that she requested to satisfy her insatiable thirst for knowledge. Her friend Emilia Chirilli, in her memoirs, evokes the 'research into family history that Carolina (Pitty) pursued, requesting information from the relevant authorities and effective offices of cousins and friends', and describes her 'breathless wait for replies' even 'in her extremely lucid old age' (Chirilli 2010: 11). Carolina also wrote poetry, and with her solid background in the classics, her verses were neither ingenuous nor naive. Her versatile, pragmatic temperament also expressed itself in less intellectual pursuits; for example, she loved growing flowers, planning new plantings, importing rare species and experimenting with her plants. Emilia Chirilli called her 'a Georgic soul. She would plant trees everywhere [...]. She used to say that someone who had planted at least one tree has not lived in vain' (Chirilli 2016:16). Her influence is still evident in the estates that belonged to her where she made many structural reforms, sinking wells, laying paths to stop the land from slipping into the sea, and planting olive and fruit trees in groves laid out with an aesthetic sense that prefigured modern-day landscape design (see Chapter 6).

Although she had shown this vivacious and curious personality from childhood, not conforming to the prevailing nineteenth-century Italian model of feminine docility (De Giorgio 1988), after her mother's early death, Carolina de Viti de Marco also experienced the exactions of women's servitude, subjecting herself to it through her sense of responsibility but without conviction and with private bitterness. She remembered, for example, her services to her brothers when they were on holiday in Casamassella, when she was 'completely monopolised by their occupations and needs' (Carolina de Viti de Marco, *Annales*); she took care of her ageing father until he died and immediately after, cared for her elder sister, a hypochondriac; and with even greater affliction, she remembered consenting, against her wishes, to marry. The husband chosen for her by her brother Antonio, in his role as paterfamilias, was Francesco Starace, a doctor from a powerful shipowning family that exported low-grade olive oil to the USA, and who was politically active in the same party as the de Viti de Marco family. It was not a happy marriage and, as we learn from Caroline's diaries, her husband's bad temper sometimes led to violence. Carolina finally freed herself from this subjection to the patriarchal order at the age of sixty, when she secured a divorce, took back her own surname and returned to the castle of Casamassella with her daughter Giulia, administering her property and that of her brother Antonio with foresight and skill for the rest of her long life. She died, still in full command of her faculties, at the age of one hundred and two.

Carolina de Viti de Marco was a shy and independent person, and although she was much less in the public eye than her brother and sister-in-law, she nonetheless shared their ideals. While, unlike Etta de Viti de Marco, she was not active in the women's movement, her commitment to feminism was implicit in her firm belief in women's values and in a style of female freedom that was private but contagious, which guided her life, both in her personal choices and in the extraordinary network of female relationships that she wove across the dividing lines of class and age. Her house was a magnet for women of diverse social origins and ages, all drawn by her personality and example, and often even taken in by her in times of difficulty. In her diary she writes that one of her favourite laceworkers, five months after her marriage, 'seeing that things were not going well, came to live with us [...] and stayed for two years' (Carolina de Viti de Marco, *Annales*). Other co-workers from the school that she had set up (which we discuss below) became faithful companions, sharing their lives with her, accompanying her on her travels and participating in her research and social life. With her daughter Giulia, she created an extended family that included local peasant women, distant relations who had been orphaned at an early age, and young townswomen searching for an alternative model. Among these was the future Latinist Emilia Chirilli who, fascinated by Carolina's broad culture, spent her adolescence and much of her life in the palace at Casamassella, recording her experiences in her *Memoirs* and her biography of the young Antonio de Viti de Marco (Chirilli 2010, 2016).

At the age of eighty, Carolina wrote for her daughters and her niece what she called her *Annales* or memories of her personal and family life,[7] which clearly represent her non-ideological but embodied feminism. In these pages, she lays down her own story and the traces of her personality, shedding light on the events that led to the key decisions of her life and portraying her most independent and authoritative forebears in a powerful female genealogy. The dedication to her daughters Lucia and Giulia and her niece Costanza clearly illustrates her purpose of transmitting to her

[7] For *Annales* see Chapter 2, footnote 13.

heirs the meaning and strength of the female presence in the history of the family and in history in general.

Carolina's sensitivity to social issues and her strong inclination towards solidarity were drawn from the De Viti de Marco family culture. Her mother Lucia had passed on to her the republican values of equality, liberty and fraternity, and her father Raffaele, also republican and anti-Bourbon, would often offer his services as a lawyer free of charge. Emilia Chirilli recalls that in the family 'there was the fixed principle [of] reaching out to people, helping them to find themselves' to cultivate their own potential (Chirilli 2016: 23–24).

This family tradition of commitment to others did not take the form of aristocratic beneficence but was inspired by a vision of social development and assistance as the promotion of the autonomy and betterment of less advantaged people. This ideal of autonomy also informed their political and entrepreneurial advocacy of the South of Italy. During his time in Parliament, Antonio de Viti de Marco contested the social assistance policies put in place for the underdeveloped areas of the South, arguing instead for financial and fiscal measures that would spur economic development. In addition to being a politician and financial theorist, Antonio de Viti de Marco was also an enlightened entrepreneur, 'one of those aristocrats who work', in the words of Cora Slocomb di Brazzà (Pucci 2016). On his estates, he planted silk, tobacco and vines, new crops challenging both the latifundists' cereal monoculture and the state's protectionism, which favoured large-scale landed property. On one domain, 'Li Veli' at Cellino San Marco near Brindisi (Apulia, Italy), he created a cutting-edge winery where he experimented with innovative methods, immunising his vines from phylloxera by grafting them with American implants, introducing modern agricultural machinery and inventing new ways of cooling the must. He reinvested the entirety of this flagship winery's profits in modernisation, at the same time putting into practice the theories reflected in many of his political speeches: that the solution to the problems of the South was not to be found in state largesse but lay in its own hands.[8] This same outlook inspired Carolina and Etta de Viti de Marco's pioneering enterprise.

[8] See Antonio de Viti de Marco (2008); see also Cardini (1985), Pedone (1995), and Mosca (2016).

5.5 The Casamassella School: A Groundbreaking Project

In 1901, Etta and Carolina de Viti de Marco opened a lacemaking school where the 'old embroidery' techniques were taught. Located in the palace at Casamassella, the school had its origins in Carolina's volunteer work among the young women of the village, helping them to weave fabrics and lace for their dowries. On one visit to her sister-in-law, Etta was so shocked by the poverty of the local families that she decided to turn the charity asked of her (as a rich American who struck people's imagination) into a project aimed at fostering the economic and social autonomy of the local population, particularly the women. This initiative represented a decisive turn towards the 'industrial' development of lacemaking which, from being a wholly domestic and traditional activity, and tending to be unpaid and repetitive, became instead a source of profits, artistic experimentation and social transformation.

In Apulia at that time, needlework for commercial purposes was practised widely and intensively in foundations for poor young women (run mainly by nuns) and in the private houses of the agricultural population. As a result of the development of the market for needle lace, there was also an increase in activity in woven and bobbin lace, which was traditionally destined for family clothing and dowries, through commissions and the peasant women contributed to the family economy with the meagre earnings from their craft. However, as Lena Mauro Airoldi, another member of the IFI, wrote in 1906, needlework was not 'industrially organised'. The commercial rationalisation and planning of production were lacking, and the workers had no contractual rights:

> the girls, coming straight from school, individually take on private orders, for which the remuneration is relatively poor. There is no cooperative association, no hourly wage, to protect their class interests and to aid the intelligent, industrious and skilful worker. (Airoldi, cited in AA.VV. 1906: 228)

Etta and Carolina de Viti de Marco's project aimed to counter the isolation and vulnerability of the women workers by training them, organising production and promoting the products. Thanks to the IFI's powerful contacts, the Casamassella School grew exponentially throughout the first decade of the twentieth century. Figures for that year show 500 students training there: a remarkable number bearing in mind the school's remoteness (AA.VV. 1906: 232). In the same period, it became internationally known and its products were shown all over Europe, and it was awarded the gold medal at the Universal Exhibitions of Milan in 1906 and Brussels in 1910. In the IFI catalogue featuring photographs of the pieces chosen for the Milan Exhibition (all destroyed by a catastrophic fire[9]), published in 1908, there was a whole section devoted to the Casamassella School. The presentation is anonymous but in all likelihood it was the work of Etta and Carolina de Viti de Marco. When outlining the organisation of the school and listing its features and qualities, they stress the cross-class nature of the students. They write:

> The School does not make any distinctions in social class or provenance. [...] We take on students from families of landowners, factory workers, agricultural workers, and also a fourth class of people, those who can look back on a happier past but have fallen victim to the crisis of unemployment and want, and often suffer from hunger without complaining. [...] The School pays the entire price of the work completed, providing thread, fabric and all the necessary raw materials. All its expenses are borne by the founders. (AA.VV. 1906: 237)

The school had its legal head office in the Orsini Palace in Rome, Etta and Antonio's home. Carolina spent long periods there, leaving her family (and thus irritating her husband) in order to study and plan new projects with Etta. Together, they carried out research in museums and private collections, acquiring samples from antique dealers and exchanging lacecraft techniques with other experts and collectors. They created their own sampler, printed vouchers in the name of the school, and invented a motto, 'singing and loving', which became their letterhead. These trips also enabled Carolina to meet and develop friendships and collaborations with some of the most brilliant feminist activists and philanthropists of the time, all regular visitors to the de Viti household. Among these were Elisa Ricci (1858–1945), a highly cultured collector of lacework and the author of studies that were crucial to cataloguing and publicising it

[9] AA.VV. (1906: 232–237). In addition to descriptions and photographs of the pieces exhibited and a list of the local committees participating in the project, this book features brief descriptions of the current state of female industries throughout the Italian regions. The presentation of the Casamassella School appears, with no title or authorship indicated, in the section on Apulia (221–237).

(Ricci 1911; Bellomo 2002); the aforementioned Carolina Amari (1866–1942), founder of the previously mentioned Trespiano and New York Schools (Lovett 1906; Palomba 2009); Lina Bianconcini Cavazza (1861–1942), president of Aemilia Ars Crafts and Lace in Bologna, a pioneering enterprise due to the quality and experimental nature of its products (Bernardini et al. 2001); and Maria Ponti Pasolini (1856–1938), a prominent intellectual who wrote for the *Giornale degli Economisti*, author of historical study catalogues designed specifically for women, and founder of the di Coccolia School near Ravenna (Baruzzi 1996; Casalena 2003; Gori 2003).

5.6 A Modern Approach to Women's Professional Training

In the wake of the success of the Casamassella School, Carolina de Viti de Marco was also asked to run the feminine section of the Art School Applied to Industry at Maglie, Apulia, Southern Italy (Alessandri 1974). This school for craft workers was founded in 1881 by an art teacher, Egidio Lanoce (Caroli 2013). In his own way, Lanoce was also a pioneer: the Apulia region was completely lacking in initiatives of this type as there were only elementary schools and elite secondary schools there, but no professional schools. Accordingly, for a long time, the Maglie school was the only such training institute in the area (Panarese 1974, 1995). Lanoce's academy was also avant-garde when compared to government educational policies following the unification of Italy. The new Italian state had set out to organise the national education system of compulsory and secondary schooling; professional training, however, was long regarded as apprenticeship or general preparation for work, and seen as being completely alien to true education, and thus left in the hands of beneficent bodies who provided it in the form of charity. It was only with the Giolitti government that a change came about[10]: from 1907 to 1908, and from 1912 to 1913, the entire commercial and industrial branch of education was reformed and rationalised: financial stability was brought to a range of schools with the assurance of government funding, and the instruction offered was standardised wherever possible. The reform

[10] Giovanni Giolitti (1842–1928) was the Prime Minister of Italy five times between 1892 and 1921.

embraced industrial schools, academies of applied arts and commercial and professional institutes for women. Thus, education in craft skills was reoriented towards the needs of industry.

At the Maglie school, aspiring craft workers were provided with the tools they needed to carry out their work autonomously, creatively and with the necessary technical mastery. They took classes in geometry, geometrical design, ornamental design, architectural design, projection and perspective, art and woodcarving. The first courses were in the crafts that the area was known for: carpentry, stonemasonry and wrought ironwork. Later, courses were set up for bricklayers, jewellery makers, copper workers, painters and decorators and sculptors (Caroli 2013). Until 1905, however, no courses were designed for women.

The launch of the lacemaking course bears witness to the increasing recognition of the technical and educational skills and groundbreaking vision of Etta and Carolina de Viti de Marco. To fully understand the innovative impact of their project, we should recall that in Italy at that time, women's technical and professional training was even scarcer than men's. An article by Clelia Fano (1907) reported on the 1903–1904 statistics from the Ministry of Agriculture, Industry and Trade, listing only 23 state-funded women's schools, while 75 were financed by other bodies or directly set up by the religious Congregations of Charity and Works, organisations over which the government had no control. Fano (1907) noted that many provinces of Italy completely lacked professional training schools for young women, and highlighted the enormous gender gap in government investment, as in contrast there were already 249 schools for young males funded by the Ministry. In addition, the few women's institutes were concentrated in the large industrial cities of Milan, Turin and Genoa, while there were virtually none in the rest of the country, as Ernestina Dal Co Viganò, director of the Normal School and an activist on the Italian National Women's Council, also protested in a memo to the minister:

> Female education and training have been severely neglected up to now: apart from the Normal Schools,[11] which have a highly specialised professional focus, apart from a few royal colleges where instruction is given only for the daughters of rich and aristocratic families, and in recent years,

[11] The Normal School (Scuola Normale) trained teachers to work in compulsory education.

a few technical schools, the government does not provide any other type of school for women; however, the needs of our society open up a wide field of activity for women. (cited in Franchini and Puzzuoli 2005: 510)

Apart from the country's industrial underdevelopment, this negligence also stemmed from a reactionary, misogynist mentality. It was taken for granted that women's work did not require professional development, as the most they needed was 'an early and precise training for the hands, to learn gestures that will later be repeated ad infinitum' (Soldani 1989: xi).

In Apulia, and throughout the South of Italy, the situation was even worse. Lena Mauro Airoldi, in her essay from the IFI catalogue cited above, noted that in many southern provinces the government had not even succeeded in setting up elementary schools for girls. And in fact, after the unification of Italy in 1861, the establishment of girls' elementary education met marked hostility in the regions, 'since illiteracy was seen as a shield protecting women from social vices, and education as a distraction from the main task they were assigned in the family: taking care of the domestic economy' (quoted in AA.VV. 1906: 226). Airoldi, however, contested the prevailing opinion that blamed the educational deficiencies of the South of Italy on the lasting backwardness of women's mentalities, pointing out that once established, the girls' schools and normal schools (which trained teachers for elementary education) were full of female pupils.

The female section of the Maglie industrial school, created by Carolina de Viti de Marco, followed the model of professionalism and modernity laid down by its founder, Lanoce. The course lasted five years and, apart from practising their craft in the workshops, students also took classes in geometrical and ornamental design. The initiative enjoyed immediate success and rapid growth, taking on 28 students in its trial year and enrolling an average of 40 per year from 1907 to 1914 (Panarese 1995: 211). Archive documents bear witness to its recognition by local government and the Ministry, with the female section picked out as a flagship project. A letter from director Egidio Lanoce to the Provincial Council requesting continuation of the school's funding, for example, points to its dynamism and productivity, highlighting Carolina de Viti de Marco's course as the prime example[12]; and in 1909, a ministerial report to the President also mentions the excellent results of the female section, with the Minister recognising its value. Numbers of female enrolments increased and began to rival those of males: by 1912–1913 there were 44 women and 57 men. A letter from the sub-prefect dated 6th March 1910 informs the prefect that 'the lacework manufactured in the school features in the permanent exhibition of the Women's Crafts Cooperative in Rome and in other permanent exhibitions in Paris and London'.[13] These brilliant results were not matched, however, by proper facilities. As extraordinary ministerial commissioner Raffaele Garzia noted on 28 January, 1907, due to constant growth in enrolments and the competing needs of the wrought-iron workshop, the women's section was housed in 'rather poor and inappropriate' areas: a basement, an entrance and a small room. It was the female students themselves who organised a festival to raise the sums needed to restructure the premises.

Despite all this and although the adventure had aroused such widespread enthusiasm, the end of the story was not a happy one. This was due to a series of factors in which public, private, political, economic and social history were intertwined. Carolina de Viti de Marco was unpopular with the Maglie aristocracy, which opposed both her brother Antonio, a member of the Radical Party, and her husband Francesco Paolo Starace, elector for the party in the area. Apart from these political reasons, the women of the local ruling-class families were also hostile to the school because its courses and competition were eroding a wide market system based on the ignorance and over-exploitation of women workers, and in which it was the women of the aristocracy and upper bourgeoisie who managed orders, distributed raw materials, set prices and wages and controlled the commercial outlets.

It was these women, then, who launched a campaign of defamation against the director of the lacemaking course, first reporting her to the government for tax evasion and then claiming that she was enriching herself from the labour of the school's craftswomen. Letters from Caroline to Etta de Viti de Marco in March–April 1911 described this

[12] Letter from the President of the School to the President of Deputazione Provinciale di Terra d'Otranto, 3 August, 1906. Archivio di Stato di Lecce, 'Provincia', III Deposito, folder 503, fasc. 2186.

[13] Letter from the Sub-Prefect of the County of Gallipoli, in Apulia. 6 March, 1910. Archivio di Stato di Lecce, 'Provincia', III Deposito, folder 503, fasc. 2186.

'obstinate, treacherous war' against her, the climate of slander, and even real intimidation.[14] The issue spread to the national political stage when word of the supposed regime of over-exploitation suffered by the Maglie workers reached the socialist deputy Anna Kuliscioff, partner of politician Filippo Turati. Advised by the economist Maffeo Pantaleoni, Kuliscioff declared herself willing to head an enquiry to shed light on the issue. To date there is no evidence, however, that the enquiry ever took place, and nothing is known about subsequent events. Finally, within a few years the Great War brought an abrupt end to the lacework market. Despite this, Etta and Carolina de Viti de Marco's work would find an unforeseen sequel in that of their daughters, as we shall see in the next chapter.

References

AA.VV. 1906. *Le industrie femminili italiane*. Milan: Rocco.

Alessandri, Giuseppe. 1974. Carolina Starace e l'arte del ricamo. *Tempo d'oggi* 2 (21): 73.

Anonymous. 1907a. Bollettino del Consiglio Nazionale delle Donne Italiane. *Vita Femminile Italiana* 1 (3): 280–293.

Anonymous. 1907b. Uno sguardo alla beneficenza romana. *La civiltà cattolica* (6 March), 58, 1 (1362): 657.

Anonymous. 1910a. Aid for Rome's Poor. *New York Times* (July 24).

Anonymous. 1910b. Marchesa de Marco Aids Italian Charity in Work. *Oakland Tribune* (August 1): 13.

Anonymous. 1912. Dans l'assistance. *Le Figaro* (April 14).

Baruzzi, Marina. 1996. Libri per un pubblico femminile: la Biblioteca storica Ponti tra modello ravennate e traduzione imolese. *Memoria e Ricerca* 7: 123–150.

Bellomo, Bianca Rosa. 2002. *Elisa di Corrado: le opere e i giorni di Elisa Ricci*. Ravenna: Società di Studi Ravennati.

Bernardini, Carla, Doretta Davanzo Poli, and Orsola Ghetti Baldi. 2001. *Aemilia Ars 1898–1903, Arts & Crafts a Bologna*. Bologna: A più G.

Buttafuoco, Annarita. 1986. *L'Audacia insolente. La cooperazione femminile, 1886–1986*. Venice: Marsilio.

Buttafuoco, Annarita. 1988. La filantropia come politica. Esperienze dell'emancipazionismo italiano nel Novecento. In *Ragnatele di rapporti: Patronage e*

[14] Carolina De Viti de Marco, Letter to Harriet Lathrop Dunham, Maglie, 20 March, 1911. Archive Carolina de Viti de Marco and Giulia Starace, Le Costaintine Foundation, Casamassella (Lecce).

reti di relazione nella storia delle donne, ed. Laura Ferrante, Maura Palazzi, and Gianna Pomata, 166–187. Turin: Rosenberg & Sellier.

Buttafuoco, Annarita. 1997. *Questioni di cittadinanza. Donne e diritti sociali nell'Italia liberale*. Siena: Protagon.

Cardini, Antonio. 1985. *Antonio de Viti de Marco. La democrazia incompiuta (1858–1943)*. Roma-Bari: Laterza.

Caroli, Dorena. 2013. Lanoce, Egidio. In *Dizionario Biografico dell'Educazione*, ed. Giorgio Chiosso and Roberto Sani, 13. Milano: Editrice Bibliografica.

Casalena, M. Pia. 2003. *Scritti storici di donne italiane. Bibliografia 1800–1945*. Florence: Olski.

Chirilli, Emilia. 2010. *Tuzzo. Preistoria e Protostoria di Antonio de Viti de Marco*, ed. Manuela Mosca, Gabriele Malinconico, and Giulia Malinconico. Bari: Cacucci.

Chirilli, Emilia. 2016. Memories. In *Antonio de Viti de Marco. A Story Worth Remembering*, ed. Manuela Mosca, 15–35. New York: Palgrave Macmillan.

De Giorgio, Michela. 1988. Signore e signorine italiane fra Ottocento e Novecento: modelli culturali e comportamenti sociali regolati da uno stato civile. In *Ragnatele di rapporti: Patronage e reti di relazione nella storia delle donne*, ed. Laura Ferrante, Maura Palazzi and Gianna Pomata, 454–480. Turin: Rosenberg e Sellier.

De Viti de Marco, Antonio. 2008. *Mezzogiorno e democrazia liberale. Antologia degli scritti*, ed. Anna Lucia Denitto. Bari: Palomar.

De Viti de Marco, Etta. 1908. Assistenza e previdenza. *Vita Femminile Italiana* 3 (3): 620–632.

Fano, Clelia. 1907. L'educazione professionale popolare femminile. *Vita Femminile Italiana* 1–3: 419–432.

Fossati, Roberta. 2010. Attiviste sociali di primo Novecento. Un mondo coeso? In *Politica e amicizia. Relazioni, conflitti e differenze di genere (1800–1915)*, ed. Emma Scaramuzza, 115–130. Milan: Angeli.

Franchini, Silvia, and Paola Puzzuoli, eds. 2005. *Archivio centrale dello Stato. Fonti per la storia della scuola. Gli istituti femminili di educazione e di istruzione (1861–1910)*, vol. VII. Rome: Ministero per i Beni e le Attività Culturali.

Frattini, Claudia. 2008. *Il primo congresso delle donne italiane, Roma, 1908. Opinione pubblica e femminismo*. Rome: Biblink.

Giannone, Antonio, Lorenzo Madaro, Mauro Marino, and Brizia Minerva, eds. 2019. *Girolamo Comi spirito d'armonia. Il poeta, l'Accademia Salentina e gli artisti dell'Albero*. Lecce: Museo Castromediano edizioni.

Gori, Claudia. 2003. *Crisalidi. Emancipazioniste liberali in età giolittiana*. Milan: Angeli.

Greetings, Joyous. 2000. *The First International Women's Movement, 1830–1860*. Oxford: Oxford University Press.

Gubin, Eliane, Leen Van Molle, and Leen Beyers. 2005. *Des femmes qui changent le monde: histoire du Conseil international des femmes, 1888–1988*. Paris: Racine.
Imprenti, Fiorella. 2012. *Alle origini dell'Unione Femminile. Idee, progetti e reti internazionali all'inizio del Novecento*. Milan: Biblion.
Lovett, Eva. 1906. An Italian Lace school in New York. *The International Studio. An Illustrated Magazine of Fine Art* 7: 13–14.
Mosca, Manuela, ed. 2016. *Antonio de Viti de Marco. A Story Worth Remembering*. New York: Palgrave Macmillan.
Palomba, Ivana. 2009. *L'arte ricamata. Uno strumento di emancipazione femminile nell'opera di Carolina Amari*. Maniago: Le Arti Tessili.
Panarese, Emilio. 1974. Egidio Lanoce e la scuola d'arte magliese. *Tempo d'oggi* 1: 4–5.
Panarese, Emilio. 1995. *Maglie. L'ambiente, la storia, il dialetto, la cultura popolare*. Galatina: Congedo.
Pantini, Romualdo. 1905. Le industrie femminili italiane: i merletti di Pescocostanzo. *Emporium* 21 (125): 389–401.
Pedone, Antonio, ed. 1995. *Antonio de Viti de Marco. Tra liberalismo economico e democrazia liberale*. Bari: Laterza.
Pieroni Bortolotti, Franca. 1975. *Alle origini del movimento femminile in Italia. 1848–1892*. Turin: Einaudi.
Pucci, Idanna. 2016. *La signora Sing Sing*. Florence: Libreria Editrice Fiorentina.
Ricci, Elisa, ed. 1911. *Antiche trine italiane. Trine ad ago e trine a fuselli. Raccolte e ordinate da Elisa Ricci*. Bergamo: IIAG.
Soldani, Simonetta, ed. 1989. *L'educazione delle donne. Scuole e modelli di vita femminile nell'Italia dell'Ottocento*. Milan: Angeli.
Taricone, Fiorenza. 1996. *L'associazionismo femminile italiano dall'Unità al fascismo*. Milan: Unicopli.
Wakefield, Edward W. 1907. Charity Organisation in Italy. *Charity Organisation Review* 21 (126): 329–333.

CHAPTER 6

The Second Generation: The Transmission of the Philosophy of Work and Assistance

Elena Laurenzi

6.1 Introduction

This chapter focuses on cross-generational transmission. Drawing on letters from family archives, it traces the evolution of a philosophy of political philanthropy across two generations as it developed beyond the model of the original project. Section 6.2 uses South African archive sources and follows the adventure of Lucia Starace, the eldest daughter of Carolina de Viti de Marco, who worked with Emily Hobhouse on an aid programme for the war-stricken Boer people. In 1908, Starace, barely eighteen, sailed for South Africa to set up a replica of her mother's school in Orange Free State, passing on the craft of lacemaking and the ideas of female emancipation and autonomy to the Boer women who lived there.

Section 6.3 tells the story of the educational therapy projects of Giulia Starace and Lucia de Viti de Marco, the younger daughters of Antonio

E. Laurenzi (✉)
University of Salento, Lecce, Italy

E. Laurenzi and M. Mosca (eds.), *A Female Activist Elite in Italy (1890–1920)*, https://doi.org/10.1007/978-3-030-87159-8_6

de Viti de Marco and Harriet Lathrop Dunham (known as Etta de Viti de Marco). In the 1950s, the two cousins created a Steiner community near Rome, affiliated to the Camphill Community founded by Karl König. There, they treated disadvantaged children suffering from polio, putting into practice their mothers' ideas on healthcare, education and social advancement. The two women then worked towards a welfare centre for the rural population of Southern Italy, intended to embody their holistic vision of healthcare, non-alienated labour, organic farming and respect for the environment. At their deaths, they ensured the survival and growth of the project by bequeathing funds to create a foundation in its name.

6.2 From Casamassella to Koppies. The Internationalisation of a Model

In March 1908, inspired by the example of the Casamassella School and the beauty and quality of its lacework, English feminist and pacifist Emily Hobhouse, internationally known for her opposition to the Anglo-Boer War, travelled to Rome to meet Etta and Carolina de Viti de Marco.

Born into a conservative upper-class family, both Emily and her brother Leonard, the first professor of sociology at the University of London, were progressive in their ideas. Emily was driven by an almost religious sense of justice, which spurred her to join the suffragist movement and later to become a socialist and pacifist.[1] At the outbreak of the Anglo-Boer War in October 1899, she publicly denounced Joseph Chamberlain's colonialist goals and the brutality of the English armies against the Boer population, demanding that Britain should uphold the principles of the rights and dignity of peoples. Moving from protest to action, she founded the South Africa Women and Children Distress Fund and set out for South Africa to visit the concentration camps, denouncing the inhuman conditions there in reports, photographs and interviews. Her South African intervention marked humanitarian activism with a strong political and symbolic charge of anti-militarism and friendship between peoples.[2] After the war, she decided on a new aid plan for the Boer population, focussing on the women, whom she saw as a force for peace and reconstruction that should be nurtured and strengthened. Undoubtedly,

[1] See Brits (2016), Hobhouse Balme (2012, 2015), Fisher (1971), and Hall (2008).

[2] See Hobhouse (1902, 1984) and Bianchi (2005).

also inspired by the economic and political successes of the Italian Female Industries (IFI), which she had become familiar with on her frequent trips to Italy, she set up a new scheme, The Boer Home Industries and Aid Society, to fund spinning and weaving schools and workshops (Gill 2012). Soon, she had set up 25 of these school-workshops in the country's main cities and towns; her dream, however, was to create lacemaking schools in South Africa based on the model of those that were flourishing in Europe. With this goal in mind, she began to travel in search of a skilled craftswoman and an English interpreter to come to South Africa and oversee the project. Finally, she came across the Casamassella School at an exhibition of its work in London in July 1908 (Macor 1908). On her subsequent visit to the Orsini Palace, she met Carolina de Viti de Marco who, in an admirably enterprising and generous spirit, proposed her eldest daughter Lucia Starace, barely eighteen at the time, for the post. Carolina recalled the beginning of Lucia's South African adventure in her *Annales*[3]:

> While I was in Rome, Etta received a visit from Miss Emily Hobhouse from London. She had seen an exhibition of our work there, sponsored by Princess Luisa, and had had the idea of setting up something similar to our school in South Africa. She was a fanatical supporter of the Boers, and in her desire to come to the aid of that war-ravaged people, had tried to introduce the weaving industry there, but had come up against insurmountable obstacles. She had put her hope in Burano lace and wished to make contact with some Italian lady who might be able to help her get her project under way. Finding Etta's address on a lacework sheet she had bought at the exhibition, she travelled straight away to Rome to meet Etta at the Orsini Palace, where she still lived. She brought with her a lovely young woman, Johanna Rood, and we had an excellent impression of both. Miss Hobhouse explained her project: she wanted to find a craftswoman skilled in Burano lace to teach it to the poor Boer women, and a young woman who spoke good English to translate for craftswoman and students. It was also clear that both women would need to be willing to travel that far. But where to find them? Etta and I both had the same idea simultaneously: Lucia! My daughter combined in one person the two abilities, and the prospect of travelling inspired anything but fear in her. It was true that

[3] As already said in Chapter 2 and 5, we refer to a series of notes that she had drafted later in life in chronological order. Archive Carolina de Viti de Marco and Giulia Starace, Le Costantine Foundation, Casamassella (Lecce).

> she was not familiar with Burano lacework but we knew that she could learn it quickly and effectively; and so, Miss Hobhouse included a stay in Venice in her programme for as long as the two girls needed for their apprenticeship. Everything, then, was organised and put in place; all that was lacking was Lucia's acceptance and her father's blessing. These were given without reserve, and Lucia arrived in Rome soon after, fired with enthusiasm for this unforeseen interesting adventure. Miss Hobhouse took care of all the arrangements, and Lucia agreed to stay in South Africa for two years to teach the Burano lacework she had learned in Venice to the young women who wanted to attend the School. The young Miss Rood would be her working companion and Miss Constance Cloete (Aunty Con) would be their chaperone and housekeeper. Lucia stayed in Rome for a few days, and on 29th March they left for Venice, which they reached safely after a short stay in Bologna. The plan was carried out exactly as projected, point by point. In Venice, Lucia learnt her new skills extremely quickly and Miss Hobhouse busied herself in providing the girls with all the entertainment they needed.

These notes reveal the modernity of Carolina, her freedom of action and open-mindedness, contrasting with the typical stereotypes of Southern Italian women. Apart from her immediate, enthusiastic acceptance of Hobhouse's idea, the qualities she encouraged in her daughter are striking: courage, independence and boldness, as opposed to obedience and submission.

It was in this way, then, that Lucia Starace embarked on a long journey to Cape Town, and from there to Koppies, a village at the heart of the Orange Free State, previously the main theatre of British operations against the Boer guerrillas. She travelled by train, crossing a wide, barren plain still showing the devastation wreaked by General Kitchener's scorched-earth policy: crops systematically destroyed, livestock slaughtered wholesale, villages and farms burnt down, springs and agricultural land poisoned.

A handful of snapshots have survived from the photographs that Lucia sent home, showing her elegant, erect and smiling, dressed in fine lace blouses in rooms decorated with doilies and flowers, seated in gardens surrounded by plants, or in the company of important friends of Hobhouse, who entertained them on beautiful estates in the wine-growing region of Constantia or in Kroonstad, nearer Koppies. The pictures are annotated on the back with rapid, vivid descriptions of the places, plants, objects and people.[4] But these superficial and intentionally light-hearted notes were doubtlessly designed to reassure her family. Setting up the school at Koppies, in fact, involved many problems. During the war the village had been razed and most of its buildings ruined and burnt down. The population were still living in corrugated iron shacks left by the British army, and it was in one of these that the two young craftswomen set up home: half of the hut served as a classroom and the other as living quarters (Brits 2016: 190–196). There was no electricity, and for this reason classes were held during hours of sunlight and the students had to move their workplaces to follow the course of the sun. Many of the students lived on far-flung farms and had no transport to the village. Thus, the two young women decided to travel on horseback to the students' homesteads to give them lessons. In the school, which replicated the educational and political model of its Italian forerunners, basic classes in more general culture—mathematics, music and French—were also given as part of an instruction programme aimed at women's empowerment.

Lucia Starace's stay at Koppies lasted the agreed two years, after which she saw her mission as fulfilled and returned to Italy. Following an unhappy marriage and separation, she settled at the Villa Carmosina at Casamassella (Apulia), which her father had inherited, opening a lace-making school and workshop there, and this became the main outlet for her irrepressibly innovative and experimental spirit. She created original designs and recorded them in technical terminology, tracing them in numbers and coloured squares on paper like musical scores, or reproducing the patterns collected by her mother Carolina on the loom. She experimented with new dying, spinning and weaving techniques, making mechanical modifications to her loom for the purpose. Production at her workshop followed a complete cycle, starting from growing the cotton and breeding sheep for wool and worms for silk, moving on to the dying and weaving of the fibres, and then manufacturing and finishing the end products. To create more exclusive fabrics, she imported a prized breed of black sheep, the Karakul, whose wool could be woven raw and undyed (Monte and Presicce 2010: 81–103). Her training was the source of the gradual spread of lacework throughout the region: today, young women

[4] A selection of these photographs has been published by the author in the webpages on the history of the Le Costantine Foundation (www.lecostantine.eu/storia) and in the photographs of Laurenzi 2018.

still practice it at home and there are high-quality workshops like that of the Le Costantine Foundation, described in the following chapter, and craftswomen often work on looms given to them by Lucia herself. Her lacemaking school at Koppies survived until 1938 under the direction of Johanna Rood, the Boer girl and assistant to Hobhouse, and a small collection of its products is kept in the Emily Hobhouse Huis, the village old people's home. It was a former student at the school, Roitjie de Wet, who started the collection when she realised that the school's products had, in addition to their economic value, historic and cultural importance as well, and she decided to preserve her own work and collect that of her former classmates. At her death, she left the collection to the old people's home where she had spent her last years. Hobhouse's memory still lives on among Afrikaners, who see her as a hero. A room is even devoted to her in the Anglo-Boer War Museum at Bloemfontein where, among other exhibits, we can see the trunk Emily took with her from England, a copy of a famous lacework made at Koppies and dedicated to the Wag-n-Bietjie Tree, and the wedding veil which, after a youthful disappointment in love, she never wore, donated in the end in homage to the women of South Africa (Laurenzi 2018).

6.3 Giulia Starace's Welfare Work and Its Sources in Catholic Modernism

If Lucia Starace was an essential link in the transmission of the needlework and weaving that had been cultivated and perfected at Casamassella, and of the entrepreneurial spirit of the Italian Female Industries, Carolina's second daughter, Giulia Starace (1895–1984), was the most direct and firmly convinced heiress of the philosophy, aspirations, ideals and models behind early twentieth-century women's political philanthropy, the culture that had inspired her mother and her aunt Etta de Viti de Marco.

Giulia was shy and reserved: there are very few photographs of her, and she is almost always captured in profile, as if fleeing from the lens. Nevertheless, many testimonies of her life and works can be gathered in the Casamassella area, where she spent her entire life, and where 'Miss Giulia' was a sort of institution. Many people, particularly among the older generation, still vividly remember her slender figure and free, audacious personality: an independent woman, skilled horseback rider, the first in the area to drive a car and hold a seat on the local council.

> The main traits of Giulia's character were her extraordinary modernity and generosity, her altruism without ulterior motives. Everyone saw her as an intrepid person. She was an excellent horseback rider. She would ride 20 or 30 kilometres on her own. She was the first women to get a driving licence, at the end of the 20s. And even in her 80s, she was still driving, not recklessly, but brilliantly, skilfully and fast.[5]

The letters preserved in her archive show her to have been an avid reader, particularly of spiritual works: the Gospel and AJ Russell's *God Calling* were her daily companions. Curious about all topics, she even studied braille. She was strong-willed and capable of taking on tasks normally reserved for men. Spartan—with a touch of the Franciscan—in her habits, she consumed only the bare essentials at the same time as she cultivated beauty, not as a luxury but as nourishment for the spirit. Surviving witnesses still vividly remember her work for the people of the village and her vision, ahead of its time, of development for the area, welfare for its people, upbringing for the young and social well-being in general. Those lucky enough to live alongside her and gain an insight into her ideas and way of life saw her as 'a guiding light', a leader along unforeseen paths towards a different style of future.[6]

Since the 1920s, in a South still suffering the consequences of the Great War and lacking any kind of state aid, Giulia Starace voluntarily offered welfare services to the local population, particularly children and the sick. She set up after-school lessons for village children whose mothers were working in the fields; she fed them and helped with their schoolwork, while at the same time educating them in the observation of nature, a love of literature, freedom and faith in one's own capacities. It was in those years that, spurred by the example of her aunt Etta de Viti de Marco, she conceived the project of a Montessori school at Casamassella[7]; and this became the kernel of a more ambitious project that would occupy her for her whole life and finally bear fruit in the Le Costantine Foundation, discussed in Chapter 7.

[5] Interview with Gabriele Malinconico (Laurenzi 2018: 211). Unless stated otherwise, the translation of the quoted texts are our own.

[6] See the interview with Maria Cristina Russo in Laurenzi (2018: 258–263).

[7] On Maria Montessori and her influence on the Italian feminist philanthropy, see the first part of this volume.

Another activity that took up much of her time was her care for the sick. She offset the lack of public health services by setting up a small emergency and first aid clinic in her own house, where she received ill people and cared for them to the best of her nursing abilities, calling in specialists to visit, and providing hospitalisation and therapy through her many contacts and friends. This was not strictly beneficence but, as Gabriele Malinconico argues, 'a kind of contact-based aid' that worked through networks of mainly affective relationships. An important part of the care she offered was her sincere sharing of people's adversity: 'People knew her. They came to her door any time they had a problem. If she could, she would solve it. But in all cases, she shared the problem, and people went away reassured'.[8] More than pity, her attitude was one of fraternal sharing encouraged by her deeply spiritual temperament. In time, she turned this spontaneous solidarity into a genuinely religious practice, although she never relinquished her secular, critical, non-confessional spirit. In the 1930s, she began to visit the hermitage situated in Campello sul Clitunno, a spiritual centre among the green mountains of Umbria,[9] where Maria Minore (born Valeria Paola Pignetti), one of the most forceful religious figures of twentieth-century Italy, had set up a pioneering ecumenical community for women.[10]

Born into a bourgeois family of Mazzinian ideas in Turin in 1875, Maria Minore had taken the veil at twenty-five, entering the congregation of Franciscan Missionaries of Mary, an order devoted to missionary work. She lived in a convent for some twenty years before deciding, with a handful of her colleagues, to start out on a deeper spiritual path, adhering more strictly to Franciscan principles. When she obtained permission from Pope Benedetto XV to leave the convent without renouncing her order, she travelled to the area of Saint Francis of Assisi's birthplace and finally found the ideal location for her project in a ruined chapel on the rugged crest of a rise overlooking the springs of the River Clitunno. She settled there in 1926, accompanied by ten of her colleagues.

The main figures helping Maria to organise the community included the Anglican Amy Turton, a key figure in the development of nursing in Italy (Turton 2002) and Clelia Allegri (known as Sister Jacopa), visually

[8] See the interview with Gabriele Malinconico in Laurenzi (2018: 211–213).

[9] Umbria is a region in central Italy.

[10] See Ceschia (2017), Morozzo Della Rocca (1998, 2013), and Borgognoni (2007).

impaired from birth, cofounder with Augusto Romagnoli of the Italian Union of the Blind, and creator of innovative teaching methods for unsighted people (Chirilli 1973). Giulia visited the community from the mid-1930s on. The letters she wrote to her mother from her frequent stays there show that her practical nature and initiative soon made her a valuable collaborator in restoring the building; and indeed, she was considered a member of the Hermitage spiritual family, a 'non-resident sister'. The sisters confided the joys and troubles of the community and its most intimate relationships to her: 'Yours is the heart more than any other to which I feel confident in entrusting the sadness of the Hermitage', Paola Casanova, community member and a doctor, wrote to her in 1956, when Sister Maria died.[11] As early as 1935, Maria Minore had sent her the card bearing an Easter lamb design that she kept for her closest comrades; and the 'Undertaking' written by Maria for the non-resident members of the sisterhood is kept among Giulia's archives:

> Undertaking.
>
> The spirit knows no distance, and Love unites the most faraway hearts. It is a fresh joy to know that one is merged in this ideal communion that brings sense and meaning to our days on earth.
>
> God is present in the human beings, in that eternal, wearying dissatisfaction that torments them, which can only be appeased by good works. The religious ideal is the most exacting undertaking and calls for the death of the old Adam and rebirth in the holy lineage springing from the new Adam, Christ. An undertaking for life, which is not merely the practice of sentimental refinement, tastes of blood and tears, not of a gratifying sweetness.
>
> Provisionally these few points [ ] may serve as the core of this undertaking:
>
> 1) To communicate amongst each other more closely, we may recite the Lord's Prayer in the morning, infusing it with the hope that we may live one not-too-distant day united in love and dedication. The Reign of Christ is the chance to fulfil the divine will that has called us to the monastic life and to a more sincere ideal of living.
>
> 2) To deepen the feeling of brotherly love, that this should not merely be a word but a reality to us. To educate ourselves to feel with others

[11] Paola Casanova, Letter to Giulia Starace, Eremo di Campello sul Clitunno, 7 July, 1956. Archive of Carolina de Viti de Marco and Giulia Starace, Le Costantine Foundation, Casamassella (Lecce).

> instead of with ourselves, forming in ourselves the sense of service to all for the joy and peace of the human community. To love with joy the children, who are always awed by that human mystery, our brothers.
>
> 3) To banish strictly from our souls the futile sorrows kindled by worldly meanness, seeking to uphold in ourselves the values whose absence we lament: to resolutely banish all idle talk, criticism, grievance and complaint, the snares set by mediocrity to impoverish us.
>
> 4) Spontaneous simplicity in all things: furnishings, clothes, language, treatment of others; complete and transparent honesty towards all: ourselves and others, superiors and inferiors.[12]

These precepts, although Giulia never explicitly professed them, shed light on her conduct and life choices and they offer us an insight into their deep, conscious spiritual roots. The Hermitage was a place of spiritual growth for her, a place for friendship and the project of a community with which she forged links of active collaboration. Aware of the spiritual, cultural and even political value of this groundbreaking experience, in later years she handed on the memory of the community to its younger members, and in the 1950s, she curated and reorganised its archives so that the spirit of its founder would not be lost.[13]

The Campello Hermitage community did not answer to any particular order or follow any specific rule. It only required its members to live in a Benedictine and Franciscan spirit of poverty, to be fraternally open to all pilgrims and to share of a non-confessional path of spiritual seeking. The community's 'unlimited family' extended to many non-resident sisters and brothers who shared its spirit from a distance, including lay and agnostic personalities and others from a wide range of faiths, among them Mahatma Gandhi (Maria di Campello and Gandhi 2017) and Albert Schweitzer, the physician, musicologist, Lutheran missionary and theologist, awarded the Nobel Peace Prize in 1952 (Maria di Campello and Schweitzer 2007).

Maria di Campello was close to Modernism, the current of spiritual renewal and religious reformism that spread widely during the first half

[12] Maria di Campello, 'Impegno' (Undertaking), dedicated to Giulia Starace. Archive of Carolina de Viti de Marco and Giulia Starace, Le Costantine Foundation, Casamassella (Lecce).

[13] As documented by the letters of the young eremite Marie-Claire Gotteland to Giulia Starace (1975–1979). Archive of Carolina de Viti de Marco and Giulia Starace, Le Costantine Foundation, Casamassella (Lecce).

of the twentieth century and which sought to return the Church to the spirit of the original Christians and orient it towards contemporary issues. She counted prominent Modernists among her spiritual friends, including the Protestant pastor Paul Sabatier, author of an influential biography of St Francis of Assisi (Sabatier 1894)[14]; Don Brizio Casciola, the Umbrian priest who inspired Antonio Fogazzaro to write his novel *The Saint* (Fogazzaro 1906); and Don Primo Mazzolari, the Lombardian prelate and patron of the Church of the Poor (Maria di Campello and Mazzolari 2007; Maria di Campello and Vannucci 2007).

These personal ties suggest that Giulia Starace, by drawing close to the spiritual experience of the hermitage community, was also following in her mother and her aunt's intellectual footsteps. As we have seen in the previous chapters, early twentieth-century feminists, and among them Etta de Viti de Marco, often had affinities with spiritual renewal and religious reform (Fossati 1997). Many important female figures were active in Catholic Modernist circles: among the most prominent were the Waldensian writer Dora Melegari, one of the movement's main champions; the writer and journalist Antonietta Giacomelli; and the educationalist Felicitas Büchner. Feminists such as Adele del Bono, Baroness Alice Hallgarten Franchetti (see Chapter 3) and Countess Maria Pasolini were frequent visitors to Italian Modernist circles and backed projects that spread its spirit. Maria Pasolini, a close friend of Etta and Antonio de Viti de Marco, organised readings and discussion groups at her house to build bridges between political economy and the social, moral and spiritual issues of religious reformism. Through these meetings, the first Modernists passed on to following generations a particular understanding of the idea of 'doing good' which embodied not only moral values but social, political and spiritual ones as well. It was specifically this political and spiritual legacy what cemented the friendship between Giulia Starace and her cousin Lucia de Viti de Marco, the third child of Antonio and Etta.

6.4 The Steiner Community of Lucia de Viti de Marco

Lucia de Viti de Marco (1900–1989) had a complex but clear-cut personality. Gifted with a will of iron, determined, fearless, strict in her

[14] On Paul Sabatier see Chapter 2, footnote 46.

judgements without being moralistic, she demanded of herself the same coherence and social awareness that she expected from others. Her carefree childhood, under the comfortable, affectionate wing of her mother and her adolescence at school in London gave way to a series of severe blows in early adulthood. Her mother died in 1939 after a long and painful degenerative illness, while her brother James, confined for many years to a nursing home, clashed bitterly with the family (see Chapter 2). Lucia was left on her own to care for her ageing father, already severely tried by being stripped of his professorship at the University of Rome and isolated by the Fascist regime (Mosca 2021), and now sad and disheartened after Harriet's death. Meanwhile, around her the storm of totalitarianism, terror and war raged. Lucia followed events anxiously: her hope in a last flicker of good sense before the outbreak of hostilities gave way to outrage when Russia invaded Finland in the so-called Winter War.

> I am in a state of anguish for the fate of poor little Finland and feel a nameless indignation with the 'allies' [...] who have not sent any aid and leave a little country of 4 million people to fight for the civilisation of the whole world... A world which inspires only horror and disgust.[15]

It finally gave way to the feeling of vulnerability and the closeness of death as the waves of deportations began. As if foreseeing the struggles that awaited her, she wrote in March 1942: 'I am rereading old letters from my friends. Who knows if I will ever see them again? It seems that everything that happens in these years is a preparation for being torn asunder'.[16]

She resisted the barbarism both indirectly—meditating, reading, corresponding with friends—and directly, through a kind of resistance that was congenial to her. Thus, rather than joining an anti-fascist organisation, she personally protected and sheltered victims of persecution. We have at least two eye-witness reports of these activities. The first is the story of a hazardous journey to Nazi-occupied Vienna in 1938 to rescue the Jewish

[15] Lucia de Viti de Marco, Letter to Umberto Zanotti Bianco, Rome, 10 February, 1940. Archive of Associazione Nazionale per gli Interessi del Mezzogiorno d'Italia (ANIMI), Rome, folder Umberto Zanotti Bianco.

[16] Lucia de Viti de Marco, Letter to Umberto Zanotti Bianco, Boscolungo Pistoiese (PT), March 1942. Archive of Associazione Nazionale per gli Interessi del Mezzogiorno d'Italia (ANIMI), Rome, folder Umberto Zanotti Bianco

doctor and Steiner educator Karl König, whose patient she had been. In his memoirs, König describes how Lucia De Viti de Marco came to his aid, drove him out of the country and hid him in her summer house at Boscolungo in the Tuscan Apennines.

> The torment and misery became noticeably worse in Vienna. The Party and the authorities soon began to pressurize me, and I knew that I would have to act quickly if I was to escape the Gestapo's web, vanishing without a trace. An Italian patient who had become a family friend the previous year travelled from Rome by car to help arrange my departure during those last weeks. Donna Lucia De Viti de Marco was still able to accomplish certain things that were beyond my possibilities. Undaunted and filled with courage, she confronted the petty tyrants. We left Vienna together on Sunday 14th August [...] Donna Lucia took me safely across the border. It was a miraculous crossing, made possible with the help of a drunken SA trooper. I had made it to Italy, escaping the murderers' clutches. (König 2008: 49)

In 1943, during the final throes of the Fascist regime, Lucia also secretly sheltered the economist Umberto Zanotti Bianco, who had come back to Rome clandestinely to take part in a conspiracy against Mussolini.[17] In his diary, Zanotti Bianco (2011) describes de Viti's failing health—he was to die on 1st December 1943—and Lucia's courage in the face of this family tragedy and the terrible last months of the war: the bombing raids, persecution of Jews and oppositionists, looting and plunder and the uncertain future of the country, split in two after the Allied landings and the chaos reigning in the capital, left at the mercy of the German troops after the flight of the government following Italy's surrender in 1943. A few months after her father's death and the end of the war, Lucia married Gino Pecorella, a noted Roman jurist. It was a passionate and mature relationship and seemed finally to bring some happiness into her life, but it was not to last, as Pecorella died suddenly a little more than a year later; and this new tragedy triggered a profound change in her life.

In her grief, Lucia decided to devote the rest of her life to alleviating the suffering of others. This choice was inspired by her spiritual guide,

[17] On Zanotti Bianco see Chapter 2, footnote 74.

Father Vincenzo Ceresi, also a Modernist, author of books such as *Il cristianesimo interiore* (Inner Christianity) and *Il mistero della povertà* (The Mystery of Poverty; Ceresi 1953, 1955), and a frequent visitor to the Hermitage community. And it was there that Lucia's project took shape. Initially, it was to be a residential care community for blind children under Sister Jacopa's expert supervision; finally, however, Lucia chose to help children affected by polio, still endemic in the country, especially the South; and, in fact, it was her cousin Giulia Starace who sent Lucia her first children from extremely poor southern families. Lucia set out not only to treat them, but also to offer them a decent life and future.

In the spacious villa at Fregene[18] that she had inherited from her husband and set up for the purpose, Lucia cared for around twenty children with polio for over a decade. They came from Apulia—through Giulia's intervention—and Umbria, sent by the Sisters at the Campello Hermitage. Lucia treated them with innovative physical methods—massage, gymnastics, homoeopathic medicines from Switzerland and Germany—and with Steiner curative education, using music, drawing, theatre and weaving as therapeutic approaches. Karl König helped her with the choice of treatments and guided her in running the little community. From Scotland, where he had settled after the flight from Vienna, he visited Fregene at least once a year to see the children, accompanied by his colleague Lotte Sahlmann; and from there he moved on to Casamassella to visit Giulia's patients. Lucia also travelled to Scotland several times to train in König's principles and techniques, which spread in those years throughout Europe, America and as far afield as South Africa.

At his curative educational centre, König taught a non-orthodox Steiner approach combined with his own ideas and experiments, mixing conventional and anthroposophical methods with complementary therapies. His system identified four areas of intervention: education in the widest sense, seen as fostering the child's social, cognitive and sensory attitudes, with a strong emphasis on emotional and spiritual needs; craft and creative activities, used as tools for stimulating neurological and cognitive growth and developing joy, faith in oneself and the sense of beauty; an individualised therapeutic approach designed to cater for the specific needs of every child and aimed at countering the constitutional and developmental imbalances that manifested themselves in their

[18] Fregene is a town in the province of Rome.

physical, cognitive, emotional and behavioural lives; and lastly, attention to daily living within a natural, harmonious environment designed to support social and emotional development. Thus, König's method set out to create a peaceful, well-balanced setting for activities that fostered the well-being of all community members. This objective was fulfilled by paying careful attention to every detail of daily life, respect for the individual and the beauty and quality of the surroundings: the buildings, furnishings and decoration; the gardens and plants; the quality of clothes and personal relations; natural, healthy food. The daily household and farming tasks were shared among all the community members with everyone contributing according to their capacities, fomenting a sense of belonging and togetherness. The therapeutic quality of the life was maintained through a healthy balance of activity and rest, social and individual activities and attention to each person's nutritional needs. Every community member was encouraged to make their own choices and to take decisions in the light of mutual responsibility and recognition of others' needs, rights and aspirations (Müller-Wiedermann 1996; Hart and Monteux 2004).

The same principles of individualised attention to each person and their relationships inspired Lucia de Viti de Marco in her own small therapeutic community at Fregene, and this made her experiment deeply revolutionary compared to the disciplinary model of healthcare prevailing at the time. Her approach encompassed all aspects of the children's lives: from strictly medical treatment to education, food and nutrition, play, celebration and rituals, growth, sexuality and emotional life, ideas and work. Lucia also kept up these relationships well beyond the children's stay at the community, following every youth after they had left, helping them to reinsert themselves back into their home lives, assisting them in complementing their education and in finding work, and taking part in the important events of their lives: engagements, marriages, births and baptisms. The end result of this long process was a positive, lasting friendship between adults.

Lucia De Viti de Marco shared all the details of her project at Fregene with Giulia Starace; we may even say that it was a kind of joint initiative. The two cousins acted in unison, exchanging advice, analysis and feedback. Lucia often wrote to Casamassella, explaining each child's progress to her cousin: the development of their relationships, their sensibility, character, inclinations, education, advances and setbacks, reactions to therapy. She sought Giulia's advice, let off steam in moments of frustration, outlined plans and decisions. Giulia, for her part, often visited Fregene, spending long periods there when she could take time off from her work, and taking care of her mother Carolina.

Their collaboration involved a clear but not rigid division of labour. Giulia worked mainly from Casamassella, ensuring communication between the families and their children and giving support to the latter when they left the community and went back to Apulia upon completion of their schooling. In the summer, she provided them with holidays at Le Costantine, in the country, or at Kalamuri, by the sea. In addition, she supplied some of the Fregene staff, such as the teacher Francesco Ottini, who lived at the villa and ran the school, through her contacts and enquiries.

6.5 Giulia and Lucia's Project: A Utopian Passion

In the 1960s, Giulia Starace and Lucia de Viti de Marco worked together on the project of a recovery education centre combining Steiner philosophy and Montessori education. Their intention was to set this centre up at Casamassella, with the aim of steering the community's development in a more sustainable, humanistic direction.

The social context of this project should be borne in mind. In the 1950s and 1960s, Salento, at the southern end of Apulia, was an extremely poor area populated mostly by agricultural labourers, manual workers and fishermen. In 1952, a parliamentary enquiry there into poverty revealed a combination of destitution and over-exploitation: over 60% of families were poor or disadvantaged; most dwellings lacked electricity and running water and only 4% had a bathroom. Infant mortality was much higher than the national average. Children's education was deficient and tended to end after compulsory schooling. More than 48% of the population was illiterate. The local tradition of splitting the agricultural property into smallholdings did not favour modernisation, and most of the workers on the land still used hoes and hand-held ploughs. Consequently, the population emigrated massively to the industrialised areas of the North of Italy and Europe, with southern emigration, already endemic since the unification of the country in 1861, becoming 'a true exodus' (Persichella 2005: 199). The rural areas were severely depopulated, and leaving the land became a rite of passage that has been described as 'existential': the majority of the agricultural population turned its back on the land and could only imagine its children's future work in industry and services. This epoch-making shift in the civilisation of the South was further spurred by state intervention since La Cassa del Mezzogiorno—the state body entrusted with the task of developing the region—had set its sights on industrialisation.

In opposition to the myth of progress embodied by state policy and private interests, Giulia Starace pursued a different type of development, put to the test not only in her own projects but also in her private life. At that time Giulia lived in the country on the estate at Le Costantine, where she had settled after her mother's death in the home that she herself had planned. One witness to this who was a frequent visitor to her house in the 1960s said:

> She was already practicing selective recycling at that time! The dishes weren't washed with detergents but only soap. All the organic waste went back to the earth. During the boom in the chemical industries, this was a revolution. I lived in an agricultural world, [...] but it was all based on chemical products. There was nothing apart from chemical products, that was the policy: the fertilisers, the herbicides. But she safeguarded and relaunched a whole world that's now our world these days.[19]

Caroline's death on 24th June 1965 also sealed the two cousins' affectionate friendship and deep spiritual communion. Their correspondence reveals that the memory of their mothers was an inexhaustible source of wisdom and affection, but it also heralded an unfulfilled task. In a letter to Giulia, Lucia writes of her conversations with Carolina on her deathbed and of the latter's blessing to both of them in their joint project of the Centre for children and youth.[20]

The strength of the links between generations, suggested at the end of the next chapter, is thus documented by Carolina's enthusiastic backing of her daughter and niece's idea. For almost ten years after her death, Lucia and Giulia continued their quest. They wrote and rewrote their wills to tie their own bequests more closely to the materialisation of an organisation that would set up and run the centre. They travelled

[19] Interview with Maria Cristina Russo, Laurenzi (2018: 259).

[20] Lucia de Viti de Marco, Letter to Giulia Starace, Le Regine (PT), 6 September, 1967. Archive Carolina de Viti de Marco and Giulia Starace, Le Costantine Foundation, Casamassella (Lecce).

for research and training purposes: in 1965, for example, they went to Switzerland and Milan, where they met Lavinia Mondolfo Sacerdote, founder of the first Steiner school in the city. Together and separately, they met experts, technicians, founders of movements, school directors and religious personalities.

Numerous letters from Giulia Starace to different organisations in Italy and abroad reveal her meticulous search for a person willing to set up the project at Casamassella, but at the same time her wish to remain independent of them all and to avoid having their rules override her own ideals. The critical notes she left in the margins of the letters she received, along with copies of her replies attached to each one, show that she also wished her heirs to understand the importance and difficulty of this search.

Lucia de Viti de Marco was also anxious to achieve this elusive objective. Her letters to Umberto Zanotti Bianco, whom she asked to take part in the project, show her awareness of its 'airy' and possibly even 'evanescent' nature,[21] but at the same time her conviction of its urgent necessity. And although the idea seemed vague, its solidity was anchored in its links to Etta and Carolina's work:

> I am sure that Casamassella could become the best children's community in our Association, as we would easily be able to set up a weaving school, a lacemaking school, an agricultural school, etc. And above all, it would bring back to life an organisation that already existed under the direction of my aunt.[22]

Realising this dream seemed to be as troublesome as giving birth to a utopia. And as the years passed and Lucia and Giulia grew old, the difficulty turned into a passion, like a desire that could not find fulfilment. Their letters bear witness to this quest that had become almost obsessive, driving Giulia and Lucia to make sacrifices in order not to whittle away the property earmarked for 'the blessed Foundation'.[23] Lucia offered her

[21] Lucia de Viti de Marco, Letter to Umberto Zanotti Bianco, 24 March, 1961. Archive of Associazione Nazionale per gli Interessi del Mezzogiorno d'Italia (ANIMI), folder Umberto Zanotti Bianco (1889–1963), Rome.

[22] Lucia de Viti de Marco, Letter to Umberto Zanotti Bianco, 1 February, 1963. Archive of Associazione Nazionale per gli Interessi del Mezzogiorno d'Italia (ANIMI), folder Umberto Zanotti Bianco (1889–1963), Rome.

[23] Lucia de Viti de Marco, Letter to Giulia Starace, 5 April, 1971. Archive Carolina de Viti de Marco and Giulia Starace, Le Costantine Foundation, Casamassella (Lecce).

services to Zanotti as a translator to raise a little money, while Giulia lived in Franciscan-style poverty to keep the assets of the centre intact. She sold plots of land to buy others where they planned to build the school. From Hermitage, various sisters wrote to Giulia telling her they would pray for the materialisation of 'this modest but great ideal' and 'everything that your mother had dreamed of, planned towards and arranged for'.[24]

Giulia died in hospital at Christmas 1983 after a long illness following a stroke. Lucia de Viti de Marco survived her by five years, but Alzheimer's crippled her towards the end. The story of enthusiasm, creativity, work, faith and hope which had united the two generations of enlightened women seemed to lose its way in the darkness and solitude of old age and death.

Through the strength of their convictions and their hope and faith in the future, however, Giulia Starace and Lucia de Viti de Marco paved the way, leaving all their possessions to the foundation that Giulia finally managed to set up, after much doubt and anguish, a few months before her death. Their wills are like bottled messages cast to the seas of posterity: alongside the dry bureaucracy of the worldly leavings, they also embodied a spiritual legacy, tying the use of their estates to the realisation of their dream of welfare and public well-being. We can witness their spirit in two texts: one is Lucia's spiritual legacy to the children who had grown up in the community at Fregene (her 'poppets'); and the other is a passage from the Foundation's Statutes, setting out its purposes.

> My dear old 'poppets,' I am writing to you all because I want you to know [that] my dream is still the same as always... To set up a little community where those of you who want to can help other needy and suffering children in the same way that we helped you [...] I'm convinced that the best gift we can bring to the world is the example we practice rather than preach! [...] You who have known the meaning of pain and suffering as children [...] are better qualified than others to come to the aid of these children and create for them (using any kind of curative treatment) a human environment where they can feel at home together like a big family (never an institution!), and where you can help them enjoy a healthy life

[24] Sister Agnese, Letter to Giulia Starace, Eremo di Campello sul Clitunno, 17 July, 1971. Archive Carolina de Viti de Marco and Giulia Starace, Le Costantine Foundation, Casamassella (Lecce).

close to nature, far from the city, from cruelty, and from the horrors of so-called progress and the robotisation of the human spirit.[25] The Foundation has as its purpose the social and cultural development of the local population through the establishment of an agriculture, craft and education centre [...]. The Centre takes as its models biodynamic organic farming, in the conviction that cultivating the earth according to natural principles and methods fosters and nourishes the balanced physical and spiritual development of human beings, and the renovation of craft production, inspired by traditional methods and aiming to restore interest and pleasure to labour, seen as factors fomenting human development. Likewise, the Centre will undertake educational work following the same principles and accompanying the individual from earliest childhood. Also, to foster physical health and protect and care for the needs of the old and the disabled, the Centre will provide, wherever possible, healthcare and social assistance and will work towards preventing and curing illness. The Foundation, in fact, is inspired by holistic ideals of human health in the physical, moral and spiritual realms, and the Centre should represent a source of well-being and advancement for the inhabitants of the area, encouraging its young people to live close to their roots in dignity and serenity.[26]

References

Bianchi, Bruna. 2005. Il Rapporto di Emily Hobhouse sui campi di concentramento in Sudafrica (gennaio - ottobre 1901). *DEP. Deportate, esuli e profughe. Rivista telematica di studi sulla memoria femminile* 2 (2): 1–10.

Borgognoni, Mariano. 2007. *Sorella Maria. Selvatica e libera in Cristo.* Assisi: Cittadella.

Brits, Elsabé. 2016. *Emily Hobhouse Beloved Traitor.* Cape Town: Tafelberg.

Ceresi, Vincenzo. 1953. *Cristianesimo interiore.* Alba: Edizioni Paoline.

Ceresi, Vincenzo. 1955. *Il mistero della povertà.* Alba: Edizioni Paoline.

Ceschia, Marzia. 2017. *Sorella Maria di Campello, la minore: eremita, cattolica, francescana. La via al* 'Sacrum facere'. Padua: Messaggero.

Chirilli, Emilia. 1973. *Contributo alla storia dell'Eremo francescano di Campello sul Clitunno. Sorella Jacopa*, Galatina: Editrice salentina.

[25] Lucia de Viti de Marco, *Testamento spirituale* (Spiritual Testament), n.d. Courtesy of Armando Foscarini, Cucumula, Lecce.

[26] Constitution of the Le Costantine Foundation, signed by Giulia Starace in 1983. Archive Le Costantine, Le Costantine Foundation, Casamassella (Lecce).

Fisher, John. 1971. *That Miss Hobhouse: The Life of a Great Feminist*. London: Secker & Warburg.

Fogazzaro, Antonio. 1906. *Il Santo*. Milan: Baldini e Castoldi.

Fossati, Roberta. 1997. *Élites femminili e nuovi modelli religiosi nell'Italia tra otto e Novecento*. Urbino: Quattroventi.

Gill, Rebecca. 2012. Networks of Concern, Boundaries of Compassion: British Relief in the South African War. *The Journal of Imperial and Commonwealth History* 40 (5): 827–844.

Hall, John. 2008. *That Bloody Woman: The Turbulent Life of Emily Hobhouse*. Truro, Cornwall: Truran Publishers.

Hart, Norma, and Angelika Monteux. 2004. An Introduction to Camphill Communities and the BA in Curative Education. *Scottish Journal of Residential Child Care* 3 (1): 67–74.

Hobhouse, Emily. 1902. *The Brunt of War and Where It Fell*. London: Methuen.

Hobhouse, Emily. 1984. *Boer War Letters*. Cape Town: Human & Rousseau.

Hobhouse Balme, Jennifer. 2012. *To Love One's Enemies: The Work and Life of Emily Hobhouse Compiled from Letters and Writings, Newspaper Cuttings and Official Documents*. New York: Columbia University Press.

Hobhouse Balme, Jennifer. 2015. *Agent of Peace: Emily Hobhouse and Her Courageous Attempt to End the First World War*. Cheltenham: The History Press.

König, Karl. 2008. *My Task. Autobiography and Biographies*. Edinburgh: Floris Books.

Laurenzi, Elena. 2018. *Fili della trasmissione. Il progetto delle donne de Viti de Marco – Starace nel Salento del 900*. Lecce: Grifo.

Macor, Emilia. 1908. Notice. *La Provincia di Lecce*, 12 July.

Maria di Campello and Primo Mazzolari. 2007. *L'ineffabile fraternità. Carteggio (1925–1959)*. Magrano: Edizioni Qiqajon.

Maria di Campello and Albert Schweitzer. 2007. *Senza varcare la soglia*. Pratovecchio: Edizioni Romena.

Maria di Campello and Giovanni Vannucci. 2007. *Il canto dell'allodola. Lettere scelte (1947–1961)*. Magnano: Edizioni Qiqajon.

Maria di Campello and Mohandas Karamchand Gandhi. 2017. *Un'amicizia grande come il mondo*. Brescia: Morcelliana Edizioni.

Monte, Antonio, and Maria Grazia Presicce. 2010. *L'arte della tessitura nel Salento*. Narni: Crace.

Morozzo Della Rocca, Roberto. 1998. *Maria dell'eremo di Campello: un'avventura spirituale nell'Italia del Novecento*. Milan: Guerini.

Morozzo Della Rocca, Roberto. 2013. *Maria di Campello. Un'amicizia francescana*. Brescia: Morcelliana Edizioni.

Mosca, Manuela. 2021. *The Decades of Silence. Antonio de Viti de Marco from 1923 to 1943*. mimeo.

Müller-Wiedermann, Hans. 1996. *Karl König, a Central European Biography of the Twentieth Century*. Edinburgh: Camphill Books.

Persichella, Vincenzo. 2005. Le trasformazioni della società dal secondo dopoguerra agli anni novanta. In *Storia della Puglia*, ed. Angelo Massafra and Biagio Salvemini, vol. 2, 194–218. Bari: Laterza.

Sabatier, Paul. 1894. *Vie de S. François d'Assise*. Paris: Libraire Fischbacher.

Turton, Amy. 2002. *Storia dell'Eremo 1921–28. Cronaca degli inizi*. Campello sul Clitunno: Eremo Francescano edizioni.

Zanotti Bianco, Umberto. 2011. *La mia Roma. Diario 1943–1944*. Manduria: Lacaita.

CHAPTER 7

The Present-Day Heritage

Elena Laurenzi

7.1 Introduction

This chapter explores the current activities of the Le Costantine Foundation, set up at the bequest of Giulia Starace and Lucia de Viti de Marco. Today the Foundation is still working in the Casamassella area close to Otranto (Apulia, Italy). It represents a real example of female excellence which continues to pursue its founders' project, reshaping it in creative and innovative ways that combine high-quality craft production with biodynamic agriculture, education and social advancement. Through field observation and semi-structured interviews with key witnesses, the chapter documents the enduring memory of the founders and how it is embodied in the Foundation's present activities.

E. Laurenzi (✉)
University of Salento, Lecce, Italy

E. Laurenzi and M. Mosca (eds.), *A Female Activist Elite in Italy (1890–1920)*, https://doi.org/10.1007/978-3-030-87159-8_7

7.2 From Past to Present

The Le Costantine Foundation, set up by Giulia Starace and by Lucia de Viti de Marco, has its home on the lovely estate that belonged to Raffaele de Viti de Marco, Carolina de Viti de Marco and Giulia Starace. The estate stretches for over 33 hectares behind the Idro river valley and includes orchards, fields of cereal crops, olive groves and an extensive Mediterranean woodland populated by holm oaks, terebinth, phillyrea, hawthorn, lentisco, myrtle and wild rosemary bushes. Here and there along the paths, one comes across evidence of the improvements carried out first by Raffaele and later by Carolina and Giulia: wells and rainwater tanks, stone watering troughs for animals, a beautiful apiary in the form of an amphitheatre, and the citrus grove, planted in a hollow surrounded by cypresses to protect it from the wind.

The manor house is a large, plain, rectangular building, occupied by offices and weaving workshops. The main entrance (bizarrely located at the back) looks out on the woodlands, the olive groves and the sea. A few metres away, in the former stables, henhouses and tool stores, there is now the reception area. It consists of a restaurant and ten large, light-filled bedrooms with disabled access. All the rooms give onto a semi-circular courtyard, with a large, flourishing carob tree at its centre, a benevolent and hospitable guardian.

The property previously belonged to Carolina de Viti de Marco, who had inherited it from her father Raffaele. She loved the estate deeply: in her *Annales* she wrote that she often went there with her father and that it was always hard for them to tear themselves away and go back to the city.[1] Her letters to her daughters are also full of references to the land's trees and flowers, and to the improvements under way. This is, then, the well-loved terrain that Carolina, according to her daughter Giulia Starace, had always planned to devote to the public good. In 1964, when she began to build the house, she buried under the first stone a note explicitly setting out its purpose, written and signed in her own hand. A copy is conserved in the archive:

[1] As we have seen in the previous chapters, the *Annales* was a series of notes that Carolina drafted later in life in chronological order. Archive Carolina de Viti de Marco and Giulia Starace.

> Today, 2nd June 1964, in the property named 'Costantine', belonging to Carolina De Viti de Marco, widow of Francesco Paolo Starace, born 15th August 1863 at Casamassella, and to her daughter Giulia Starace, was laid, in the name of God and His holy protection, the first stone of their house, which will also house children in need of special care. The house will rise in this place, made especially beautiful by its woodlands and views – although distant – of Lake Alimini and the Adriatic Sea. We pray to God to bless all the present and future inhabitants of this house and this place that Raffaele De Viti de Marco, father of Carolina, loved so much. With special thanks to Lucia de Viti de Marco Pecorella, Carlo Papadia and Franco Astuto, who, in loving collaboration, made it possible to achieve this goal.[2]

Giulia Starace moved into the house when her mother died in 1965. She was already elderly, but in her remaining twenty years she stubbornly pursued the project, which finally took shape, as we have seen, in the Foundation bearing the estate's name.

Gabriele Malinconico, a friend of the De Viti-Starace family, who spent many months on the estate as a child, recalls how the house was when Giulia Starace was living there. He remembers Giulia explaining to him the approach to landscaping that she had worked on with her mother Carolina. They had considered not only the land's productivity, but also the aesthetics of the landscape and its effects. Following Steiner's ideas, they had endeavoured to maintain a balance between fullness and emptiness, between crop fields and orchards or woods to create a feeling of space and meditative calm.[3]

The main entrance, at the back of the house, has an elegant fan-shaped staircase, although it is barely used, and access is normally through what was previously the service entrance. In Giulia's time, this meant coming straight into the kitchen (now an exhibition space for the workshop's fabrics). This direct access to a private family area was a clear sign of the owner's personality. She did not receive people formally, but ushered guests into a house that was permanently open to all, sharing its domestic life with them. The kitchen had wood-burning ovens and a three-metre

[2] Carolina De Viti de Marco, copy of the note deposited under the first stone of Le Costantine, 2 June, 1964, Archive Carolina de Viti de Marco and Giulia Starace, Le Costantine Foundation, Casamassella (Lecce). Unless otherwise stated, the translations of the quoted texts are our own.

[3] See the interview with Gabriele Malinconico, in Laurenzi (2018: 211–213).

extendable table where guests gathered to eat, and Gabriele Malinconico remembers the liveliness of these meals with Giulia, his own family, and the group of children from Fregene, taken in and cared for by Giulia in the summer months. The area that is now the weaving workshop was once the living room. Its wide window has a superb view reaching as far as the small town of Giurdignano, and the horizon is framed by two high, flourishing pine trees. Malinconico recalls that, when the electricity company put posts at the point where the lines of perspective meet, Giulia protested strongly, writing many letters to call for their removal, but without success. On the upper story of the house there were numerous guest bedrooms, each with a private bathroom, which was unusual for those times; Giulia wanted every guest to be able to come and go at will and to enjoy their stay at Le Costantine without being disturbed or without disturbing others.

Today, as stipulated in its statutes, the Le Costantine Foundation combines craft production, biodynamic agriculture, education and social advancement. The textile workshop bears the name 'Amando e cantando' (Singing and loving), given to it by Giulia, and it has been in operation since 2003. There, the craftswomen weave natural fibres on traditional wooden four-framed looms. Their work follows traditional methods with completely handsewn finishing, but there is a wide space for experiments in research, design and the choice and treatment of materials. Apart from rugs, tapestries and blankets, loom-woven and hand-finished in the traditional way, the artisans are constantly creating new products: scarves and stoles in cashmere, linen and silk; bags, household accessories and jewellery. Working with teachers from the Polytechnic University of Bari,[4] they also support students in their research into weaving with unconventional, recycled or treated fabrics. The excellence of their craft has won the workshop a leading position within its own niche market, with products exhibited at prestige outlets in Italy and France and featuring on the covers of the sector's most important magazines and journals. Their work was recently selected by Dior for its Cruise 2021 collection, and woven pieces made with Le Costantine fabrics were shown in the magical setting of the Piazza del Duomo in Lecce (Apulia). Dior's creative director, Maria Grazia Chiuri, was attracted not only by the quality of the

[4] Bari is the capital of Apulia. The Polytechnic of Bari is an Italian scientific and technological university institute. The disciplines contained in the fields of architecture, engineering and industrial design are the subject of study and research.

products, but also by the history of the Foundation, where high-quality craftwork is interwoven with women's traditional savoir-faire and the aims of advancement and emancipation for women:

> In November I travelled to Puglia to get to know the local craftspeople and work with them. On this journey I discovered incredible craftspeople, such as those of the Le Costantine Foundation, run by the women of the area working on the creation of fabrics. They produce amazing fabrics representing all the different local traditions, woven on handlooms. It is important to celebrate this type of work, particularly because of the idea, not only in Italy but also throughout the world, that these products are normally women's domestic work, rather than being truly creative productions. (Jana 2021)

The Dior Spring 2021 fashion show makes the perfect ending to our story of this far-sighted project, with its awareness of the value of women's traditional knowledge; a story of women's solidarity and complicity mobilised through the strength and freedom of their creativity (Frisa 2020).

One important factor in the originality and inspirational power of this enterprise is that its statutes direct it towards caring for the local environment and disadvantaged people. Entrepreneurial action and social initiative rather than clashing nourish and boost each other, pointing us along the path to sustainable development.

The Foundation also produces biodynamic oils, grains and vegetables, approved by Demeter, another successful brand that was launched in 1927 by farmers experimenting in Steiner agricultural methods. Sewing, fertilisation and harvesting follow the lunar cycle, and chemical fertilisers and pesticides are replaced by natural methods that support the vitality and fertility of the soil: organic farm compost, vegetable fertilisers, crop rotation and vegetable- or mineral-based pesticides.

The Foundation also offers professional training aimed at fostering the local economy and culture, with a wide range of courses from weaving to dressmaking and tailoring, gardening, organic and biodynamic farming, cake- and bread-making, street food and diversity management. Another important initiative of the Foundation is the education it provides for children and adolescents, mainly from refugee minorities, who are at risk of dropping out of school. In this way, through vocational training, Giulia and Lucia's mission of assisting and guiding disadvantaged children is fulfilled, helping them find a path to self-fulfilment and a job through which, instead of emigrating in search of work, they can put down real roots in the area.

7.3 The Living Space of a Community

What was Giulia Starace's home in the last years of her life is now taken up with workbenches, blackboards, files, desks, looms and beautifully exhibited multicoloured textiles. The rooms and corridors are constantly bustling with tourists, purchasers, friends dropping in to say hello, workers, collaborators on various projects, teachers, students, guests, researchers, walkers, meditators, peace and nature lovers staying over for a few nights, neighbours and local people paying ritual visits on church festival days. One thing that stands out is the informal, almost domestic atmosphere in which all the activities are carried out, while at the same time fulfilling criteria of professionalism and excellence. This family-style atmosphere envelops not only personal relationships but also the organisation of the work itself. One example of this style is the flexibility with which roles and spaces are arranged. The rooms communicate with each other through doors that open onto the wide corridors, so that the tasks of the different people working there are largely shared. The spaces can also vary their function whenever necessary and are often changed out of all recognition. The classroom next to the workshop, for example, where training courses are given in winter, becomes the exhibition area open to the many tourists who visit the Foundation in summer. Every June, the benches and blackboards are removed, the large loom is reassembled and the cupboard full of rugs is opened; scarves and bags are hung from the walls, and tapestries laid out on the shelves.

The weaving workshop, where the work is done to the rhythmic sound of the looms, is also a creative area where materials, models and designs are studied, tried out and discussed, and a training room where the master craftswomen patiently and skilfully teach the ancient and contemporary art of weaving to students often from far afield. The workshop is also the heart of the Foundation, a social space where visitors, clients and friends mix, and where news circulates, old stories are told and improvised parties take place.

The activities in these multi-purpose spaces are also varied and flexible: they share in the protean nature of care work. The weaving courses, for example, give rise to a network of relationships that are kept up and cared for through time, so that the training goes well beyond the limited period that students spend on the course. This flexibility and rigour are even greater in the education of children and adolescents in difficulty. The teaching in this case goes well beyond the aims of vocational training in the narrow sense, and includes psychological and physical support from specialists working with the teachers, and post-course guidance in the working world offered by teachers and tutors in collaboration with the host communities and a wide network of relationships with local entrepreneurs and reception organisations.

In general, the work tasks, although accomplished to a high, sometimes extremely high level of professionalism, are not rigidly set within narrow confines of objectives and competences. Bridging figures and all-rounders are the norm: people who can move on different levels and in different areas, taking on varying roles and functions without losing sight of the Foundation's many different faces and purposes.

The all-round figure par excellence is Lucia de Vito, daughter of one of the children hosted at Fregene, and today a worker at the Foundation. Lucia fulfils a range of different functions depending on the season: tutor in winter and receptionist in summer, trainer when necessary, secretary, organiser, telephone operator and always the first port of call for any need, demand, request or report. More than a role, hers is a presence: a watchful and constant presence that enables her to act outside the stipulations of her contract. Lena Pajano, the teacher who manages the weavers with tact and skill, is another similarly versatile employee. Lena also has personal links to the history of the Foundation, as her father, Camillo, worked for Giulia Starace until her late old age. Then there is Francesco de Cicco, driver, supervisor and factotum, who carries out the essential task of mediating between the tutors and the children, acting as a member of the group, almost an older brother.

The President, Maria Cristina Rizzo, supervises all the Foundation's activities and keeps its different areas in contact with each other. She does not control from above but participates from within: in the weaving workshop, she plans the products with the weavers and then promotes them to the outside world; she prepares and organises hosting arrangements along with those who are responsible; she programmes the educational activities and courses with the teachers and trainers and follows the children's progress closely. She views her role through the optic of maternal love, finding in these 'other children' a reason for living and a source of joy, after losing her own son in a tragic accident.

The way the Foundation recruits staff is also interesting. Mostly, as our interviewees testified, staff members are taken on through co-optation or personal contacts, mainly family and friends. Many of the personnel, as we have seen, have personal histories closely linked to that of the Viti de Marco-Starace project. However, this choice of taking on staff through proximity should not be confused with nepotism, a well-known and much-studied phenomenon in the history of some regions of the South of Italy, where access to jobs is often clientelist and non-transparent, and this creates a corrupt social atmosphere characterised by a lack of civic sense and the weakness of the law (Banfield 1958; Gribaudi 1994; Alcaro 2009). The links of loyalty and trust nourishing the Foundation's recruitment tend in the opposite direction, since they embody an awareness of the common good and a willingness to carry out tasks that go beyond the legal formalities of the contract. All the interviewees spoke of the staff's attitude of responsibility. The official rules have less weight than the organic ties between the members of the community, which are the measure of both their commitment and their autonomy. Professionalism, however, is still the essential qualification for employment at the Foundation, and the rights and duties of all working relationships are well defined. In all, this process is very far from the wild deregulation of advanced neoliberalism.

To attempt a definition of the way of working that we have sketched above, we could borrow the notion of 'community economy', a term coined in the 1950s by the entrepreneur Adriano Olivetti for an industrial context (Olivetti 1952; Ferrarotti and Gemelli 2015; Ferrarotti 2016; Cadeddu 2016). This 'inappropriate appropriation', although originally applied to a setting totally distinct from the Foundation, can help us to delineate an experience whose characteristics do not fully correspond to those of the social market economy and the solidarity initiatives that have been widely studied in the last thirty years (Mau 2003; Van Hook 2004; Felice 2009). Here we are not only defining a model that combines profit-making with the common good. The specificity of the Foundation's economy cannot be understood outside the ties (professional, cultural, family, friendship) that bind its people together and motivate their work for the success of their common enterprise.

This feeling of belonging to a community, even when it gives rise to inevitable frustrations and conflicts, is fed by a fundamental reciprocal satisfaction (and in some cases, happiness) and a shared sense of responsibility. Many interviewees stressed this basic aspect of the Foundation, which emerges not only in their honesty but also in the generosity with which they offer their services and share others' problems.

The memory of the founders is an essential component in this community economy. Theirs is both a living presence that binds, more tightly than any legal statutes, the services of the people who form part of the Foundation, and an inherent value that ensures the market value of its products.

7.4 Reflections on What Is Transmitted

Transmettre n'est pas donner un objet constitué, mais faire de soi-même un lieu de passage, un vecteur dans une dynamique de devenir, puisqu'on ne peut transmettre qu'à partir de ce que l'on a reçu. Christiane Vollaire[5]

At the end of this long skein, then, we come back to its binding thread, the key issue of transmission. This is a strand that, as it has passed through time, has interwoven with countless others to form the extraordinary story of our central characters, and which reaches well beyond their deaths to the present day, forcing us to ask certain questions.

What is being transmitted through the stories that we have reconstructed? If it is a project, as we suggested at the outset, in what sense can we say that it is the same project? What connects such diverse experiences as Carolina de Viti de Marco and Harriet Lathrop Dunham's school at Casamassella, Lucia de Viti de Marco's Steiner community, Giulia Starace's dream of a Montessori house for children, and the Le Costantine Foundation? Clearly there are family ties; but this is not an enterprise handed down from mother to daughter to perpetuate the household economy. It is not a model to be reproduced or an idea to be materialised, and still less an ideal to which we should raise an altar, perhaps made of granite, like most altars. What passes along these threads is something more alive; something both subtle and tenacious.

[5] 'Transmitting something, rather than handing on an already constituted object, means turning yourself into a channel, a vector in a process of becoming, since you can only transmit on the basis of something you have received' (Vollaire 2007). Thanks to Fina Birulés for pointing me to this text.

It is a civic (and therefore political) sense of the common good; it is an attitude of responsibility towards the world (*amor mundi*); it is engagement and co-engagement in others' lives (not only of human beings, but also animals and plants); it is the awareness of care and its delicacy, complexity and wisdom; it is an idea of work that aims for excellence not only in its products but also in its processes and relationships; and it is the principle that people are more important than procedures and profits.

None of this is organised in a set of commandments or a theoretical system. There is no sign of a manual, articulated approach or legacy—if we leave aside Giulia Starace's Foundation's statutes. What is transmitted primarily, and what continues to be transmitted even today, above and beyond any formal ties, is rather an experience, or better, the distillation of an experience: a way of being in the world, a style that unites our central characters despite their diverse personalities, bringing their actions into harmony with each other. It is something that is communicated almost without words, by contact—or even by contagion. And since these are lived experiences (differing also in this way from experiments), they do not have the crystalline purity of ideas, but rather the hybrid nature of living organisms, in which the parts only work when acting together in harmony, and this is the only thing that gives drive and energy to the whole.

An example is the Casamassella School. It emerges clearly, when we study its history in both the public and private realms, that Carolina de Viti de Marco's initiative did not only transmit technical skills or a pure model of social entrepreneurship; together with these things, she offered, warmth, affection, personal freedom and the ability to go beyond preestablished roles and limits. Carolina herself avoided—not without difficulty, as we have seen—the 'enforced division of women's social destiny' that condemned nineteenth- and twentieth-century women to being either wives or 'old maids' (De Giorgio 1988: 455). Instead, she created a family-style working environment that was an alternative to the factory or subaltern domestic labour. In this space, the qualities of domesticity and patience which, according to a still-persistent prejudice, are essential to learning needlework, were not transmitted, or did not involve any kind of submission. We only have to think of the short passage from the *Annales*: after five months of marriage, 'since things were not going well', one of Carolina's best-loved craft workers 'came to live with us [...] and stayed for two years'. Of course, I do not wish to argue that the Casamassella Palace was a den of subversive feminists where women were urged to leave their husbands. But in contact with Carolina, the freedom she had won and had always enjoyed, independently of organised groups and slogans, was transmitted to those who lived and worked with her; and first of all to her daughters, who in turn, and not by chance, escaped from the 'enforced division' of women's roles: like her mother, Lucia spent almost half her life separated from her husband, and Giulia was not seen by her compatriots, still less by her friends, as an 'old maid'. It may be said that this has nothing to do with the school and its transmission. Yet this is not the case, since the reason that the Casamassella School inspired the following generation—both Lucia Starace on the experimental, technical and entrepreneurial side and Giulia Starace and Lucia De Viti de Marco from the welfare and the spiritual perspectives—was that it was not only a technical training institute and therefore a school of excellence, but also a complex experience, both personal and political, in which extraordinary designs, fabrics and colours were produced at the same time as extraordinary (out of the ordinary) relationships among women and lifestyles that combined daring and invention with humility and discretion.

This story tells of initiatives that were conceived and carried out in a predominantly family environment and transmitted through channels of affection, care and moral authority. Yet among the prime movers, personal commitment did not exclude an awareness of the political value of their work and a desire to give it continuity. For this reason, their experience and their practice evolved into a project. But here we should also make a proviso. What they imagined and planned did not have the requisite features of a conventional project: rationality, stability, internal consistency, well-defined objectives, a cost and profit analysis. It flowed; it was uneven and discontinuous. We have seen it change its shape often, while always remaining recognisable: taking on different guises, changing its name and responding to passionate, sometimes even obsessive, quests. This divergence from rational planning norms may appear a deficiency, perhaps new proof of the old prejudice that women's minds are unsuited to public life. I would argue, in contrast, that the highly political essence of this project consists precisely in that it follows no preconceived model or finite, definitive theory. It is open to constant reinterpretation by its heirs; and these make it their own, taking part in it and bringing it back to the world.

We are far, then, from the mental experiments of the great utopians (old and new) who defined the smallest details of their projects on the basis of a rationality that was granite-like because it was pure and uncontaminated by reality. Here, on the contrary, a completely feminine awareness of reality and freedom was given life: a practical awareness that pits the idea against the roughness, resistance and sudden collapses of the chosen terrain; a political awareness that bringing someone or something into the world means letting it live its own life, since 'one can only transmit something by giving up one's power over it and delivering it into the power of another' (Vollaire 2007). From this point of view, the undefined or perhaps 'airy' nature of the project and its debatable fortunes and failures do not disprove its political value for the present day.

Furthermore, the story we have told challenges us to accept the value of a form of political transmission through experiences and ideas that have no ideological pretentions. They may be 'small, simple, modest ideas, that cannot raise any great flag of revolt', as Amelia Rosselli (1907: 17) wrote of the Italian Female Industries; yet they can effect a revolution in everyday life and making deep and lasting changes. From this perspective, the initiatives of the women presented here belong to the 'practical feminism' characterising the early twentieth-century women's movement and described by Amelia Rosselli (1907: 16) as a political attitude that, rather than focussing on a grand idea, 'grasps the still nebulous image and shapes its contours with a humble art'. The reference to art is interesting, since it frames politics as *praxis*: as a creative, experimental exercise mobilising ideas and actions that are embodied in relationships. From this standpoint, transmission is not simply a handing on, but is also itself *praxis*, process and transformation: an 'inheritance without testament', in Hannah Arendt's favourite phrase from René Char, a legacy that the receiver responds to without having to accept it completely.

While the Le Costantine Foundation has inherited and carried on the project of its two founders, it is not a slavish copy, but a free, creative and responsible one. A sense of the shared world; caring for the environment and those living in it; an idea of work that aims for excellence not only of its products but also in its processes and relationships; an attitude of responsibility towards the world; the importance of people over processes: the values of this ideal heritage transmitted across the two generations of women studied here are not only expressed but also further developed at Le Costantine. What ensures the endurance of this legacy is not only (and not so much) compliance with the objectives laid out in the statutes but the cultivation of the memory of those women who wished for the place, imagined it and, to a certain extent, experienced it.

The interviews showed that the memory of the founders is still present for the current staff (certainly more for those who had known them in their lifetimes, but for the others as well), and the ways that this influences their organisation of their work and relationships, their attitude towards the services they offer and their awareness of the value of the Foundation's products. This memory is therefore a source of meaning, and through it, each person feels that they are part of a common endeavour, that their work is not limited to earning a salary but is a contribution (in terms of beauty, knowledge, and care) to the *civitas*, the world. Memory is thus the binding force that nourishes the ties within the community and drives creativity and personal fulfilment, since the example of the founders proffers freedom and requires effort at the same time.

In this story, tradition functions as the inspiration for change, and the past clarifies our understanding of the present and, at the same time, it nourishes our imagination and our political actions aimed at changing the future. The relationship between the three dimensions of time is thus in constant movement. Rather than following the traditional linear view of transmission in which the past consigns its heritage to the present in a single direction, a virtuous cycle is set up in which the present looks to the past not as a foundation or a binding rule but as a fund of experience and knowledge that can be reactivated and reanimated, and the past in turn illuminates the present not in the flat light of a set of instructions but with flashes of experience that inspire and nourish the political imagination.[6] Thus, the 'silent labourers' of a small village in the deep South of Italy can also become a source of inspiration to us, 'like so many little sparks spreading a beneficent light within their own small circle' (Rosselli 1907, 17).

References

Alcaro, Mario. 2009. La favola del "familismo amorale" del Sud. *Critica marxista* 6: 21–25.

Banfield, Edward Christie. 1958. *The Moral Basis of a Backward Society*. Glencoe: The Free Press.

Cadeddu, Davide. 2016. *Humana Civilitas, Profilo intellettuale di Adriano Olivetti*. Turin: Edizioni di Comunità.

[6] On this paradigm of history, see Didi-Huberman (2009).

De Giorgio, Michela. 1988. Signore e signorine italiane fra Ottocento e Novecento: modelli culturali e comportamenti sociali regolati da uno stato civile In *Ragnatele di rapporti: Patronage e reti di relazione nella storia delle donne*, ed. Laura Ferrante, Maura Palazzi, and Gianna Pomata, 454–480, Turin: Rosenberg & Sellier.

Didi-Huberman, George. 2009. *Survivance des lucioles*. Paris: Les Éditions de Minuit.

Felice, Flavio. 2009. *L'economia sociale di mercato*. Soveria Mannelli: Rubbettino.

Ferrarotti, Franco, and Giuliana Gemelli. 2015. *Adriano Olivetti, Un imprenditore di idee*. Turin: Edizioni di Comunità.

Ferrarotti, Franco. 2016. *La concreta utopia di Adriano Olivetti*. Bologna: EDB.

Frisa, Maria Luisa. 2020. L'indicibile fortuna dell'essere donna. Una Conversazione con Maria Grazia Chiuri. *Flash Art*, 349, Available at https://flash---art.it/article/maria-grazia-chiuri (26 June 2021).

Gribaudi, Gabriella. 1994. Il paradigma del "familismo amorale". In *Fra storia e storiografia. Scritti in onore di Pasquale Villani*, ed. Paolo Macrì and Angelo Massafra, 337–354. Bologna: Il Mulino.

Jana, Rosalinde. 2021. Maria Grazia Chiuri racconta la natura "magica" dell'ultima collezione Dior Cruise 2021. *Vogue*, July. Available at https://www.vogue.it/moda/article/maria-grazia-chiuri-dior-cruise-2021-lecce-intervista (26 June 2021).

Laurenzi, Elena. 2018. *Fili della trasmissione. Il progetto delle donne De Viti de Marco – Starace nel Salento del 900*. Lecce: Grifo.

Mau, Steffen. 2003. *Moral Economy of Welfare States*. New York: Routledge.

Olivetti, Adriano. 1952. *Società, stato, comunità. Per un'economia e politica comunitaria*. Milan: Edizioni di Comunità.

Rosselli, Amelia. 1907. Femminismo pratico e femminismo teorico. *Vita femminile italiana* 1 (3): 16–20.

Van Hook, James C. 2004. *Rebuilding Germany: The Creation of the Social Market Economy 1945–1957*. Cambridge: Cambridge University Press.

Vollaire, Christiane. 2007. Lost in Translation. Sur la Question de la Transmission. *Catalogue Transmettre, Espace 36*, Saint-Omer, September. Available at www.christiane-vollaire.fr/index.php?/philosophieesthetique/lost-in-translation (26 June 2021).

PART III

Arts, Politics and Transmission: Methodological and Historiographical Considerations

CHAPTER 8

The Signs of an Art

Marisa Forcina

8.1 'Good Work' and the Art of Democratic Happiness

With the title 'The Signs of an Art', our proposal is not to offer an aesthetic system or revolution or to argue that handmade lacework and other such craft products are forms of art. Although such arguments were advanced over the course of the twentieth century—when new forms of household decoration, industrial architecture and photography aspired to the status of art—it is not our intention here to trace the signs of art in weaving or lacemaking, however legitimate that might be. Neither is it our purpose to validate needlework as a creative endeavour or as a relationship between form and content—a relation which, as Benedetto Croce (1947: 12) writes,[1] affords insight into the *a priori* synthesis inherent in all philosophical activity. In contrast, what we wish to do here is to shed some light

[1]Benedetto Croce (1856–1952) was an outstanding Italian philosopher, historian and politician. An idealist in philosophy, a liberal in politics, he is mainly known for his aesthetic theory.

M. Forcina (✉)
University of Salento, Lecce, Italy

E. Laurenzi and M. Mosca (eds.), *A Female Activist Elite in Italy (1890–1920)*, https://doi.org/10.1007/978-3-030-87159-8_8

on the project of the art of work well done, and to show how this was theorised and practised as a way of life by particular women and advocated as an authentically political project by writers whose work has become all too quickly forgotten. What interests us here, then, is to explore the way that the idea and practice of working well became a symbol and paradigm of emancipation and a project of freedom for those who were involved and also for their social and geographical circumstances.

The purpose behind the studies in the previous parts of this book is to focus on specific locations and on persons who lived in and loved these areas, and to bring their stories back to the place, and also to show the broad political significance of these stories within the international context at the turn of the twentieth century. As we have already seen, the women studied in this volume were no strangers to this international context. These were years when there was widespread debate about how to change society; in other words, about the art of creating a radically new society. The signs of this art were already visible in the new centrality that women's work and relations between the sexes acquired among the bourgeoisie. New models of subjectivity and relationships revealed the revolutionary possibility that a woman's existence need no longer be tied to that of her husband, and women finally began to glimpse the prospect of a new and unprecedented self-fulfilment in living the single life. This was a revolutionary, epoch-making development, even more so since this self-fulfilment also represented both a social fulfilment and a positive change for society as a whole.

So, if we find a series of unmarried women in the female line of the de Viti de Marco-Starace family, this is not the result of a succession of 'misfortunes', but rather it is due to a new congruence, which shifted the bourgeois vision of female liberty based on money and the power of the family towards a new vision of freedom that had worked at its core. Single women had already begun to assume the central role in realising this new idea. They founded schools and workshops, showing that it was possible to transform industrial production into cooperative associations with a different style of relationships between workers; relationships that could materialise in the real world the notion that happiness, at least, if not the means of production, could be redistributed.[2]

[2] The research of Rosanna Basso (1999, 2000) was particularly helpful with regard to the region of Salento (Apulia, Italy) where the de Viti de Marco-Starace family was

The idea that work, citizenship and happiness could be a shared and central concern, that they could be the foundation stones of a new politics, has an important place in the history of political thought and the theory of democracy in particular. We may recall, for example, the broad lines of the concept of happiness formulated by Kant at the end of the eighteenth century, combining the universal and the particular in an idea of subjective happiness that has its culmination in the affirmation that 'people are unwilling to give up their universal human desire to seek happiness in their own way' (Kant 1793/1991: 83).

Kant's overarching theory, however, saw the social contract as being conditioned by law, i.e. the rational and universal notion that each individual's freedom is defined in its limitation by that of the other ('negative freedom'); yet the idea of subjective happiness that he clearly seems to assert, and which was enshrined politically in the American Constitution as the right to happiness, contradicts this. There is the same distance between Kant and the American Constitution as that existing between the rational universality of the subject's rights when subordinated to a state and politics seen as the public dimension of the subject-citizen's private fulfilment. In Kant, it is universal reason that prevails over the quest for happiness and which dictates the principles of politics. Yet, despite this claim to universality, the Kantian subject is still split: it is the bearer of liberty as man, the possessor of equality as subject, the owner of independence as citizen, the seeker of happiness as an individual. And it is a subject further divided into male and female, a difference reproducing that between freedom and subordination that is recomposed—though only instrumentally—in the reciprocity of the 'use' of the body in marriage (Pateman 1988). The false equality of this reciprocal 'use' emerges on the woman's side even more patently than in the exchange of freedom for security and protection in political theory.[3]

In contrast, a different, female sensibility, matured by experience and history, enables Hannah Arendt to define 'public happiness' as the recompense for the risks and sacrifices required not by personal interests but

based, in the southeast of Italy. In these studies, Basso shows how some early twentieth-century female figures made schools and teaching the means of realising unforeseen styles of emancipation for themselves and for society as a whole. This is in line with what we showed in the first two parts of the present book.

[3] Regarding this subject, which has been the basis of theories of power from Hobbes up to the present day, the studies of Arienzo and De Luca (2019) are particularly interesting.

by public ones, stemming from our acting together as citizens. This is because, she argues, it is only by operating in our shared world and enjoying the happiness and freedom of revealing ourselves and acting in a non-solitary way that we can discover our common public interests and transcend, when necessary, our limited private ones. In 1963, stressing the links between public happiness and public freedom, Arendt formulated a further clear definition of democracy:

> what we today call democracy is a form of government where the few rule, at least supposedly, in the interest of the many. This government is democratic in that popular welfare and private happiness are its chief goals; but it can be called oligarchic in the sense that public happiness and public freedom have again become the privilege of the few. (Arendt 1963: 269)

Arendt's definition of democracy places at its centre a type of private happiness that can be extended to the common world. This idea was foreseen and given a functional form by many women at the beginning of the twentieth century, as we have seen in this book. These women embodied the awareness that subjection could be turned into emancipation through their own work rather than by campaigning for rights or equality, and this form of work could give rise to welfare for the people at the same time as both individual and social subjective happiness. They knew that there is no moral freedom without economic freedom; yet they also knew that women's economic freedom heralded a new era if it had not been won through heredity, property or a secure marriage, but rather conquered through a new model of work capable of producing new social models and, very soon, new acquisitions of rights. As in Arendt, the political project and its recognition derive from an awareness gained through experience.

In short, new and revolutionary models of women's liberation that privileged economic over political freedom took root between the late nineteenth and early twentieth centuries. And women were fully aware that they would access this freedom not through marriage or heredity but by ensuring that their own work was recognised, increasingly aspiring to assert its value as 'good work', work well done, work that carried the signs of art within it. A new art.

8.2 A New Art

The signs of this art, which ranged from needlework to social work, became for many women the outward traces of another kind of art: that of cultivating themselves. This was an art that they practised not to please others but an art for themselves. Indeed, in one single action, they learned to identify and cultivate their recognition of themselves and their social relationships. And these signs, well understood, were openly embodied in the culture of the time and in some of its texts, which turned these new social situations into political projects.

It was during those years that Chernyshevsky's novel *What Is to Be Done?* (1863), one of the most important expressions of Russian populism, was published. It saw revolution as emanating from the transformation of relationships between men and women and, rather than a class struggle, a *rapprochement* between the popular and educated classes. Chernyshevsky channelled his anti-utopian, practical revolutionary passion into his criticism of conventions and his vision of equality between the sexes and the ethical-social formation of personal behaviour. These ideals are symbolised in the book by a needlecraft workshop that produces high-quality linen products, through which the heroine, Vera—meaning 'faith' in Russian, representing revolutionary faith—builds her own emancipation and that of her co-workers, founded on the belief that we can also redistribute happiness through work. Thus, her objective was not to realise economic and social equality alone, but also equality in the sense of real and equal access to happiness, expressed explicitly in the phrase: 'There can be no full happiness without full independence'.[4]

In contrast to Romantic literature, which had inextricably linked happiness to love—or, as in melodrama, love and death—Chernyshevsky's novel separates them and turns emotions into political actions. If love is the desire to make the loved one happy, then the awareness that love cannot exist without freedom leads Chernyshevsky to turn romantic love into friendship and solidarity in the name of freedom. In the novel this transformation is described as

> a grand secret, it is good to avail oneself of it, and it does not take great skill to do so. All that is required is a pure heart and an honest soul, and

[4] The quote continues with: 'Poor women, how few among you have this happiness!' (Chernyshevsky 1863/1989: 357).

> the present idea of the rights of a human being with regard to the freedom of the one with whom you live. (Chernyshevsky 1863/1989: 362)

As previously in Filmer's seventeenth-century text *The Patriarch* (1680), which had theorised human governments through the model of the patriarchal family, at the dawn of the twentieth century the new model of social and political revolution was theorised by Chernyshevsky, once again through the mould of the family. Here, however, the model was not a patriarchal rule; rather, it was women's emancipation that became the new paradigm. This was a new form of freedom and a new social conscience that women had shown they had developed through work. It should also be noted that the political thought of the two writers was not an empty project, but the translation into the theory of an already existing social fact, an objective recording of the lives of people they had personally witnessed. Chernyshevsky states this openly, criticising the hypocrisy of the bourgeois way of life: 'Now, among those whom we call the people of the present, it is quite different. They, after being united by love, become brightened and warmed more and more by the poetry of it the longer they live together' (Chernyshevsky 1863/1989: 362). At the centre of this new life, presented as the model for the new revolutionary political project, the author places women, with their subjective dedication to working with others—just as was already occurring in some aspects of contemporary reality. This social dimension was a complete departure from the individualistic paradigm that had limited women's labour to caring for their families. To this first element another was added, broader and more general: that of women's competence in work displayed to others, a work demanding dexterity and skill and eliciting the acknowledgement of a well-crafted product. Women's conscientious concern to 'work well' became, then, an impulse towards the good, towards well-being and therefore towards the well-being of others as well. It was in this way that many women, like the second De Viti de Marco-Starace generation studied in this book (see Chapter 6), turned their attention to caring for others, their initiatives giving shape to a holistic vision of well-being. As in Chernyshevsky's novel, where Vera, after leaving the workshop to her colleagues, chooses medicine and healthcare as the scenario of her intervention in the world, Lucia de Viti de Marco and Giulia Starace saw their care of polio-affected children not as an individualistic act of charity and subjective attention towards others, but as a positive intervention in the common world, a political action contributing to the life of their own home region. It was a political project focussed on overcoming the pain of an impoverished area and the pain of its inhabitants who suffered from illness, and it was devoted to staving off neglect and decline. This political tie to the land, experienced as both a geographical and a spiritual place, was far removed from any type of regional identity politics.

8.3 Tracing the Signs of a Defeated Art

In political terms, everything that Chernyshevsky had advanced as revolutionary action in *What Is to Be Done?* was buried by Lenin's manifesto, which had the same title (Lenin 1902) and which was resolutely centred on the concepts of the revolutionary party and its hegemony, both of which were far from the feminine subjectivity in play in Chernyshevsky's text. Lenin's aspiration—which was inherited by the Italian Marxist philosopher Antonio Gramsci[5]—was to make change possible by equipping the working class with a unified national organisation directed from a single centre, driven by a programme and ruled by a statute. This was a different path to social renewal and socialism, in which the new world would not be created by the knowing work of subjects, but by organising them, with the transformation process carried out by a single subject: the party. It was a completely different story, and one that contributed to silencing and isolating all other experiments that linked social transformation to work and women's active and individual presence.

In contrast, these new studies of women's political action, the changes that they set in motion and the arts that they practised and in which they believed, open up new vistas and unforeseen destinations. The relationship with the voices of women from the past—most of whom are excluded from the narrowly political canon—is constructed not in terms of hierarchy but through everyday equality based on trust. This follows Hannah Arendt's reading of politics, which teaches new historians of political thought to steer clear of all forms of scholastic pedantry: an approach that, as Ferruccio Focher (2000: 144) writes,[6]

[5] Antonio Gramsci (1891–1937) founded the Communist Party of Italy in 1921 and was its leader until 1926, when he was imprisoned by the Fascist regime. During his eleven years of imprisonment, he wrote his famous *Prison Notebooks* (Gramsci 1948–1951/2011).

[6] Unless stated otherwise, the translations of the quoted texts are our own.

> seeks in other writers not so much what they intended to say at the moment when they expressed themselves – an impossible undertaking, and also futile today – but all that they do say or could say, seen from the standpoint of our present needs, with freedom from hallowed but worn-out frames of interpretation and with the understanding that it is impossible to use these [...]. It is not a question, of course, of arbitrarily updating rediscovered authors [...] but of an open dialogue with them, of the fruition in time of their timeless words.

The merit of the studies in this book is that they reveal how the women we focus on consciously sought to drive the transformation of a specific place: a political process, then, but one that did not rely on any form of institution or party-political strategy. This is especially true of the project of the two sisters-in-law Carolina and Etta de Viti De Marco and their daughters Giulia Starace and Lucia de Viti de Marco, analysed by Elena Laurenzi in the second part of the book. The relationships among these women were not just affective but they were nourished by a deep spiritual and practical sharing of their love of their homeland. What Laurenzi reconstructs is an amply documented civil passion and a love of subjective freedom that was not afraid to manifest itself through care and affection. The story of one of the cousins' concern for the other, advising her to take care of herself and not to isolate herself, does not only represent anxiety. Their frequent use of English was not xenophilia, but rather a recourse to Etta's language, which took on a political and symbolic value as a measure of balance and self-care. As we have said, self-care is also a political project for the care of the common world; and for this reason, the memory of their mothers was not only a psychological haven, a source of wisdom and inexhaustible warmth, but it also set them a task to fulfil. When over the decades, Lucia de Viti de Marco and Giulia Starace laid plans and worked together, buying and selling plots of land, negotiating, trying to save the Casamassella palace from sale, writing and rewriting their wills to find the best way to bind their own assets to the idea that had so much difficulty taking shape, they were doing all this to carry out this assignment, to accomplish an action that they knew to be a political task.

The story of this network of women enables us, even obliges us, not only to reread the history of Italy, but also to completely revise the ideas that have too often represented the southern Italian regions, as a place of economic and cultural backwardness and geographical and existential isolation. What we find there, in contrast, is the heart of a network of international friendships and contacts bound together by their deeply felt joint political endeavours, inspired by pacificism and a desire for sustainable economic and political development, nourished by readings in French and English, and embodied in the study and practice of innovative approaches to farming (biodynamic agriculture) and healthcare (Steiner's holistic approach to treating illness). These networks of friends and relations were comprehensively shaped as a political project for self-transformation and the transformation of their common world.

The 'signs of art' are therefore the signs of art of composing a life,[7] which is at the same time the political art of transforming one's own environment and leaving traces of oneself in it. Lucia de Viti de Marco and Giulia Starace cultivated their mothers' project of positive change for the region, in which the friendship uniting them was also a spiritual communication and the search for sharing happiness with their compatriots, beginning with those less fortunate than themselves. It is a project that has been handed down across the generations and which, although not always unchanged—unlike a structure or institution—has always represented a political faith and a determination to positively transform the world. Thus, the case study presented in the second part of this book reconstitutes a strong, enduring tie between generations, which has never been abandoned because of any possible isolation or the lack of necessary backing. In these women's lives and creative work, everything is framed, as in Carolina de Viti de Marco's diary (*Annales*),[8] in the sober creativity of everyday life and in an awareness of, and care for the environment. Their lives show the manner in which they freely and knowingly placed themselves at the centre of a moral revolution; and this is an art that women have practised with coherence and freedom in a congruent pursuit of action and relationships with the world.

[7] See Bateson (1989). This essay is an interesting autobiographical account, in which the identity of the self is 'composed' and defined at the end of the life story, and not put forward as a model or choice of identity.

[8] Archive Carolina de Viti de Marco and Giulia Starace, Le Costantine Foundation, Casamassella (Lecce).

8.4 The Signs of Political Work: The Art of Composing a Life

The projects described in this book are not utopian or visionary dreams or vague, impractical women's aspirations; rather, they express a deep sense of politics emerging from a specific cultural context. The web of relationships woven by the women studied here composes a space which can be articulated in Hanna Arendt's political terms: as a space that is political because it enables the revelation of the *who*—the person—and not the definition of a *what*—a thing. As in every political operation, this revelation also contains an underlying uncertainty. Uncertainty is in fact the medium in which human beings and their mutual affairs are steeped. It is lacking, however, in utopian visions, which are founded on projects (if only to the project of history), just as it is lacking in organisation-building, founded on the certainty of solid 'winning' factors. Instead, it has the characteristic uncertainty of the ancient oracles, who—as Arendt says, paraphrasing Heraclitus—'neither reveal nor hide in words, but give manifest signs' (Arendt 1958: 182). Thus, we see the manifest signs of art that cultivates a deep sense of politics and guides concrete actions.

The relationship with the world, then, was always strong and present in these women. Besides, their particular choices embodied a moral revolution that changed the habits of their social environment even though these might be isolated and, in political terms, non-winning actions. And in fact, they left an important and still undeveloped legacy since their initiatives were open to the future from the start. The testimonies gathered by Elena Laurenzi[9] provide evidence of this revolution, even in terms of their usual low-toned speech that did not inconvenience anyone, which also became habitual among the common people who surrounded them. This is only one of many examples of a moral revolution that spread by contagion—as argued by Simone Weil (1970), who also believed that good is infectious. These moral choices were made with a deep political sense, evidenced by the lacemaking schools and the Steiner community for children with polio, which put their vision of active citizenship and social justice into practice. We should also emphasise the fact that at that time, moral choices, which are clearly related to individual freedom, were

[9] The complete texts in the original language (Italian) of the interviews can be found in Laurenzi (2018).

not seen as solitary or subjective decisions or as the uncritical performance of duty. In fact, while it is true that the desire and the care behind these women's actions stemmed from their moral choices, it is also especially true to say they also encompassed feminist ideas and that they were consciously political actions aimed at transforming social relationships and the world as a whole. Thus, they combined moral and political revolution.

We should also remember that in France in the first five years of the twentieth century, Charles Péguy had called for a new political project with a phrase that would very quickly become much more than just a slogan: 'the revolution will be moral or not at all'. Péguy's aim, to conquer all forms of lies and ideology in politics with the truth, which led him to found the journal *Cahiers de la quinzaine*[10] represented the programme for and promise of a further revolution: that of the realisation of social justice.

8.5 Popular Art, Socialist Art, Arts and Crafts

The importance of this type of research, then, is not in giving a clear account of a personality or personalities, exemplary beings who remain prisoners of their own example in the end; and nor is it in the endeavour to understand every aspect of who they were, which would be the same as condemning them to the solitude of their excellence. Neither is it, lastly, in the description of the many qualities they had and may have shared with others. In short, our aim here is not to set a level or measure of emancipation based on common denominators such as money, the acquisition of rights or a presumed superiority of spirit.

In contrast, what is important in the art of this type of research is that it enables us to explore a series of political issues that were debated—or only acted on—at the end of the nineteenth century and the beginning of the twentieth. We already discussed the first issue, how to bring about the revolution, when we outlined the differences between the political theories of the two texts titled *What Is to Be Done?* And in mentioning the second issue, the idea of the need for a moral revolution, we have touched on something that merits further analysis.

[10] The journal *Les Cahiers de la quinzaine* was founded in 1900 in the wake of the Dreyfus affair. The poet Girolamo Comi (1890–1968), son of Baron Giuseppe and Costanza de Viti de Marco (Carolina's sister), had many issues of the *Cahiers* in his library.

There remains the issue of the arts of weaving and lacemaking themselves. This is a practical question that is interwoven with the theoretical one of popular art, which at that time was identified with social or socialist art. And it was in fact precisely at the end of the nineteenth century that the crisis of art caused by its increasing commercialisation gave rise to the debate on art for all, an art that could promote social reform and become a source and sign of welfare and emancipation. William Morris, a writer who deserves to be better known, was one of the most prominent theorists of this tendency.[11] Morris wished craftspeople to become artists once again; he was convinced that the craft methods of the Middle Ages, a period that he had studied in depth, were the only way to create an art of the people. Mediaeval art, the art that had built the great cathedrals, had never needed any author's signature, is based rather on the good work of each craftsman. Morris, like Péguy, counterposed the poor quality of profit-based production with the excellence and personal fulfilment inherent in what he called 'good work'. In his view, art should be accessible to all, without hierarchies of merit. In 1888, he was among the founders of the *Arts and Crafts Exhibition Society*, a hub for the promotion of new ideas, whose members, all artist-craftspeople, exhibited their work regularly.

A firm opponent of mass production, Morris advocated techniques and procedures that he had unearthed in old books and which he personally experimented with in a manner similar to what the leading figures of the Italian Female Industries (IFI) were doing with lacemaking. Eleanor Marx, the daughter of Karl Marx, also worked with Morris and his daughter May, who were among the first English Marxists. By the end of the nineteenth century, however, Morris' project was losing ground. The arguments of *his* journal *Commonweal, the mouthpiece of the Socialist League, were not enough to stem the rise of both anarchism and the new party organisations.* Eleanor Marx committed suicide, and Morris' ideas on socially harmonious ways of producing art and collective wealth, for example by exchanging services with no waste in labour or materials, did not prosper. In the end, his vision of socialist values and principles, which he propounded in countless lectures, meetings and essays, was swept aside by the debate on the need for a revolutionary organisation.

[11] William Morris (1834–1896) has not been studied as much as he deserves. Miguel Abensour is one of his best commentators (2009, 2014).

8.6 A Landscape as a Finely Woven Lace

Charles Péguy, in a perceptive and poetic passage, noted the demise of the idea of art that he believed in, seeing it as the basis of an alternative project, charged with history and culture and radically socialist at the same time. Péguy uses the metaphor of the Ancient Greek trireme to represent the art of the people: an art that would be socialist insofar as it would socialise labour, producing work that would be authentic and superbly crafted because it was reiterated and precise, as fine as lacemaking and guided by the principles of a fairer and thus more honest society, like the 'fineness of a finely-woven landscape'. He writes that:

> Marvel of precision, born of an exacting people, a people of navigators, masterpiece of precise cut and curve, the ancient galley has foundered. Foundered the perfect lines, the precise inventions, the inventions of a people of geometricians, the first people of geometricians. Foundered the perfectly designed rigging, the just camber of the beams, the bends, the lengthening, the lightening, the shafts, the ingenious, industrious, subtle but always just and justified curvatures of the flanks. Whether they be the flanks of a vase or of a trireme, this nautical vase, the same perfection, the same perfect accuracy, the same truth, the same just curve of the nautical curvatures. Rectitude, perfect rectitude of the lines, the same perfect straightness, so to speak, and even, yes, truly, the same rectitude, the same perfect rectitude even of the curves, the same (perfect) honesty of the curves: honest truth, subtle nonetheless, almost too ingenious, industrious, inventive, *polymetis* itself. Precision of the nautical curves, my dear Mille, and not only that: I would go as far as to say the aeronautical curves. [...] By the straight and cutting intention of the line, penetrating, energetic, piercing, plunging, by the direct camber of the prow, going straight, plunging into the horizon, straight into the far-flung horizon, by this sort of intention, this perforating aim of the prow's purpose. By the straightness of the steering. By that rectitude, by that rightness. By that linear and perforating aim. By that perforating tension towards the infinite [...] [B]orn in these times, whatever we do, whatever we have, we are unfortunately permeated, polluted, penetrated (with barbarism) with the modern and with modernism. As if it were an idea, to add something to exactness. As if with adding the word *perfect* to exactness, we added to it, we could add to it something, give it some further virtue, give it some kind of increase [...] Delicacy (of a lacework) without exclamations, without exclamation points, without grand words. And which has shown a hundred times that it could rediscover everything that is great (or greater)

in greatness, all that is deep (or deeper) in the depths of human nature. (1953: 274)

It is interesting to note the repeated terms here: precision, perfection, rectitude, industrious, accurate, exact, value, growth, depth, honesty, justice. The fineness of a finely woven landscape.

This, then, is also the finely woven landscape that forms the backdrop to the stories described in the present volume, where we discover the reality of regions peopled by highly educated women, free to live their own lives, without men if they chose, women skilled in creating businesses and welfare initiatives, linked by international friendships, lovers of literature, motivated by a thirst for knowledge, intellectually curious enough to learn languages not widely studied at that time, capable of studying weaving and lacemaking techniques rigorously and then handing them on, founders of schools that, more than being simply places for learning techniques, also quickly became places where students learned to live in a society with a sense of their own economic and moral autonomy.

A finely woven landscape, where the signs of the art of living are almost a series of clues or suggestions, rather than hard and intimidating tests. These suggestions bring new meaning to art and politics, and instead of a programme, they leave a heritage of signs. The heritage that this story hands down to us, then, is above all a symbolic one: it consists in the fact that these women, and others like them, succeeded in thinking the unthinkable and putting it into practice—for example, sending an eighteen-year-old daughter to South Africa, encouraging a polio-stricken child to ride a horse or a bicycle, replacing the costs and complexities of fixed industrial capital with the non-cost of a needle and then building an industry with this needle. This is the unthinkable realised by a female genealogy, their art of opening themselves to the possible.

I would like to conclude by citing the French philosopher Françoise Collin (1999), who finds art in every action knowingly accomplished by a woman. Collin argues, apparently against the evidence, that every woman artist is a feminist, regardless of her sources of inspiration, her conscious ideology or the artforms she adopts. Every woman artist, simply by registering her traces in the universe of signs, by cracking it open or by enriching its techniques, even when not upsetting it spectacularly, achieves the same thing: that women are no longer spoken about but speak, no longer seen but see.

It is for this reason that women's artworks, studied and offered to us in this book, are so precious, regardless of whether they express themselves on their position as women or not. And the works of infinitely more numerous women, more numerous every day, are also equally precious, realised in forms that have not yet received the verdict of time as to whether they will be seen as masterpieces. If every work is feminist, it is because it testifies to an affirmation even though it might not manifest specifically 'female' characteristics. It is a protest even when it is not protesting.

And so, exploring the lived experience, the personal and affective lives of these women, is not a sentimental choice, but it helps us to discover, through the pre-political domain, the political meaning of action, and it enables us to leave the stereotypes behind, to go beyond the tyranny of models, towards a reading of history that, between objectivity and subjectivity, does not forget its contexts, even when they are not victorious ones.

The political aspect of this reading is not its dating of events with which to construct memory, but its restoration of the political features of difficult choices, while simultaneously avoiding both the appeal of heroic gestures and the anonymous accumulation of biographical data. It is an art that allows us to specifically narrate the contours of a landscape that is also composed of existential categories, where history is not the tracing of external events that lend solidity to the lives of individuals, but where instead, memory, identity, time, experience and the inner life give substance to the outer and to political choices that simply listen to and understand the words of others, opening new foundations and bringing new rights and institutions and new finely woven landscapes.

References

Abensour, Miguel. 2009. *Pour une philosophie politique critique: itinéraires*. Paris: Sens & Tonka.

Abensour, Miguel. 2014. *La communauté politique des 'tous uns': désir de liberté, désir d'utopie*. Le Kremlin Bicêtre: Editions Belles Lettres.

Arendt, Hannah. 1963. *On Revolution*. New York: Penguin.

Arendt, Hannah. 1958. *The Human Condition*. Chicago: Chicago University Press.

Arienzo, Alessandro, and Stefano De Luca. 2019. *Protego ergo obligo. Ordine, sicurezza e legittimazione nella storia del pensiero politico*, Pisa: Edizioni ETS.

Basso, Rosanna. 1999. *Stili di emancipazione*. Lecce: Argo.

Basso, Rosanna. 2000. *Donne in provincia, Percorsi di emancipazione attraverso la scuola nel Salento tra otto e novecento*. Milan: Angeli.

Bateson, Mary Catherine. 1989. *Composing a Life*. New York: Grove Press.

Chernyshevsky, Nikolay. 1863/1989. *What Is to Be Done?* New York: Random.

Collin, Françoise. 1999. Visibilité et representation. In *Je partirais d'un mot. Le champ simbolique*, 23–24. Paris: Fus Art.

Croce, Benedetto. 1947. *Breviario di estetica*. Bari: Laterza.

Filmer, Robert. 1680/1991. Patriarcha, or The Natural Power of Kings. In *Patriarcha and Other Writing*, ed. Johann P. Sommerville. Cambridge: Cambridge University Press.

Focher, Ferruccio. 2000. Hannah Arendt, gli autori e la tradizione infranta. In *Libertà e teoria dell'ordine politico*. Milan: Angeli.

Gramsci, Antonio. 1948–1951/2011. *Prison Notebooks*. New York: Columbia University Press.

Kant, Immanuel. 1793/1911. On the Common Saying: This May Be True in Theory, but It Doesn't Apply in Practice. In *Kant's Political Writings*, ed. Hans Siegbert Reiss. Cambridge: Cambridge University Press.

Laurenzi, Elena. 2018. *Fili della trasmissione. Il progetto delle donne De Viti de Marco-Starace nel Salento del Novecento*. Lecce: Grifo.

Lenin, Vladimir Ilyich. 1902/1988. *What Is to Be Done?* Harmondsworth: Penguin Books.

Pateman, Carole. 1988. *The Sexual Contract*. Stanford: Stanford University Press.

Péguy, Charles. 1953. Pierre Mille. In *L'esprit de système*. Paris: Pierre Mille.

Weil, Simone. 1970. *First and Last Notebooks*. London: Oxford University Press.

CHAPTER 9

Female Biographies and Family History: An Approach to Social and Political History

Anna Lucia Denitto

9.1 Introduction

The life stories of Harriet Lathrop Dunham, Alice Hallgarten, Cora Slocomb, Carolina de Viti de Marco and the intergenerational story of the De Viti de Marco-Starace families reconstructed in this book prompt some more general considerations about the political history of women and the most stimulating approaches to investigating it.

It is not our intention to examine the intense scientific discussion on these issues, which has often been interwoven with the extremely lively debate between women's history and gender history. On this debate, Ida Fazio—when recently introducing the Italian edition of Joan W. Scott's book, *Gender and the Politics of History* (1988)—offered an interesting historiographic overview of the various seasons that have marked international studies, highlighting the different meanings, theoretical grounds, developments, juxtapositions and products of women's history and gender history (Fazio 2013, 2016). After years of sharp

A. L. Denitto (✉)
University of Salento, Lecce, Italy

E. Laurenzi and M. Mosca (eds.), *A Female Activist Elite in Italy (1890–1920)*, https://doi.org/10.1007/978-3-030-87159-8_9

theoretical and methodological contrast, today, it is felt that there is a need to overcome the dualism of these two scientific standpoints and to bring them together. This could allow an even more effective contribution to be made in challenging stereotyped methods and interpretative criteria, and to consolidate the approaches to research in cultural, political and social history, starting from the interweaving of public and private spheres, between individuality and citizenship. This debate also stimulates the exploration of new research paths and the systematic, in-depth investigation of documents and archives to trace the presence, role and words of women.

The latest studies published in Italy often mention the historian Gianna Pomata's critical note of 1993 on the use of the historiographic concept of 'gender' and its complicated relationship with women's history. Pomata stated that:

> The first task in the history of women is not, in my opinion, to deconstruct the male discourse on women, but to overcome this dearth of facts about their lives which has made historiography so unreal, so lame, so poor, would I say. (Pomata 1993: 1021)[1]

The exhortation to overcome the scarcity of facts on the life of women has enabled Italian historiography to be less unreal and less shaky, and to produce interesting results both on the theoretical and methodological plane, as well as that of research (Rossi Doria 2003), opening up new issues and new paths.[2]

The political history of women has also moved in this direction. After the political shift that sprang from the great changes in the years 1989–91, there has been a renewal of research into the political dimension of the female presence in history, which risked being submerged and overshadowed by research in social history.[3] Accordingly, it was felt that there

[1] Unless stated otherwise, the translations of the quoted texts are our own.

[2] To interpret power relations in women's history and plural and asymmetrical social relations, the concept of patronage indicated in the pioneering book by Ferrante et al. (1988) is still valid.

[3] Anna Rossi Doria points out that 'the alarm' about the loss of the political dimension of women's history was sounded in the journals *Past and Present* and *Annales* by distinguished historians, respectively Joan W. Scott and the leading French scholars of women's history, about 'the return to a certain 'political history' or rather 'history of the political'' (xvi).

was a need to try out new paths of analysis and research in order to 'give shape to the silence of women'; this is a silence that, as Anna Rossi Doria (2007: ix) writes, 'is particularly oppressive in the political sphere, which for a long time, together with the law, was the place of the greatest exclusion of women'. As far as the contemporary age is concerned, it is a matter of reconstructing the challenging, rocky paths by which women, in different Western countries, with different timing and methods, have achieved 'individuality and citizenship, which are closely connected' (ix).

In a recent work summing up the history of Italian women in the early twentieth century, Perry Willson justifies the choice of chronology in her reconstruction with the need to highlight the importance of the political dimension without necessarily overlooking the social, cultural and economic aspects. She points out that 'politics has been an important force for change in gender relations (although certainly not the only one)' in a society like that of Italy marked by 'a particular mix of modernity and tradition' (2010: 1). The book reconstructs the history of civil and political rights of Italian women's material conditions over two centuries and therefore the transformation of relations between the sexes in said country. It reveals the difficult, winding path Italian women had to face in adapting and transforming their behaviour, buffeted between the opposing forces of aspirations towards new social and cultural models on the one hand, and loyalty to the bonds of family and caregiving on the other. It was a totally original pathway in 'a fascinating mix of modernity and tradition' (Willson 2010: 189). The historian aims to combine the focus on the processes and timing of the transformation of society with the habits and responses of local societies, which differ considerably in the various territorial contexts. However, she specifies that she was not able to make a deeper analysis at regional level of the cultural, economic, social and political processes, which have 'multiple specificities' and which affect 'many aspects of women's lives' (Willson 2010: 2).

As a matter of fact, further research studies are desirable in order to expand Willson's useful summary, and to adopt a differentiated and comparative analysis of women's actions in different territorial and socio-cultural contexts. Such an analysis is necessary—for example—in order to avoid the danger of levelling and over-generalising on the North-South dichotomy, seen in terms of development-backwardness.[4] It can

[4] On this point, see the interesting review by Gribaudi (2012: 296) on Willson (2010).

also be particularly productive to trace women's political history by reconstructing individual and collective paths through biographical analysis and family history.

Starting from these introductory considerations, in the following pages we will tackle three main themes, within which the interpretation of the female protagonists of this book will be positioned: the contribution that family history and biographical analysis have made to women's political history; the issue of backwardness/development, tradition/modernity; the relation between history and memory. The aim of this chapter is twofold. Its first goal is to demonstrate the potentialities of family history and biographical analysis in reconstructing women's political history, using family archives and women's writings. The second and more general aim is to show how women's history can help to revise stereotypes and established interpretations of Italian history, going beyond a vision of the nation's history as marked only by excelling or only by lagging behind (Benigno and Mineo 2020).

9.2 Individuals and Citizens: The Contribution of Family History and Biography to Women's Political History

The latest studies encourage us to recombine social history with political history, focussing on the various public and private spaces where women's participation unfolds. To do so, they urge us to reconstruct the figures of women in their public/private experience, in a generational, relational perspective. One interesting contribution in this direction applied to Italy is that of Mori et al. (2014), who reconstruct

> the processes of female participation that the birth [of the nation] triggered and accelerated [...] what it meant for Italian women, the varied spaces where they were establishing an active role, not only and not mainly political, in the making of contemporary Italy. (15)

The stated aim of the book is to revise deep-rooted stereotypes about male power and about the 'woman tied to her body', and to give priority to 'a close connection between gender history and women's history, between social history and cultural history' (Mori et al. 2014: 18). To retrace this story, to 'explore in a new way the social, and therefore historical, construction of the male and the female' the curators chose 'generation' as the concept capable of 'undermining' the separate study of the public/political sphere as opposed to the private sphere. Accordingly, they pay special attention to defining and flexibly historicising the category of 'generation', and to including some female biographies in the generations, which allows them to 'reintroduce the individual into the historical account' and 'enhance the plural nature of women and men' (19). Therefore, the generational approach, chosen as the hermeneutical key, is interwoven with the biographical angle, designed to trace and accentuate the presence of the many women, often unknown, in the different periods of the history of Italy since unification.

Both perspectives are present in this book, in the reconstruction of the life stories of Harriet Lathrop Dunham, Alice Hallgarten, Cora Slocomb, Carolina de Viti de Marco and the young women of the De Viti de Marco-Starace family, the sisters Lucia and Giulia Starace, and their cousin Lucia de Viti de Marco. Their interpretative approach has produced original, unexpected results on the political role played by these women in contexts and ways that cannot be attributed to the most established interpretations of existing historiography, which give priority to the more developed and dynamic geographical areas and women's political militancy in parties and trade unions. Equally unpredictable were the links between the experiences of women, so different and yet so similar in their cultural and political aspiration towards a social protagonism which was also political. The women examined here reveal life trajectories that were complex and pluralistic in terms of the paths they took to assert their individuality. Think, for instance, of Carolina de Viti de Marco, and her difficult decision to separate from her husband after years of marriage within the distrustful male-dominated context of the periphery of south-eastern Italy; or of her stubborn defence of her educational role in female vocational training in a predominantly male school like the Art School Applied to Industry (see Chapter 5). At the same time, the biographies of these women demonstrate their participation and protagonism in the social field, their ability to promote employment and welfare activities, which would prove to be enduring over time, and decisive for the autonomy of the weaker members of society. In other words, they indicate the journey undertaken both to be individuals and to become citizens. With great cogency, Mori et al. argue that:

> We are convinced that individual stories can illuminate general themes by providing perspectives that result in knowledge: the focus on single experiences redefines and recomposes those same opposing pairs that women's history has challenged, such as public/private, presence/absence, inclusion/exclusion. The lives of people dwell in all these spaces, and history that can take this into account is capable of breaking down the traditionalisms and artificial fences between the political, the cultural, the social, making historical time intersect with the time of lived experience. (2014: 19–20)

For some time now, the attention of historiography has been drawn to the scientific potentialities of biographical analysis, though with an urgency to avoid facile infatuations and glorification of the subjects investigated. There has been a great demand to adopt it in the field of women's history (Loriga 2006; Varikas 1996; Casalena 2012). The biographical dimension enables the network of family and social relations to be reconstructed, along with the paths of cross-fertilisation between historical-cultural models and subjective experience. It also allows us 'to observe the ways each individual is positioned and moves in the social space, continuously changing it' (Calanca 2004: 205). In the essays presented in this volume, biographical analysis is interwoven with family history, in order to study family strategies and reconstruct social relationships. Today, we have moved beyond the studies initiated by Peter Laslett and which circulated all over Europe during the 1970s and 1980s, favouring a quantitative investigation of family structure (Laslett 1968; see also Salvatici 2009). The focal point of theoretical reflection and research is currently the relational world of which the family is part. A fundamental contribution in this direction was made by Levi (1985; see Lanaro 2011), who, as Franco Ramella writes,

> proposed replacing the study of the structures with the analysis of family strategies, which requires the reconstruction of the relations external to the domestic group, without which it is hard to grasp the meaning of choices, because it is precisely the relations established with the outside world that are the tool of the strategies. (2000: 7)

It is therefore necessary to use a different viewpoint in studying the family 'to make it a way of studying society'.

Hence the need to adopt a relational perspective both on the internal analysis of the family and on its relations with civil society. For the first aspect, it is therefore possible to reconstruct the relations between the sexes and the relation between the generations, which 'enables the plurality of forms of relations to be interpreted as hubs in a multiplicity of generational stories that are constantly being interwoven' (Calanca 2004: 205). For the second aspect, the danger to avoid is that of levelling the role of the family and seeing it as the 'central institution in civil society', without grasping the 'biunivocal' process between family and civil society. On this point, Paul Ginsborg (2010) points out that either some members of the family become part of civil society or elements of civil society 'enter' the family. Therefore, rather than adopting the traditional division between the private and public spheres, what is stressed is the analysis 'of the modes of connection between families and civil society'. It is no coincidence that the more recent orientations in historiography indicate the need to study the relationship between the family and historical change and specifically the links between individuals, families, civil society and the state (Asquer et al. 2010). Such perspectives and orientations, as we have said, become a productive key to understanding the history and political culture of women who are found to have unexpected roles, strategies and knowledge in the study of the social relations that families had with each other and with other individuals.

The focus of the analysis in the essays of this book is not only on women, but on the relational world to which they and their families belonged; the relations formed with society became the main instrument in their political strategies. What emerges is a spider-web of local and supra-local relations that reveal a complex, dynamic social reality at a European level, in both the private and the public spheres. A clear international profile also emerges, not so much due to the geographical origin of some of them (as in the case of the Americans Harriet Lathrop Dunham and Cora Slocomb, or the American of German Jewish origin Alice Hallgarten), but in their cosmopolitan background and the fact that they all took part in the cultural and political ferment of the age: women's emancipation, feminism, pacifism and anti-colonialism.

Their biographies and the complex interweaving of their local/national/international relations provide food for thought on the link between women's history and world history. However, world history has aroused more bewilderment than agreement out of a fear of annulling or underestimating the differences and specificities typical of women's history (Capuzzo and Vezzosi 2005). Hence the proposal to adopt instead a transnational approach that considers a multiplicity of areas and contexts, their connections and their interrelations (Capuzzo and Vezzosi 2005; see also Di Fiore and Meriggi 2011). World history is however a spatial perspective that enables us to overcome political boundaries and the Eurocentric approach, and to bring together the multiple interconnections between different worlds in which the early twentieth-century feminist activists operated and wove the threads of a female internationalism (see Baritono 2007; Bini and Testi 2009). This concerned the themes of peace, emancipation, feminism, work, the liberation of the weak—whether women, children or the disabled—both in the industrialised societies of Europe and North America, and in the more backward areas of southern Europe and South Africa. This is illustrated here by Cora Slocomb's work in favour of the first international movement for peace and disarmament, the founding of the American Council of Women, the campaign against the death penalty (Chapter 4), or Etta and Carolina de Viti de Marco's commitment and support for the activities assisting the Anglo-Boer populations promoted by Emily Hobhouse in South Africa, where the worst consequences of European nations' imperialist policies were being played out. The two sisters-in-law did not hesitate to encourage the departure of the young Lucia Starace, Carolina's eldest daughter, who was only eighteen, for a village in South Africa to promote the establishment and running of a lace school, greatly desired by Emily Hobhouse (see Chapter 6). They were therefore giving her an opportunity to experience cultural growth outside the common schemes prevailing in the aristocratic and upper-middle-class world to which they belonged. As Part II shows, Carolina and Etta de Viti de Marco handed down their values and political experience to their daughters, who then adapted the spaces, themes and political practices of their activity without betraying the fundamental values of their mothers. Thus, there emerges a female and feminist elite, active even in the contradictory, outlying reality of Italy, in a long-term perspective that enables us to know not only their political activity but also the political culture of women committed to peace, opposed to discrimination and marginalisation, who were fighting for women's rights and social liberation.

The first generation of women studied in Part I share the broad cultural and political yearnings that characterise the 'new woman' of the early 1900s: the battle for emancipation and the vote, 'practical feminism' that inspired their feverish social, welfare and educational activities, with a strong awareness of being both a woman and a mother capable of transforming the family and society. But they also shared the fragility of their human existences. We only need to recall Cora Slocomb's mental anguish, which constrained her for almost forty years, isolating her from the intense world of entrepreneurial initiatives and social activities she had undertaken. We might also consider the short life of Alice Hallgarten, an untiring supporter of the pedagogist Maria Montessori and her method, who died when she was only thirty-seven after promoting and establishing numerous activities, schools for children and weaving workshops, faithful to her philosophy of life of giving work and education rather than alms (Chapter 3). And finally, we might think of the degenerative illness suffered by Etta de Viti de Marco during her final years, which were marked by devastating family tragedy (Chapter 2). The exception was Carolina de Viti de Marco, who had a long life that was nonetheless troubled (Chapter 5). In her memoire, she outlined that long line of values, practices, feelings and aspirations which—in different forms—are visible in the lives of her daughters, Lucia and Giulia Starace, and her niece, Lucia de Viti de Marco. In this second generation, the biographical and generational interpretative key makes it possible to reconstruct a female activism that was manifested between the 1940s and the 1960s and totally different from that of their mothers in the early 1900s, to which however it is anchored. The political, cultural and social aims of the first generation have taken on new forms but they are still nurtured by an engagement with the cultural springs of modernism, religious reform and the innovative health and education theories of Steiner and Montessori (Chapter 6).

The stories of these women reveal a man/woman and husband/wife relationship reinterpreted as complicity and/or otherness. Cora Slocomb's husband, Count Detalmo Savorgnan di Brazzà, shared his wife's values and entrepreneurial initiatives, supporting her by acting as the secretary of Italian Female Industries (IFI), of which she was president (Chapter 4). Etta de Viti de Marco carried on an intense cultural and relational activity to support and promote the scientific and political work of her husband, Antonio de Viti de Marco, an esteemed economist and deputy elected several times to Parliament (Chapter 1). Leopoldo Franchetti gave full moral and economic support to the welfare and educational initiatives promoted by his young wife Alice Hallgarten (Chapter 3). Carolina de Viti de Marco, on the other hand, like her daughter Lucia, did not hesitate to break up the marriage when faced with the authoritarianism of their respective husbands, which made their lives difficult as women and citizens (Chapters 5 and 6). The mother/daughters/sons relationship in the case of Carolina and Etta de Viti de Marco is also worth reflecting upon and their presence/absence was due to their political and entrepreneurial commitments, but also to their great interest in the upbringing and education of their daughters—albeit delegated to carefully guided tutors—and the respect shown for their choices in life.

In short, they had difficult lives, lives committed to affirming their individuality and to achieving a social and political role of their own, but also to transforming the situation in which the protagonists operated, and to creating life and work opportunities for women and the more vulnerable. Accordingly, they reveal the existence of strong networks of national and international relations, the participation as protagonists in the emancipation movement of the early 1900s, and above all, the endorsement of work, especially the art of embroidery and weaving, as an instrument of autonomy for women and for their emancipation.

9.3 Backwardness/Development, Tradition/Modernity: Philanthropy and the Origin of the Welfare State

One of the common threads linking these cosmopolitan upper-class women is the philanthropic activity they promoted and carried out between the late nineteenth and early twentieth centuries, which in some cases was revived and updated by their daughters and granddaughters between the 1940s and the 1960s. They generally operated in poor rural areas, such as Friuli in northern Italy in the case of Cora Slocomb, Umbria in Central Italy for Alice Hallgarten, and Salento in the extreme periphery of southern Apulia for Etta and Carolina de Viti de Marco and their descendants. In those areas, far removed from the ongoing industrial development, new opportunities were experienced and activities and initiatives were undertaken for the emancipation and education of the most vulnerable members of the population. Some of these women (such as Alice Hallgarten and Harriet Lathrop Dunham) also lived in a family atmosphere imbued with the cultural and political drive of their respective husbands, engaged in the battle for the development of Southern Italy, such as Leopoldo Franchetti and Antonio de Viti de Marco. This book allows their numerous activities to be reconstructed, as well as the role they played from generation to generation, always moving between the local, national and international spheres. These are important results in terms of scientific research, and they are all the more significant insofar as they concern the social, political, cultural and economic dynamics that characterised seemingly marginal situations, as in the case of the school founded by Carolina and Etta de Viti de Marco in Casamassella, a rural centre in the south of Apulia. These results help to introduce a new perspective and to overcome the stereotypes and *clichés* regarding the backwardness of the South from the liberal age to today, on its isolation and its place on the cultural and social periphery.

In the last thirty years, Italian historiography has produced innovative contributions on southern history, inviting us to use the concept of 'complexity' when interpreting the dynamics of the South and to adopt three different levels of analysis in studying and making sense of it: the history of the real processes that marked the South during the various stages of Italian history; the construction of the 'Southern question', based on the thought and political struggle of some of its protagonists[5]; and Meridionalism, a cultural movement and political project in favour of the South. More recent studies have reconstructed the picture of Southern Italy, analysed and interpreted in a European and international dimension, investigated in its territorial and social nuances, considered a reality 'in motion', pressured by drives for and against change. Some historians[6] have constantly rejected the false claims that the South is backward and immobile, and have invited historians, observers and politicians to adopt a 'cross-eyed' view in order to grasp, on the one hand, the changes and transformations of Southern Italy during its more than one hundred and fifty years of history since unification,[7] and on the other, the persistence and continuity between the South's level of development and that of the rest of Italy.[8] Specific attention has been paid to the study of the southern and Apulian upper middle classes, highlighting the existence not only of backward, parasitic landowning and professional categories, but also the widespread presence of a productive, active bourgeoisie at a European

[5] These included Pasquale Villari, Leopoldo Franchetti, Giustino Fortunato, Gaetano Salvemini, Francesco Saverio Nitti and Antonio de Viti de Marco.

[6] Specially Galasso (1983).

[7] The unification of Italy took place in 1861.

[8] See Lupo (2015), Cassese (2016), and Pescosolido (2017). For Apulia, see Denitto (2005, 2007).

level in the professions, participating in the great changes taking place and engaged in innovative processes of political, economic, social and cultural transformation (Rizzo 2015, 2016). The study of the case of the De Viti de Marco-Starace families published in the second part of this book, which reconstructs the innovative initiatives introduced by Etta and Carolina de Viti de Marco and the dogged opposition they encountered, highlights the difficulties and resistance to change on the part of the most backward circles of southern society.

Philanthropic activity was one of the main paths chosen by the feminist movement of the early 1900s. The women examined here took part in the process of emancipation and the first wave of feminism: in the case of Cora Slocomb and Harriet Lathrop Dunham, they were active protagonists, holding public offices. In Italy, there was a composite, pluralist movement marked by the presence of such different orientations, ideas and tendencies that the writer Sibilla Aleramo evoked the myth of Tower of Babel to indicate the feminist question.[9] The women active in the movement promoted multiple initiatives and had different cultural and political backgrounds, ranging from the suffragist spirit, more committed to claiming political and civil rights, to the maternal or social spirit, which gave political depth to the traditional female activities of care, assistance and education. The Italian emancipationists were bourgeois and aristocratic; among them, there was a significant presence of feminists from other countries, especially the United States. It is not surprising that the Italians were greatly influenced by theories developed abroad, especially in the Anglo-Saxon world. The contact and exchange networks were often informal and were also built up through friendships or at elite social events. In this sense, a leading role was played by gatherings in salons where the upper-middle class and aristocrats socialised (De Giorgio 1992; Buttafuoco 1997; Gazzetta 2018). The collaboration, also through the various associations that had been created in the meantime, lasted through the first decade of the twentieth century. Willson indicates a date and an event that marked the peak of the movement's political visibility and its theoretical and cultural elaboration, but also the origin of 'an irreparable fracture' and the end of the collaboration between Catholic and secular emancipationists: this was the first national conference of Italian women,

[9] This is an expression mentioned by Willson (2010: 25). On the use of terms such as 'emancipationism, 'feminism' or 'first-wave feminism' in Italian historiography, see Willson (2019).

organised by the National Council of Italian Women (CNDI) in April 1908. Many of the activists in the CNDI shared and pursued the aims of the Italian Female Industries (IFI, see Chapter 1). It is this very connection, previously overlooked, that links the experience of the protagonists of this book, notwithstanding the fact that they were involved in different areas, and that their social, cultural and friendship networks were close in some cases and very distant in others. Embroidery, seen as a social enterprise and a political activity in the broad sense, is what indicates their capacity for action, work, transformation and innovation. Their experience combines philanthropy and work, activities pursued by the CNDI, and which are generally regarded as 'a means of social control that could prevent unrest' (Willson 2010: 36). For a correct interpretation of the philanthropic activity promoted by the feminist movement, it is in fact necessary to take up and develop Annarita Buttafuoco's reflections on methodology and research. Many years ago, the Italian historian was already arguing that the activities promoted by practical feminism were anything but traditional and that they had to be reconstructed in their daily practices. She also maintained that assistance was designed to reduce social deprivation and to open the way to civil and political rights for women. In other words, she pointed to the culture and emancipationist practise of practical feminism as the genesis of the welfare state in Italy.[10]

One of the distinctive features of practical feminism, and more generally of the 'new woman' of the early 1900s, was the social value attributed to motherhood, and the association of motherhood with the concept of citizenship. Studies on the social commitment of women in the early 1900s actually refer to the theme of motherhood, linking it to the concept of citizenship and interpreting the numerous activities promoted for employment, the vote, and education of the weaker individuals in society as 'maternalistic practices [...] at the origin of the welfare state'.[11]

Undoubtedly, the public enhancement of maternal feeling accompanies the transition to the modern female ideal type envisaged for the 1900s: the strong, active woman, engaged in social work but also a well-informed mother. (Mori et al. 2014: 23)

[10] See Buttafuoco (1997, 1988). On the importance of the methodological and scientific contribution of Annarita Buttafuoco, see, among others, Rossi Doria (2001), Gabrielli (2001, 2002), and De Clementi (2016).

[11] See Mori et al. (2014) who refer to the stimulating analyses that were proposed in this direction at the beginning of the 1990s by Thane and Bock (1991).

This was the same perspective in which Maria Montessori's activity was seen with her 'pedagogy as social motherhood' (De Giorgio 2014; Babini 2014).

In the life experiences of the protagonists of this volume, there is a dynamic coexistence of tradition and modernity; they focussed on embroidery and craftsmanship, sectors generally considered traditional and linked to pre-modern lifestyles, but they imbued them with roles, function and meaning for the social, economic and political transformation of women, even the poorest, as Marisa Forcina underlines in her contribution to this book (Chapter 8). Cora Slocomb promoted a large enterprise in Friuli, one of the poorest parts of northern Italy, offering her skills, her international network of friends and the dynamism of her Anglo-Saxon cultural background to the work ethic and individual rights. She was profoundly convinced—like Etta and Carolina de Viti de Marco and Alice Hallgarten—that work was an important stimulus for the emancipation and dignity of women, especially the poor and exploited. Embroidery was seen as a major factor for the training of women and their entry into the world of work through the cooperatively organised embroidery schools she founded for the production and subsequent marketing of the products in Europe and the United States (Chapter 4).

Such strengths, as Laurenzi states in Part II, debunk the stereotype of embroidery as a traditional activity and of craftsmanship as an expression of a pre-industrial society, and they highlight its transformative function for female workers and for the artefact, incorporating innovation and tradition. We only need to think of the originality of the embroideries designed by Cora Slocomb with the skill and taste she had acquired in Munich and her ability to develop the manual skills of the young women in her schools where ancient working methods were used. We can also reflect on the creative effort and original research for designs by Etta and Carolina de Viti de Marco, who stubbornly claimed the intellectual property rights to the lace designs used in the girls' section of the Art school applied to industry. As we have seen, many of the activities established in Friuli, Umbria and Apulia did not fizzle out with the death of their founders; in some cases, they were resumed and updated in initiatives designed to promote the recovery of those crafts, still combining tradition and innovation and enhancing traditional and territorial vocations from a glocal perspective.

Finally, it must be said that even though the women studied here were forward-thinking democratic members of the elites of the enlightened aristocracy and upper-middle classes in business and the professions, they struggled to deal with the emergence of mass society and the leading role claimed by collective movements. However, they are indicative of the existence of a female bourgeoisie, which was a factor of change in its international openness, cultural relations, entrepreneurial activity and social commitment. These women managed to implement processes of social and cultural transformation designed to transform the philanthropic action they had undertaken into an activity of employment and support for working-class women as a prelude to culture and to 'welfare' policies (Gemelli 2014; Nunin and Vezzosi 2007).

9.4 History and Memory

The scientific and methodological results presented and discussed in this book were based on the use of an extremely rich documentation, in many cases unpublished, sourced from libraries and archives, both public and private. Of fundamental importance for the analytical perspectives chosen were family archives, in their capacity as repositories of individual and family memory. Family papers are indispensable when reconstructing the intricate networks of family and social relationships, as well as of inter-family relationships, while also revealing the individual subjective paths taken by its members. The archives of aristocratic and upper-middle-class families contain different kinds of female writings, essential for reconstructing the often-hidden traces of women's political actions (Contini and Scattigno 2005; Guidi 2004; Zarri 1999).

In the various case studies presented in this volume, the different ways these women wrote are illuminating, ranging from letters and correspondence to diaries, autobiographies, family memories, through public interventions, literary, historical and scientific writings. They allow us to analyse various levels of the subjectivity of their authors and their presence in civil society as well as their intense social, intra-family and personal relationships. The letters and correspondence in particular are exceptionally valuable sources for the history of women and, more generally, for historical research, and therefore they need to be analysed with methodological rigour and subjected to critical analysis and contextualised interpretation. Their analytical potential offers scholars the possibility of capturing the mood of women, reconstructing their feelings, desires, dreams, illusions, weaknesses, contradictions and pains. The papers in the family archives are very rich in this sense; suffice it to mention, for example, the writings by Cora Slocomb (quoted in Chapter 4), or the *Annales* written by Carolina de Viti de Marco (see Chapter 5).

Equally useful for the long-term reconstruction of the actions of the women dealt with in this book, and for reflecting on the social, cultural and political heritage of their 'political' action, are the testimonies and interviews here mentioned.[12] But in this case, we need to examine the relationship between memory and historical knowledge, pointing out that they are not the same thing. Memory is necessarily subjective, whether it be individual or group memory. It is selective, instinctive and disorganised. Segments of memory arrange themselves in the long past, which yields different traces or sources. Memories arouse emotions and involvement. History is founded on an effort to achieve scientific knowledge; it analyses sources and puts forward possible interpretations with the primary aim of understanding the past. It requires an in-depth analysis. It is a process of constantly growing knowledge (Bloch 1949). History and memory feed on each other and must therefore proceed hand in hand, especially when faced with today's situation, which seems to have lost any long-term vision and depth of analysis. Historians assign a central role to memory, which is considered an essential element of the individual and collective identity.

Delving into memory is one of the fundamental activities of present-day individuals and society. One of the most intriguing historians of the twentieth century, Jacques Le Goff (1977/1992: 99), writes that:

> Memory, on which history draws and which it nourishes in return, seeks to save the past in order to serve the present and the future. Let us act in such a way that collective memory may serve the liberation and not the enslavement of human beings.

But celebratory rituals, media simplification and political exploitation can lead to separate memory and, therefore, to intolerance or, at the other extreme, to indifference. Anna Rossi Doria's methodological and historiographic reflections on this point are stimulating. She has on many occasions (especially in her work on women and the Shoah) stressed the importance of the relation between the present and the past, but she has also expressed concern about the public use of history, the fragmentation

[12] Collected by Elena Laurenzi in her study (Laurenzi 2018).

of history into a myriad of individual memories, into separate pasts that end up fostering separate memories, opposing and identitarian, undermining the compactness of historical interpretations (Rossi-Doria 2012, 2017). The collection of testimonies presented by Laurenzi in this book (Chapter 7) is an example of how to successfully revive the subjective and collective memory that has accumulated around the protagonists of this story over time. In conclusion, through historical knowledge and memory we can trace the heritage of ideas and community bonds in which women have played a political role in the broad sense. In other words, it can help build a culture of social possibility and a system of plural cultures, working to overcome indifference, rediscover pride in one's roots and encourage the participation of women and men in the democratic life of the community.

References

Asquer, Enrica, Maria Casalini, Anna Di Biagio, and Paul Ginsborg, eds. 2010. *Famiglie del Novecento. Conflitti, culture e relazioni*. Rome: Carocci.

Babini, Valeria P. 2014. Maria Montessori. Liberare la madre: la pedagogia come maternità sociale. In *Di generazione in generazione. Le italiane dall'Unità a oggi*, ed. Maria Teresa Mori, Alessandra Pescarolo, Anna Scattigno, and Simonetta Soldani, 167–179. Rome: Viella.

Baritono, Raffaella. 2007. Femminismi in un contesto globale. Appunti per un'analisi storica e una riflessione teorica. *Contemporanea* 10 (4): 721–730.

Benigno, Francesco, and E. Igor Mineo, eds. 2020. *L'Italia come storia. Primato, decadenza, eccezione*. Rome: Viella.

Bini, Elisabetta, and Arnaldo Testi. 2009. Introduzione al tema Femminismi senza frontiere. *Genesis* 8 (2): 1–14.

Bloch, Marc. 1949/1954. *The Historian's Craft or Apology of History*. New York: Knopf.

Buttafuoco, Annarita. 1988. La filantropia come politica. Esperienze dell'emancipazionismo italiano nel Novecento. In *Ragnatele di rapporti: patronage e reti di relazione nella storia delle donne*, ed. Lucia Ferrante, Maura Palazzi, and Gianna Pomata, 166–187. Turin: Rosenberg & Sellier.

Buttafuoco, Annarita. 1993. Tra cittadinanza politica e cittadinanza sociale. Progetti ed esperienze del movimento politico delle donne in Italia liberale. In *Il dilemma della cittadinanza*, ed. Gabriella M. Bonacchi and Angela Groppi, 104–127. Rome-Bari: Laterza.

Buttafuoco, Annarita. 1997. *Questioni di cittadinanza: donne e diritti sociali nell'Italia liberale*. Siena: Protagon.

Calanca, Daniela. 2004. Percorsi di storia della famiglia. *Storia e Futuro* 5: 203–210.

Capuzzo, Paolo, and Elisabetta Vezzosi. 2005. Traiettorie della "World History." *Contemporanea* 8 (1): 105–134.

Casalena, Maria Pia. 2012. *Biografie: la scrittura delle vite in Italia tra politica società e cultura (1796–1915)*. Milan: Bruno Mondadori.

Cassese, Sabino, ed. 2016. *Lezioni sul meridionalismo. Nord e Sud nella storia d'Italia*, Bologna: Il Mulino.

Contini, Alessandra, and Anna Scattigno, eds. 2005. *Carte di donne. Per un censimento regionale della scrittura delle donne dal XVI al XX secolo*. Rome: Edizioni di Storia e Letteratura.

De Clementi, Andreina. 2016. Buttafuoco, Annarita. In *Dizionario biografico degli italiani*. Rome: Treccani.

De Giorgio, Michela. 1992. *Le italiane dall'Unità a oggi. Modelli culturali e comportamenti sociali*. Rome and Bari: Laterza.

De Giorgio, Michela. 2014. Madri del "secol nuovo". Sfide, lotte, scelte. In *Di generazione in generazione. Le italiane dall'Unità a oggi*, ed. Maria Teresa Mori, Alessandra Pescarolo, Anna Scattigno, and Simonetta Soldani, 139–166. Rome: Viella.

Denitto, Anna Lucia. 2005. Alle origini della Puglia contemporanea. In *Storia della Puglia*, ed. Angelo Massafra and Biagio Salvemini, 102–122. Rome and Bari: Laterza.

Denitto, Anna Lucia. 2007. Insediamenti e geografie amministrative dall'Unità alla Repubblica: il caso della Terra d'Otranto. In *Storia e misura. Indicatori sociali ed economici nel Mezzogiorno d'Italia (secoli XVIII-XX)*, ed. Renata De Lorenzo, 87–128. Milan: Angeli.

Di Fiore, Laura, and Marco Meriggi. 2011. *World History. Le nuove rotte della storia*. Rome and Bari: Laterza.

Fazio, Ida. 2013. A 25 anni dalla prima traduzione italiana de *Il "genere": un'utile categoria di analisi storica*. In *Joan W. Scott, Genere, politica, storia*, ed. Ida Fazio, 7–27. Rome: Viella.

Fazio, Ida. 2016. Il "genere', un'utile categoria di analisi storica. Il saggio di Joan W. Scott 25 anni dopo. *Italia Contemporanea* 281: 154–166.

Ferrante, Lucia, Maura Palazzi, and Gianna Pomata, eds. 1988. *Ragnatele di rapporti: patronage e reti di relazione nella storia delle donne*. Turin: Rosenberg & Sellier.

Gabrielli, Patrizia. 2001. *Questioni di femminismo e di cittadinanza. Leggere Annarita Buttafuoco*. Siena: Università degli Studi.

Gabrielli, Patrizia. 2002. Protagonists and Politics in the Italian Women's Movement: A Reflection on the Work of Annarita Buttafuoco. *Journal of Modern Italian Studies* 7 (1): 74–87.

Galasso, Giuseppe. 1983. Gli studi di storia della famiglia e il Mezzogiorno d'Italia. *Mélanges de l'Ecole française de Rome. Moyen-Age, temps modernes* 95 (1): 149–159.

Gazzetta, Liviana. 2018. *Orizzonti nuovi. Storia del primo femminismo in Italia. 1865–1925*. Rome: Viella.

Gemelli, Giuliana. 2014. La filantropia al femminile. In *Genere e storia*, ed. Cesarina Casanova and Vincenzo Lagioia, 189–196. Bologna: Bononia University Press.

Ginsborg, Paul. 2010. Scrivere la storia delle famiglie del Novecento: la connettività in un quadro comparato. In *Famiglie del Novecento. Conflitti, culture e relazioni*, ed. Enrica Asquer, Maria Casalini, Anna Di Biagio, and Paul Ginsborg, 15–38. Rome: Carocci.

Gribaudi, Gabriella. 2012. Review of Perry Willson's *Women in Twentieth-Century Italy*, Palgrave, Macmillan 2010. *Il mestiere di storico* 2: 296.

Guidi, Laura, ed. 2004. *Scritture femminili e storia*. Naples: Clio Press.

Lanaro, Paola, ed. 2011. *Microstoria. A venticinque anni da 'L'eredità immateriale.'* Milan: Angeli.

Laslett, Peter. 1968. *The World We Have Lost*. London: Methuen and Company.

Laurenzi, Elena. 2018. *Fili della trasmissione. Il progetto delle donne De Viti de Marco – Starace nel Salento del Novecento*. Lecce: Grifo.

Le Goff, Jacques. 1977/1992. *History and Memory*. New York: Columbia University Press.

Levi, Giovanni. 1985. *L'eredità immateriale*. Turin: Einaudi.

Loriga, Sabina. 2006. La biografia come problema. In *Giochi di scala. La microstoria alla prova dell'esperienza*, ed. Jacques Revel, 201–226. Rome: Viella.

Lupo, Salvatore. 2015. *La questione. Come liberare la storia del Mezzogiorno dagli stereotipi*. Rome: Donzelli.

Mori, Maria Teresa, Alessandra Pescarolo, Anna Scattigno, and Simonetta Soldani, eds. 2014. *Di generazione in generazione. Le italiane dall'Unità a oggi*. Rome: Viella.

Nunin, Roberta, and Elisabetta Vezzosi, eds. 2007. *Donne e famiglie nei sistemi di welfare. Esperienze nazionali e regionali a confronto*. Rome: Carocci.

Pescosolido, Guido. 2017. *La questione meridionale in breve. Centocinquant'anni di storia*. Rome: Donzelli.

Pomata, Gianna. 1993. Histoire des femmes et "gender history" (note critique). *Annales ESC* 4: 1021.

Ramella, Franco. 2000. La storia della famiglia nella storiografia europea: alcuni problemi. *Theomai* 2, available at http://www.redalyc.org/articulo.oa?id=12400209.

Rizzo, Maria Marcella. 2015. Ascesa e crisi del notabilato in Puglia. *Itinerari Di Ricerca Storica* 29 (2): 65–122.

Rizzo, Maria Marcella. 2016. Ingegno e "sentimento" al servizio del territorio: Filippo Bacile di Castiglione (1827–1911). *Itinerari Di Ricerca Storica* 30 (2): 219–232.

Rossi Doria, Anna, ed. 2001. *Annarita Buttafuoco. Ritratto di una storica.* Rome: Jouvence.

Rossi Doria, Anna, ed. 2003. *A che punto è la storia delle donne in Italia: Seminario Annarita Buttafuoco.* Rome: Viella.

Rossi Doria, Anna. 2007. *Dare forma al silenzio. Scritti di storia politica delle donne.* Rome: Viella.

Rossi Doria, Anna. 2012. Memoria e racconto della Shoah. *Genesis* 11 (1–2): 231–251.

Rossi Doria, Anna. 2017. Narrare e rappresentare una storia. *Genesis* 16 (2): 104.

Salvatici, Silvia, ed. 2009. The World We Have Lost di Peter Laslett. *Contemporanea* 12 (4): 743–770.

Scott, Joan W. 1988. *Gender and the Politics of History.* New York: Columbia University Press.

Thane, Pat, and Gisela Bock, eds. 1991. *Mothers of a New World. Materialist Politics and Origins of Welfare State.* London: Routledge.

Varikas, Eleni. 1996. L'approccio biografico nella storia delle donne. In *Altre storie. La critica femminista alla storia*, ed. Paola Di Cori, 349–369. Bologna: Clueb.

Willson, Perry. 2010. *Women in Twentieth-Century Italy.* New York: Palgrave Macmillan.

Willson, Perry. 2019. Confusione terminologica: "femminismo" ed "emancipazionismo" nell'Italia liberale. *Italia Contemporanea*: 209–229.

Zarri, Gabriella. 1999. *Per lettera. La scrittura epistolare femminile tra archivio e tipografia. Secc. XV-XVII.* Rome: Viella.

CHAPTER 10

A Feminine and Feminist Story of Transmission

À. Lorena Fuster and Fina Birulés

10.1 Introduction

Any serious attempt to explore in depth the notion of transmission requires the mobilisation of very complex general themes linked to the status, the power and the powerlessness of history and memory as it is referred to in some of the essays included in this volume. However, if, as a way to begin our reflections, we were to focus on clarifying the notion of transmission from the point of view of experience rather than wading into the production of a state of the art that exceeds our possibilities and thwarts our expectations, it would seem that its origins have become lost over time. We could define transmission as a very mundane initial realisation of the primacy of memory that is required to cope with life in the world. In this regard, transmission responds to the human need to free oneself of the burden of having to start anew each time.

Regardless of the more or less conscious desire for transmission that characterises all periods of history, the greatest realisation of the sense of

À. L. Fuster (✉) · F. Birulés
University of Barcelona, Barcelona, Spain

E. Laurenzi and M. Mosca (eds.), *A Female Activist Elite in Italy (1890–1920)*, https://doi.org/10.1007/978-3-030-87159-8_10

transmission as an activity, in contrast to history or memory, seems to be related to its social importance in terms of practical usefulness or sociocultural reproduction. Whether it be in oral or written form, more or less stylized, in the context of the family, profession, community or society, transmission is the process we use to try to pass on the knowledge (or goods) acquired within the various fields of experience from one generation to the next, from the most practical to the most theoretical: skills, methods, content, goals, values as well as relationships.

However, if, on the one hand, transmission seems to be linked to necessity, it should also be noted that—at a time when, as Hannah Arendt points out (2002: 8), we must constantly re-establish the link between past and present because it is no longer guaranteed by the continuity of tradition—transmission appears to be particularly linked to freedom and contingency. Like any other action, transmission does not entail an implicit guarantee of success, since it takes place within the scheme of actions and relationships of the world. Moreover, the possibility of transmission is based on a relationship between two poles that must come into play if movement is to occur: one that transmits and one that receives. Accordingly, neither the relationship nor the actions necessary for transmission can be taken for granted, because the conditions and dynamics of desire that are required for the process of transmitting something to take place do not always exist. Beyond these conditions, which suggest a very interesting and as yet unexplored performativity that is characteristic of transmission, it is also necessary to take into account what is transmitted, because as pointed out by historians who challenge and deny the prejudice of *passive* reception, what is being received, even when there is a desire to inherit, is filtered by the schemes of the recipient, and very often it is adapted to present circumstances in a more or less creative manner (De Certeau 1984). The Belgian feminist philosopher Françoise Collin reiterated this idea, in her lucid reflection on transmission, when reflecting upon the management of the legacy of the feminism of the 1970s; she states that it is the new generations who must decide whether they want this legacy, and they must pick the parts they most care about and decide what they would like to do with them (Collin 1986, 2004).

It is no coincidence that precisely at the heart of this feminism of the late twentieth century we see a reflection emerge from an observation of the non-transmission of women's thoughts and gestures as part, on the one hand, of a generalised exclusion of women from history and, on the other, of their relegation to a role as mere transmitters of 'the repetition of the same': loving, giving birth, feeding, dressing, caring for (Collin 2004). However, following this diagnosis, and without lingering for too long on denunciation, some theorists have embarked upon the task of searching for, recovering and reconstructing the histories, making transmission possible. The materials transmitted are often so fragmented that, as Simone Weil states in relation to the reconstruction of the spirit of civilizations destroyed by barbarity, this reconstructive work requires a tremendous effort of the imagination that allows the materials that have been passed down through the centuries to speak to us (Weil 1960: 54).

This effort of the imagination, which combines a reconstructive and interpretative task, has been necessary in order to build a set of conceptual and methodological tools suitable for dealing with the materials, whether ancient or contemporary, to be recovered with the aim of transmitting them without ironing out any rough edges or imperfections, that made them unique when they were created, or submitting them entirely to the interests of the present.

Over the course of the study and analysis that we have carried out as scholars of female philosophical thought over a period of three decades, we have uncovered and articulated a series of conceptual tools that have guided and given direction to our research on the works of women thinkers and their transmission. Our reason for presenting them here is to see whether they might also apply to the other female figures dealt with in this book, such as the various generations of women in the De Viti de Marco-Starace family, Cora Slocomb or Alice Hallgarten, who had an influence on their time through their work and their thinking, and who might inspire our actions and reflections today. And we introduce them with the caveat that their application should not be conceived in chronological order, nor should they be seen as alternatives. Indeed, their desirability lies in the possibility of them being used in a simultaneous and non-ideological fashion, in other words, each one should be used whenever required and not *a priori*, because otherwise we would run the risk of losing sight of the specificity and richness of the object of our study.

Even though we find at the present more and more cases of female figures from other eras and places being recovered within what we might call cultural feminism, reflections on transmission are still few and far between. The thoughts that we set out here take their lead from the reflections of Françoise Collin and they are based on the following issues: the exclusion of women from the canon, the centrality of women's distinguishing experiences in their contexts through the clues and traces in which they emerge and are manifested, and finally, the possibility of conceiving that collective of unique females as part of a hidden tradition.

10.2 Reflections on Exclusion from the Canon

10.2.1 Non-Existence or a Lack of Tradition?

When Western women were finally able to access universities and the various fields of knowledge on a massive scale during the second half of the twentieth century, some did so with a desire for dialogue, but they were astonished by the (almost) total absence of female figures from the canon of the various disciplines, which were used as a device to maintain and transform what is considered tradition.

Tradition has been usually seen as a chain uniting each generation to a specific aspect of the past, thereby allowing humans to be guided in their present and their future. Tradition provides continuity, it constitutes itself as a form of memory insofar as it 'selects and names, which hands down and preserves, which indicates where the treasures are and what their worth is' (Arendt 1968: 5). However, tradition consists of both forgetfulness and memory: it is a system of choices that allows us to judge all that is new and then decide what is worthy of being transmitted.

Thus, the assumption reflected in the canon is that women have not occupied themselves with the elaboration of thought or been involved in many areas of knowledge, nor have they been greatly relevant in the business world or indeed the working world in general.

The question regarding the presence of women in the area of knowledge and the reconsideration of history from a gender perspective opened up a number of approaches and methods for reflection and research that had not been explored prior to that moment. On the one hand, the lack of attention to and assessment of female experiences and the traditional spaces of women was reiterated, and the causes for the political and epistemic hierarchies that sustain this lack of consideration were criticised. On the other hand, the truth is that women have been present in all the disciplines down through the ages but, generally speaking, their work, their practices and their name have not been transmitted. This fact is also reflected in the essays included in this volume, and one of the goals of the book is to investigate the work and initiatives of some relatively unknown female figures from the early twentieth century in order to include and situate them in a given canon.

In this sense, one of the most common objections raised by feminist theorists within the various fields of knowledge is the non-inclusion of women in the canon, the ideological device par excellence that forms the catalogue of what is worthy of being transmitted. This criticism gives rise, almost automatically, to calls for the inclusion of the work of women as a mechanism for bringing them into the institution of knowledge. Thus, and particularly at the beginning, much of the legitimacy of the women's knowledge came from a reading of their works that attempts to prove that they comply with the positive values that the canon uses to decide what is worthy of passing into history and what is not. In other words, there has been an effort to make recognition, which undoubtedly can be a condition for transmission, subject to women fulfilling the same critical principles as those that make up the canon. Seeking recognition by trying to meet the criteria according to which something is made intelligible and valuable is the most immediate way of conceiving the reestablishment of a certain historical, historiographical, social, epistemic justice that resembles equality. However, the other side of the coin is that this reinforces the authority of the canon and consequently its values, whatever they may be, its effective power of exclusion and of creating inequality, as well as, as we will see later, its power of neutralisation when it eventually includes some female output under a scheme that introduces women as an anomaly or exception.

10.2.2 *The Introduction of Women as an Anomaly or Exception*

When it comes to making a real commitment to researching women's work and writings, it emerges the fact that historically it seems that the first scheme through which the presence of women became acceptable in fields and catalogues that are supposed to be exclusively masculine is that of affirming the exceptionality of one woman among all other women. A unique figure stands out among the others, who would perfectly fulfil a narrative that recognises them as women while also spurning them. In this resolute scheme, a woman who is accepted into these traditionally masculine areas and qualities is a person who is the exception to the norm of femininity that prevails in her time, and accordingly she tends to be considered less female than her contemporaries. When we transpose this everyday social practice to the area of knowledge, it almost seems as though the presence of empowered, original and creative women in history can only be analysed in terms of the anomaly or exception that confirms the rule. In turn, we note that these exceptions are quickly redirected to figures that place them in the context of their relationships with important men: this is the figure of the 'best disciple of' or 'wife of' or 'daughter of' or the role of mere commentator. Even if we recognise the effectiveness of this type of recovery, we will realise that the way of telling history does not change, but rather that this simply adds an appendix of excellent women to the usual way of transmitting the past. Accordingly, our focus is centred on casting doubt on this mechanism of recognition which is very much in vogue at the present time and which tends to recover individualities that emerge as rare examples of their species and their time. Moreover, we consider that it is a case of a past tailored to the demands of the present where only some isolated figures fit in while the others are discarded or ignored. If the logic of approaching what has been done, thought and said by women is based on exceptionalism, we do not see any possible transformation of culture in general, nor indeed of the canon of the disciplines. This becomes even clearer at times such as our own, when cultural institutions and the canon are already willing to integrate 'the others' following a logic of quotas. Thus, we see how a series of judged minorities are incorporated as exceptional in order to allow the canon to continue as an authority that satisfies new in vogue discourses. This is the minimum price to be paid for circumventing the danger of overhauling the criteria on which this canon is built. Furthermore, and as we have observed in the works of the women, they are almost always subjected to a process of prior normalisation to allow them to fit in with the times and with what is politically correct.

10.2.3 Introducing the Difference

For this reason, not only has it been important to work from the diagnosis of subordination, but also to highlight the variety and complexity of relationships that the studied women maintain with the traditions managed by the canon at any given time. Hence, the research conducted in the present volume suggests and emphasises the creative and ambiguous relationships that some of these female elites have maintained both with tradition and with transmission practices that are typical of the different areas in which they have worked and moved, a space that ranges from manufacturing work, in both the domestic and the social space, to the space of economic or political thought.

This approach also characterises the sort of rereading and interpretation that we have carried out, because in researching the relationship between women and tradition, we have not limited ourselves to pointing out the shortcoming, wound or need for assimilation. Rather, we insist on the value of women's contributions and legacies, introducing their difference in the world and their unique positions of recognition and freedom as opposed to what is given by tradition and the duty of transmission. This approach allows us to show and foreground the limits or myopia of the canon itself.

10.2.4 Let Them Be

This, in turn, has become a source of inspiration for rethinking the very ideas of tradition and transmission. In a world that did not treat them as equals, the women who first entered the spaces of knowledge or traditionally masculine activities (whether it was philosophy, economics, politics, art, industry or business, without prejudice to the specificity of each of these sectors), however, had to draw strength from their unique status, their eccentricity. This is precisely the reason why their work, their output, their life and their projects can be considered an expression of great freedom. This is the case of twentieth-century thinkers such as Hannah Arendt, Simone Weil, María Zambrano and Suzanne Langer; but it is also the case of the women studied in this volume. In addition to showcasing a female knowledge which, under the sign of what Forcina calls the art of a work well done (Chapter 8), erases the rigid border between art and craftsmanship, the women of the De Viti de Marco-Starace family, Alice Hallgarten Franchetti and Cora Slocomb di Brazzà were able to initiate and develop pioneering and transformative experiences of work and education, guided by the goal of female emancipation and social justice.

If we return to the question of the canon for a moment, beyond any differences between them, all these women seem to be aware that they will not be included in the canon, and yet they do not give up on their desire to satisfy their need to think, speak, write, experiment and innovate. And they do so without any fear of making mistakes or falling from grace as demonstrated by the reconstructions of their trajectories carried out in the chapters of this book. This attitude of not allowing themselves to become obsessed by cases of authorization and legitimacy and to dare to take responsibility for doing something by themselves is also very inspiring for those of us whose work is devoted to trying to rewrite the histories from a critical position. Perhaps, this does not mean spending our energy on achieving institutionalisation through recognition, but rather investing it in letting them be, in recovering their work and their writings in order to put them into circulation. Throughout these decades, we have learnt that if we take the initiative and manage to assume responsibility for recovering and spreading the thought and work of women with all its potent uniqueness, this already has an impact on the alleged innocence of a certain imaginary of the neutral. This has been achieved firstly by creating a space for conversation and resonance among a majority of women and, at the same time, by creating a gap that allows the emergence of an institutional place where they can be heard by those who want to listen. If, on the other hand, we succeed in circulating their writings outside the confines of academia and in places where the canon is of little importance, but where knowledge is required to deal with issues of the common space that affect us, for example in political activism, this also opens up other very powerful possibilities for transmission.

10.3 Reflections on the Clues of Female Experiences

10.3.1 Recording an Awareness of One's Own Place and Value: Granting Authority

As it has been already said, during these years, we have been able to see how female philosophers, academics and political activists, businesswomen, philanthropists, etc. were aware of the non-central position they occupied, and of the fact that if they did not want to limit themselves to serving as ventriloquists of a legacy that did not fully belong to them, they had to draw strength from their position on the margins. Those margins are not the outside, but rather they are a sort of liminal zone between the interior and exterior of institutions, tradition and the circles of power. However, and quite contrary to what one might conclude by following the *cliché* that associates this marginality with a reduced awareness of their own value, these women did attach great importance to their own thoughts and actions. Their experience of the margin offered them the possibility of not having to become the guardians of any orthodoxy and to feel sufficiently free to convey their thoughts and actions through innovative paths, exposing themselves to other languages and the innovative trends of their day, without abandoning the tradition in which they were trained. In the case of the women studied in this volume, they remained in dialogue with the currents of modernisation and transformation of educational, health and religious theories, turning them into mediators and promotors of the actions of individuals such as Maria Montessori, or Rudolf Steiner.

Aware of the fact that transmission was not guaranteed, they invested a lot of their energy in circulating their output through unexpected channels that gave them visibility and publicity. Thus, we can highlight channels like correspondence or the press, as well as the world exhibitions, where their words and their products found visibility and a great deal of recognition. This was the case of the works of Cora Slocomb at the International Exhibition held in Chicago in 1893.

In this regard, and even taking note of their marginal position, another heuristic premise of our work has consisted in placing the focus on women who, in their position of authority, were regarded as activists, teachers, leaders and communicators, but also as founders of institutions such as the Casamassella School of the De Viti de Marco-Starace family (Chapter 5) or the Le Costantine Foundation, the centre for agricultural, artisanal and pedagogical activities that was established by Giulia Starace (Chapters 6 and 7), Alice Hallgarten's Umbrian Canvas Laboratory (Chapter 3) or Cora Slocomb's seven lace schools (Chapter 4), or indeed the Italian Feminine Industries (IFI) in which many of them were involved (Chapter 1). These institutions were created with the aim of promoting the economic and political emancipation of women as well as the social and cultural improvement of persons who were born in impoverished areas as a consequence of capitalist economic models. As far as content, form, methodology and tools are concerned, the essays gathered in this volume insist on emphasising the actions and thoughts of these women and their teaching work outside the strictly academic realm, reiterating the example that has been lived and not preached, and using very diverse means, but introduced through philanthropy at the point where the labour, educational, social and political spheres intersect.

A large part of the changing viewpoints that we have worked with, and which we have dissected thus far, feed off the political link that unites us to the feminism of the 1970s. This radical insurrection movement existed 'on a different plane' (Lonzi 1982: 52) in relation to the classical grievances of modern feminism, opening up new scenarios for reflecting on and questioning the experience of women. Oppression was condemned, but a special emphasis was placed on the need for a political work on the symbolic and an unblocking of the symbolic transmission that presupposes treating women as individuals capable of generating and creating, and not as specimens of a gender relegated to reproducing life and transmitting this reproduction.

In coherence with this need for the transformation of sense, for providing the context and the conditions for making sayable, thinkable and performable things which did not participate of the hegemonic symbolic, the political importance of transmission is emphasised and there is a strong commitment to the creation of a female genealogy for the transmission of women's work.

It is not merely a question of undertaking archaeological work to recover what has not been dealt with, even though that does carry some value in its own right. It is about showing that these women are capable of responding to questions that are still open today or which have just been raised from other languages and other historical contexts. Moreover, they often make it possible to illuminate the blind spots of current debates.

Furthermore, with the rise of feminist theory, the origin of which already confirmed the complexity and richness of the feminisms of the final decades of the twentieth century, a space opened up for questions relating to the possibility of speaking about female thought and practices or themes that have been a cause for reflection for us, such as the type of tradition that might exist among the figures excluded from the tradition. All this research has an experimental and incomplete nature, and we must highlight the extent to which it permeates the texts included in this book, which combine a thorough search of the archive, a procedure of hypothetical reconstruction, and an interpretative work that seeks to give general meaning to particular deeds.

It is worth remembering that this is not aimed at inclusion in the canon, but rather it is about putting women's thought and work into circulation so that once they have been introduced into the world, they can allow us to relate differently with each other, with ourselves and with the world itself.

10.3.2 The Evidential Paradigm: Making Sense

In this subsection we will refer briefly to some research that has been key in terms of defining our methodology. First of all, we must mention Carlo Ginzburg's evidential paradigm (1992), which states that an analysis of social relationships and their density can be achieved if the scale of observation is reduced; it is a matter of observing a small or particular point while raising general questions. This involves recovering fragments of the past that have escaped examination by both practitioners of hegemonic history and contemporary commentators. In this resides the significance of the figures studied in this book and their work, often unknown or forgotten, and quite frequently unpublished in the case of those women who left us a written legacy.

When the sources of hegemonic history systematically silence or distort social or cultural reality, there are reasons to return to the archives in order to search for relatively unknown documents, thus ensuring that we do not continue travelling along well-trodden paths with their prefabricated images of the past (Birulés 2015: 112). These documents, fragments of the past, can open up gaps that offer us an opportunity to develop new hypotheses of the history of women and the transmission of their thought and actions, as well as of other general histories, as shown in the work carried out by the scholars of this volume in which the entrepreneurial actions of some of these women is linked to a rereading of the *cliché* of the backward South or reconsiderations of industrial development in Italy (see Chapter 9). This type of approach allows the creation of a space of inscription that opens up the possibility of reading their contributions not as isolated cases that emerge only to disappear, but with some continuity and in relation to other initiatives. These forms of reading, rereading and interpretation that take the signs of deleted or erased experiences into account, make it possible to establish new areas of research. In this way, by putting their works into circulation, in the various meanings of the word, and fostering dialogue around the texts, a previously unexplored, rich and dynamic corpus is created.

As a result of the recovery of documents of a very varied nature through archive work, we have regarded the marginal and minor productions—less studied and less recognised—as well as the informative, literary and epistolary didactic texts, as privileged observation points for studying women's special relationship with the notion and practice of transmission, and this book is a testament to this. In a similar fashion, we believe that we can find valuable tools in these materials that will help us address the challenges of our time, and drive us towards reconsidering what is at play in the transmission of knowledge, in the practices of a globalised world, within a life space where different traditions, and very diverse forms of relationship with them, coexist.

10.4 Reflections Based on the Idea of a Hidden Tradition

10.4.1 A Female Tradition?

One of the questions that we pose within the context of our study devoted to women thinkers is the following: can we speak of a tradition of female thought? In the context of this volume, which deals with something as characteristic of the female tradition as lacemaking, we can associate this question with another related one: can we speak of a tradition of female activism and social commitment?

At the beginning of this chapter, we claimed that tradition is a system of choices that allows us to judge all that is new, and to decide what is worthy of being transmitted. Accordingly, there is always the danger that something will be forgotten if its significance cannot be integrated into the traditional system: this has been the case of women philosophers, academics and political activists, businesswomen, philanthropists, etc. whose works, even though they assumed the responsibility and the task of transmitting and putting into circulation a knowledge that changed their world, have not been transmitted. However, as this book shows, we can discover a sort of 'hidden tradition' among these women, in the sense in which Hannah Arendt (2007) uses this expression to refer to figures who are not fully included in the world: non-Hebrew speaking, Jewish poets, writers and artists, pariah figures who took the message of emancipation more seriously than anybody expected.

We can hypothesise this hidden tradition, but not in reference to the women who form part of the collective of those who have been excluded from everywhere. Rather, we must search among female intellectuals, activists, philanthropists, among women from various intellectual, economic and social elites, who have been inadequately researched until now because nobody considered them 'as one of their own'. These women represent pure products of emancipation, a minority phenomenon back in their own day. It is also worth remembering that in many cases their access to culture and education was conditioned by a certain 'masculinization'. But perhaps, in the case of the activists studied here and in contrast to women philosophers, masculinization is deconstructed *a posteriori*, with the explicit empowerment of feminine practices and their values.

In the case of the women philosophers of the early twentieth century, we have decided to resort to the notion of 'hidden tradition' because there are very few links between the great but isolated women who have affirmed their willingness to think. However, we continue to speak of 'tradition' because the same basic conditions of uprooting and the absence of easily traceable links have resulted in and provoked a similar basic reaction of freedom. In the case of entrepreneurial and activist women, such as those of the De Viti de Marco-Starace family, Slocomb or Hallgarten, perhaps we could speak of a 'hidden tradition' in another sense: unlike most (women) philosophers, they have been true to the female, so to speak, unhidden tradition, Indeed, they have been loyal to one of the few traditions allowed to women since ancient times: the tradition of weaving and caring. However, what is unprecedented is that they moved it away from the domestic space to which it had been relegated to the social space of work and they even transformed it into a political project.

10.4.2 The Given Tradition and the Reappropriated Tradition

Even though the change that reappraised and established the market possibilities for lace was the Arts and Craft movement promoted by two men, John Ruskin and William Morris (see Chapter 1), lacemaking is deeply female when considered as a tradition. As far as women working with threads is concerned, the *Iliad* was the first instance in the Western literary tradition where weaving was recorded as a sort of epithet of female work: it was the occupation of mortal women regardless of their class, but also of goddesses. For women, this would be the given tradition, the inherited or imposed tradition. However, despite being part of what was imposed and therefore interpretable as a sign of oppression, what is given can also be lived, revisited or reappropriated in its ambiguity as a place of freedom and creativity. As we see in the stories of Lucia Starace, Etta, Cora and Alice, by weaving and innovating in their ways of making patterns, women have been able to exercise their creativity even though they were denied spaces for study and representation. This is why contemporary artists such as Judith Chicago or Gadha Amer use weaving in their work as a female sign of artistic creativity that speaks of the exclusion of women from the field of art, albeit under very different circumstances. When considering the symbolic dimension of the task of weaving, it is interesting to consider one of the many mentions that Homer makes as a distant forerunner of the various valences of this art. In this case, the poet assigns Helen the task of recording her own time as he describes her engaged in the embroidering scenes of the Trojan War, in other words, an event of which she is an essential part, and which is still in progress (Homer 1924: 3, 125 ff.). Helen does with threads what Homer does with words: she shows her time through her own *Iliad*.

Moreover, mythology, the symbolic universe that nourishes this first Western epic poem, also includes the story of Arachne, who challenges the goddess Athena to a weaving contest to determine who is the best weaver. Because of the disproportion inherent to the desire to better the goddess at something, and the added fact of weaving scenes from the lives of gods that are demeaning for them, Athena transforms Arachne and all her female descendants into spiders, the lineage of animal weavers that will make weaving their home and the place from which to get food. Turning weaving into the workplace with its symbolism, and into a practical place where they can obtain sustenance, seems therefore to be a fate inscribed in the representation of this art. In any case, and stretching the thread of Forcina's reflection even further (Chapter 8), we could say that these stories are preludes of some 'signs of this art, which ranged from needlework to social work'. And because it was traditionally a women's task, unlike philosophical work, the power of the female genealogy is practised and recognised within the area of weaving, which has to do with the knowledge of woman associated with what has usually been seen as a private domain and which has passed through what Luce Irigaray refers to as a plane of the vertical relationship between women, the intergenerational genealogical, but also in the horizontal plane of the relationship between equals and/or peers (1993: 97–115). In such matters, transmission operates, materially and symbolically, in both directions.

10.4.3 A Tradition to Be Created or Reconstructed?

As we have already mentioned and emphasised as a fundamental point in the essays included here, the women studied in this volume are pioneers in something that did belong to them by tradition: they caused this knowledge and these practices to pass through the social and public world, thereby transforming them into a collective enterprise and a source of work and value. What is more, they converted it into a political project. In this regard, we can say that the female emancipationists of the early twentieth century took explicit advantage of female values (caring, maternity, affection, empathy, etc.) to support the political presence of women and their capacity for transformation (Laurenzi 2017). Their thought did not take place mainly through intellectual work, but rather it was linked to politics as the practice of weaving relationships, as a praxis, and in this case as a form of art, as a creative exercise.

From this perspective, we can also speak of a hidden tradition insofar as it has been neglected by the dominant historiography and that it still seems to be unknown for several reasons:

1. Although the most likely is that there are some bonds between these elites that stretch beyond the family relationships that unite, for example, the women of the De Viti de Marco and Starace families, these have not been explored in depth, so that the extent and intensity of these networks cannot be fully grasped.
2. Beyond explicit relationships, linked to a common militancy or friendships, we find some coincidences in their gestures, the causes of which are still pending investigation to a large extent.
3. It remains unclear in which tradition they inscribed their original conception of the struggle for female freedom as being inseparable from caring for the world and the people who inhabit it. Consequently, their political culture, beyond the classical party logic, is expressed through philanthropy in a shared passion for innovation within education, health, reformism, religious and pacificist, abolitionist and anticolonial movements.

The industrial revolution that began in the latter half of the nineteenth century caused a social transformation with far-reaching consequences, including the loss of the conditions for satisfying basic material and spiritual needs (food, housing, health, childcare, the transmission of knowledge and education, a sense of belonging and recognition etc.), which were linked to the social dynamics of the family, guilds, traditional civil and religious communities. Human vulnerability was exposed then in an unprecedented manner, as its exploitation affected large numbers of people. It is an awareness of this human vulnerability as well as the vulnerability of the common world, together with the faith in the possibilities of action and knowledge, that seems to lie at the root of the activism of women such as those studied in this volume, as well as others with whom they coincided in various formal and informal networks at a national and transnational level. These figures played a leading role in the gradual secularisation of charity and the conformation of a type of female activism and social commitment that would continue being transformed in the early twentieth century as seen, in particular, in the ideas of welfare forwarded by Etta de Viti de Marco, Cora Slocomb di Brazzà, Giulia Starace or Lucia de Viti de Marco. Their moral and political commitment is materialised in their leading role, or collaboration with philanthropic initiatives that marked a departure from the models of Christian charity and paternalist state welfarism. It is also materialised in the fact that they played an active role in the foundation of institutions that encouraged empowerment and individual development through practical and theoretical training like those devoted to educating women (cultural and professional training focused on work in industry), childcare institutions (the first kindergartens for the protection of children), the various end-of-century leagues for peace whose actions were also targeted at the education of women, etc. In this regard, the gradual institutionalisation of benefit systems by the state culminating in the welfare state or mutual work insurance societies coexists with these self-organised associations which in turn favoured another type of relationship between women.

Therefore, we need to persevere with the task of opening spaces to record what these women did through the creation of genealogical networks and affiliations that are improbable if we follow the patriarchal rationale of the canon. This transmission work will help to prevent the presentism that characterises our time from removing them from the new alternative ways of presenting the history or histories of institutions and concepts. But in order to do this, we must be capable of registering the change; we must incorporate it so that transmission really does occur. Together, we have managed to create a female corpus that other women can refer to or indeed that anybody can refer to. This corpus will remain alive if we feed from it, refer to it, quote it whenever we act, think and write. Thanks to the work of many women, and in contrast to the feminist scholars of the past, whenever we ask ourselves about what women did in the past, we do not find ourselves facing the silence that resulted from total erasure. Only by not ignoring everything that has been done and by being capable of resisting the temptation to make ourselves out to be the first women to have come up with certain ideas or to have carried out certain business ventures will we manage to honour the beginnings. To honour the beginnings that the inaugural strength of these women gave rise to is to create culture, taking into account the past, the present and the future.

References

Arendt, Hannah. 1968. Tradition and Modern Age. In *Between Past and Future. Eight Exercises on Political Thought*, 17–40. New York: The Viking Press.

Arendt, Hannah. 2002. *Denktagebuch, 1950 bis 1973*, ed. Ursula Ludz and Ingeborg Nordman. Munich: Piper.

Arendt, Hannah. 2007. The Jew as Paria: A Hidden Tradition. In *Jewish Writings*, 275–297. New York: Schocken Books.

Birulés, Fina. 2015. Las filósofas y la tradición. In *Entreactos: En torno a la política el feminismo y el pensamiento*, 107–128. Buenos Aires: Katz Editores.

Collin, Françoise. 1986. Un héritage sans testament. *Les Cahiers Du Grif* 34: 81–92.

Collin, Françoise. 2004. Le féminisme pour quoi faire? Genèse et formes d'un mouvement. *La Revue Nouvelle* 11: 9–25.

1984.De Certeau, Michel. 1984. *The Practice of Everyday Life*. Oakland: University of California Press.

Ginzburg, Carlo. 1992. *Clues, Myths, and the Historical Method*. Baltimore: Johns Hopkins University Press.

Homer. 1924. *Iliad*. Cambridge: Harvard University Press.

Irigaray, Luce. 1993. *An Ethics of Sexual Difference*. Ithaca: Cornell University.

Laurenzi, Elena. 2017. Dal passato al futuro. La trasmissione del progetto politico attraverso una genealogia femminile nella prima metà del secolo XX. *Historia Magistra* 24: 34–58.

Lonzi, Carla. 1982. *Sputiamo su Hegel*. Milan: Gammalibri.

Weil, Simone. 1960. L'agonie d'une civilisation vue à travers un poème épique. *Écrits historiques et politiques*, 53–67. Paris: Gallimard.

Index

A

Abensour, Miguel, 202
Adam, Thomas, 7, 161
Alcaro, Mario, 182
Aleramo, Sibilla, 8, 218
Alessandri, Giuseppe, 146
Allegri, Clelia, 160
Amadori, Rosi, 10
Amari, Carolina, 77, 78, 136, 146
Amari, Michele, 136
Amer, Gadha, 239
Anstruther-Thomson, John, 33
Anthony, Susan B., 115, 120
Arendt, Hannah, 21, 186, 193, 194, 197, 200, 228, 230, 233, 238
Arienzo, Alessandro, 193
Aronica, Ferdinando, 69, 70
Ascoli Nathan, Lilih, 109
Asquer, Enrica, 213
Astuto, Franco, 177
Attila the Hun, 100
Augello, Massimo M., 44

B

Babini, Valeria P., 87, 220
Bacile di Castiglione, Gennaro, 37
Bakałowicz-Aloisi, Giuseppina, 10
Bakałowicz, Stefan, 10
Ballerini, Elisabetta, 85
Bance, Rosamunde, 85
Banfield, Edward Christie, 182
Barbella, Maria, 115, 125
Barberini, Henriette, 54
Barbetta, Maria Cecilia, 69
Baritono, Raffaella, 214
Baruzzi, Marina, 146
Basso, Rosanna, 192, 193
Bates-Batcheller, Tryphosa B., 74, 79
Bateson, Mary Catherine, 199
Bearzi, Dorina, 96
Beckert, Sven, 2
Bedeschi, Lorenzo, 71
Beillard, Corinne, 8
Bellomo, Bianca Rosa, 146
Benigno, Francesco, 210
Bernardini, Carla, 146
Besso, Marco, 3, 134

E. Laurenzi and M. Mosca (eds.), *A Female Activist Elite in Italy (1890–1920)*, https://doi.org/10.1007/978-3-030-87159-8

Beyers, Leen, 38
Biagioli, Giuliana, 84
Bianchi, Bruna, 154
Bianconcini Cavazza, Lina, 146
Biggi, Maria Ida, 39, 49, 53
Bini, Elisabetta, 214
Birmingham, Stephen, 61
Birulés, Fina, 6, 22, 183, 237
Bisi Albini, Sofia, 9, 68, 76, 77
Bistoni, Vittor Ugo, 67, 72, 74, 81
Bloch, Marc, 222
Bo, Carlo, 39, 71
Boccini, Giuseppe, 66
Bock, Gisela, 219
Bodio, Luigi, 48
Bonaparte, Napoleon, 100
Bonghi, Ruggiero, 96
Bonsanti, Alessandro, 43
Borghese, Scipio, 39
Borgognoni, Mariano, 160
Bovio, Giovanni, 117
Bowles, Joseph, 82
Breschi, Danilo, 64
Brits, Elsabé, 154, 157
Bronson Rucellai, Edith, 77
Buchanan, Hellen, 39
Buchanan, James A., 39
Buchner, Felicitas, 68, 73, 74, 79, 81
Bufacchi, Enrica, 2
Buseghin, Maria Luciana, 17, 60, 63, 64, 66, 67, 69, 71, 72, 74, 76–82, 84–86
Bussey, Gertrude, 3
Buttafuoco, Annarita, 8, 13–15, 134, 135, 218, 219

C
Cadeddu, Davide, 182
Caetani, Leone, 48
Calanca, Daniela, 212, 213
Caldani, Enrichetta, 64
Cammarota Adorno, Gaetano, 64
Cammarota Adorno, Sofia, 64
Capek, Mary Ellen, 8
Capuzzo, Ester, 60
Capuzzo, Paolo, 213, 214
Cardini, Antonio, 41, 43, 45–47, 51, 143
Carluccio, Carolina, 139
Carman, Jillian, 11
Carmignani, Marianna, 11
Caroli, Dorena, 146, 147
Casalena, Maria Pia, 146, 212
Casalini, Maria, 213
Casciola, Brizio (Don), 69, 70, 163
Cassese, Sabino, 217
Castronovo, Valerio, 44
Cavell, Edith, 49
Celli, Angelo, 63
Ceresi, Vincenzo, 166
Ceschia, Marzia, 160
Chamberlain, Joseph, 154
Chernyshevsky, Nikolaj, 21, 195–197
Chicago, Judith, 239
Chirilli, Emilia, 35, 53, 139–143, 161
Chiuri, Maria Grazia, 178
Cini, Giorgio, 39, 51
Cloete, Constance, 156
Colajanni, Napoleone, 35
Colgate, Florence, 137
Collin, Françoise, 4, 7, 21, 204, 228, 229
Comi, Girolamo, 140, 201
Contini, Alessandra, 221
Conti Odorisio, Ginevra, 13, 14
Converse, Florence, 81
Corbin, Austin, 115
Cordelli, Chiara, 7
Corder Denser, Angela, 109
Corder Denser, Giuseppe, 109
Cornero, Giuseppe, 64
Corrigan, Michael Augustine, 48
Creighton, Mandell, 37

Croce, Benedetto, 140, 191
Curie, Marie. *See* Skłodowska, Marie Salomea

D

Dal Co Viganò, Ernestina, 147
Dana, Nathalie, 78, 86
Danieli, Lisa, 42
Danzetta, Vittoria Luce, 77
Darmstaedter, Eleonore, 62
Daumard, Adeline, 2
Davanzo Poli, Doretta, 146
Davidoff, Leonore, 2
Day, Abigail, 117, 120, 124
De Certeau, Michel, 228
De Cicco, Francesco, 181
De Clementi, Andreina, 219
De Felice, Renzo, 36, 40
De Giampietro, Massimo Ludovico, 67
De Giorgio, Michela, 16, 141, 184, 218, 220
Del Bono, Adele, 163
De Luca, Stefano, 193
Denitto, Anna Lucia, 21, 46, 207, 217
Devins, John B., 115
De Viti Anguissola, Antonio, 139
De Viti de Marco, Antonio, 17, 18, 31, 33, 35, 134, 139, 142, 143, 154, 163, 215–217
De Viti de Marco, Carolina, 19, 33, 36, 54, 133, 139–142, 144–150, 153–155, 161, 162, 169–171, 176, 177, 183, 184, 199, 207, 211, 214–216, 218, 220, 222
De Viti de Marco, Costanza, 201
De Viti de Marco, Etta. *See* Dunham, Harriet Lathrop
De Viti de Marco, Lucia, 19, 20, 52, 153, 163–165, 167–172, 175–177, 183, 185, 196, 198, 199, 211, 215, 242
De Viti de Marco, Raffaele, 139, 176, 177
De Vito, Lucia, 181
De Wet, Roitjie, 158
Didi-Huberman, George, 187
Di Biagio, Anna, 213
Di Fiore, Laura, 214
Di Meco, Lucina, 5
Douglas-Hamilton, Mary, 82, 83, 85, 86
Ducommun, Elie, 117, 119, 122
Dunham, Catherine Skinner, 32
Dunham, Elisabeth Howland, 32
Dunham, Grace Louise, 32
Dunham, Harriet Lathrop, 17, 19, 31, 32, 133, 150, 154, 183, 207, 211, 213, 216, 218
Dunham, Helen Bliss, 32
Dunham, James Harvey, 32
Dunham, Lilian Howland, 32
Duse, Eleonora, 38, 39, 49, 51, 53
Duvenek, Frank, 124

E

Edison, Thomas, 115, 116
Einaudi, Giulio, 52
Einaudi, Luigi, 34, 37, 44, 47, 52

F

Fabiani, Anna Angelica, 81
Faina, Eugenio, 83
Fane, Violet. *See* Montgomerie Currie, Mary
Fano, Clelia, 147
Fazio, Ida, 207
Fedeli, Anna, 85
Feez, Susan, 38
Felice, Flavio, 45, 182
Fernández de Alarcón, Roca, 2

Fernández, Pura, 2
Ferrante, Laura, 5, 208
Ferrari, Cesare, 127
Ferrarotti, Franco, 182
Ferrero, Guglielmo, 37, 39, 40, 43, 44, 45, 46
Filmer, Robert, 196
Fisher, John, 154
Flanagan, Maureen A., 2
Flour, Els, 3, 134
Focher, Ferruccio, 197
Fogazzaro, Antonio, 64, 68, 163
Fontanesi, Harriette, 11
Forcina, Marisa, 16, 21, 68, 73, 220, 233, 240
Fortunato, Giustino, 63, 64, 217
Foscarini, Armando, 172
Fossati, Roberta, 3, 17, 66, 70–73, 88, 134, 163
Foster, Rebecca Salome, 115
Franchetti, Leopoldo, 18, 63, 65, 68, 85, 215–217
Franchetti, Ludovica Valeria, 67
Franchini, Silvia, 148
Francis of Assisi (Saint), 160, 163
Frattini, Claudia, 3, 135
Frisa, Maria Luisa, 179
Fröbel, Friedrich Wilhelm, 82
Fuster, Àngela Lorena, 6, 22, 68

G

Gabrielli, Patrizia, 219
Galasso, Giuseppe, 217
Gallarati Scotti, Tommaso, 64
Ganci, Salvatore Massimo, 35
Gandhi, Mohandas Karamchand, 123, 162
Garibaldi, Giuseppe, 139
Garland, Hannibal Hamlin, 39
Garzia, Raffaele, 149
Gazzetta, Liviana, 218
Gemelli, Giuliana, 182, 221
Geraldini, Arnaldo, 41
Ghetti Baldi, Orsola, 146
Giacomelli, Antonietta, 70, 163
Giammattei, Emma, 2
Giannone, Antonio, 140
Gill, Rebecca, 155
Ginori, Carlo, 137
Ginsborg, Paul, 213
Ginzburg, Carlo, 236
Giolitti, Giovanni, 146
Giretti, Edoardo, 44, 45
Gnoli, Domenico, 86
Gnoli, Umberto, 86
Gori, Claudia, 9, 16, 135, 146
Gotteland, Marie-Claire, 162
Gouverneur, Virginie, 53
Gramsci, Antonio, 197
Greetings, Joyous, 3, 134
Gribaudi, Gabriella, 182, 209
Griscom, Lloyd C., 48
Gubiani Gallo, Amalia, 140
Gubin, Eliane, 3, 134
Guidi, Laura, 5, 11, 221
Guidi, Marco E.L., 44

H

Hadrian (Emperor), 87
Hall, Catherine, 2
Hallgarten, Charles/Karl, 61, 62
Hallgarten, Eleanor Rose, 63
Hallgarten Franchetti, Alice, 9, 17, 59, 87, 134, 163, 233
Hallgarten, Ida, 63
Hallgarten, J. Adolph, 60, 61, 63
Hallgarten, Julius, 61
Hallgarten, Lazarus, 61
Hallgarten Nordheimer, Walter, 60
Hall, John, 154
Hart, Norma, 167
Harvey, Robert, 4

Heine, Johann Heinrich, 107
Heraclitus, 200
Hitler, Adolf, 52
Hobhouse Balme, Jennifer, 154
Hobhouse, Emily, 38, 153–156, 158, 214
Holmes, Diana, 2
Howe, Elliott Maud, 35, 37
Howe, Julia Ward, 35, 37

I
Imprenti, Fiorella, 135
Ingersoll, Robert Green, 115
Ingoldsby, Kit, 82
Irigaray, Luce, 240

J
Jagow, Gottlieb von, 38
James, Henry, 33
Jana, Rosalinde, 179
John, King of England, 101
Johnson, Joan Marie, 2, 8
Josz, Aurelia, 74
Juston-Sabatier, Louise, 71

K
Kant, Immanuel, 21, 193
Kaplan, Ann, 4
King, Martin Luther, 123
Kitchener, Horatio Herbert, 156
König, Karl, 154, 165–167
Kramer, Rita, 16, 38
Kuliscioff, Anna, 41, 150

L
Lama, Luisa, 87
Lamberini, Daniela, 13
La Mothe, Berta, 81, 84
Lanaro, Paola, 212
Langer, Suzanne, 233
Lanoce, Egidio, 146, 148
Larsen, Ruth, 2
Laslett, Peter, 212
Lathrop, Harriet Winslow, 32
Latter, Lucy R., 81–83
Laurenzi, Elena, 19, 133, 153, 157–160, 169, 175, 177, 198, 200, 220, 222, 223, 241
Lee, Lucy, 32
Le Goff, Jacques, 222
Lenin, Vladimir Ilyich, 197
Leonard (Saint), 111, 154
Levi, Giovanni, 212
Liszt, Franz, 62
Lloyd George, David, 52
Lombardo Radice, Giuseppe, 84
Lombroso, Cesare, 43
Lombroso, Gina, 43
Lonzi, Carla, 235
Loriga, Sabina, 212
Lovett, Eva, 146
Luck, Minnie, 137, 138
Lupo, Salvatore, 217
Lustiger, Arno, 63

M
Maccheroni, Anna Maria, 85
Macor, Emilia, 155
Madaro, Lorenzo, 140
Malinconico, Gabriele, 159, 160, 177, 178
Mancina, Claudia, 13
Maraini Guerrieri-Gonzaga, Maria, 38
Marcello, Andreana, 99
Marchetti Bullough, Enrichetta, 53
Marchetti Montemaggi, Malwida, 78
Marconi, Guglielmo, 48
Marcuzzi, Angelica, 127
Maria di Campello. *See* Pignetti, Valeria Paola

Marino, Mauro, 140
Martelloni, Francesco, 48, 53
Marx, Eleanor, 202
Marx, Karl, 202
Mauro Airoldi, Lena, 144, 148
Mau, Steffen, 182
May, Hope Elizabeth, 123, 128
May, Maude G., 86
Mazzini, Giuseppe, 41, 70, 139
Mazzolari, Primo, 163
Mazzola, Ugo, 35
McJones, Walter, 39
Mead, Molly, 8
Melegari, Dora, 9, 163
Meriggi, Marco, 214
Merril, Jenny, 87
Meysenbug, Malwida von, 41, 69, 72
Mezzomonti, Elisa, 41
Miller, Tom, 33
Mineo, E. Igor, 210
Minerva, Brizia, 140
Minghetti, Marco, 79
Mondolfo Sacerdote, Lavinia, 170
Monte, Antonio, 157
Montemartini, Giovanni, 45
Montessori, Carolina, 84, 87
Montessori, Maria, 38, 76, 80, 81, 83, 84, 87, 159, 215, 220, 235
Monteux, Angelika, 167
Montgomerie Currie, Mary, 39
Mori, Maria Teresa, 210, 211, 219
Morin, Edgar, 128
Morozzo Della Rocca, Roberto, 160
Morris, William, 11, 21, 202, 239
Mosca, Gaetano, 52
Mosca, Manuela, 17, 33, 46, 48, 53, 143, 164
Mozzoni, Anna Maria, 13
Müller-Wiedermann, Hans, 167
Murri, Romolo, 39, 71
Musci, Leonardo, 65, 67, 70
Mussolini, Benito, 52, 165

N
Nathan, Ernesto, 10, 70
Nathan, Liliah, 10
Nietzsche, Friedrich, 41
Nigris, Naomi, 127
Nitti, Francesco Saverio, 217
Nobel, Alfred, 121
Nordheimer Hallgarten, Julia, 70
Nordheimer, William, 61
Noudelmann, Françoise, 4
Nunin, Roberta, 221

O
Oddone, Ines, 13
O'Donnel, Marion, 87
Old Traveller. *See* Hallgarten Nordheimer, Walter
Olivetti, Adriano, 182
Orlando, Alda, 42
Ottini, Francesco, 168

P
Paderewski, Ignacy Jan, 32
Page, Thomas N., 43
Pajano, Lena, 181
Palazzi, Maura, 208
Palmieri de Marco, Costanza, 139
Palomba, Ivana, 9, 137, 146
Panarese, Egidio, 146, 148
Pantaleoni, Maffeo, 33, 35, 44, 45, 150
Pantini, Romualdo, 137
Papadia, Carlo, 177
Papafava, Francesco, 45
Paradiso, Massimo, 35
Pareto, Vilfredo, 44, 45
Pasolini dall'Onda, Angelica, 35, 43
Pasqui Marchetti, Maria, 64, 66, 67, 71–73, 78, 80, 81, 84
Pateman, Carole, 193
Paull, John, 3

Pavanelli, Giovanni, 44
Pazzini, Claudia, 86
Pecile, Gabriele Luigi, 96, 104, 105, 125
Pecorella, Gino, 165, 177
Pecorella, Marco, 177
Pedone, Antonio, 143
Péguy, Charles, 21, 201–203
Pellizzi, Camillo, 36, 40
Persichella, Vincenzo, 168
Pescarolo, Alessandra, 9, 210
Pescosolido, Guido, 217
Pestalozzi, Johann Heinrich, 82
Pettit, Henri, 118
Pezzino, Paolo, 64
Pieroni Bortolotti, Franca, 13, 15, 135
Pignetti, Valeria Paola, 160
Pironi, Tiziana, 16
Pirzio Biroli, Giuseppe, 127
Pomata, Gianna, 4, 208
Ponti Suardi, Antonia, 109
Presicce, Maria Grazia, 157
Prezzolini, Giuseppe, 44, 45
Proust, Marcel, 40
Pucci, Idanna, 18, 93–95, 117, 120–122, 128, 143
Puzzuoli, Paola, 148

R
Ramella, Franco, 212
Ranieri di Sorbello, Romeyne Robert, 77
Ranieri di Sorbello, Ruggero, 86
Rasponi, Angelica, 36, 37
Ravà, Bice, 83
Reich, Rob, 7
Ricci, Elisa, 11, 145, 146
Richards, Laura E., 35, 37
Rizzo, Maria Cristina, 181
Rizzo, Maria Marcella, 218
Roesler, Franz Maria, 42
Rogari, Sandro, 64
Rolland, Romain, 37
Romagnoli, Augusto, 161
Rood, Johanna, 155, 156, 158
Rosenbaum, Julia, 2
Rosselli, Amelia, 9, 12–15, 186, 187
Rossi, Adele, 140
Rossi Doria, Anna, 13, 208, 209, 219, 222
Ross, Janet, 37
Ruskin, John, 11–13, 138, 239
Russell, Arthur James, 159
Russo, Maria Cristina, 159, 169
Ryan, Eilish, 32, 33

S
Sabatier, Charles Paul Marie, 39, 66, 67, 71, 73, 80, 88, 163
Saccavini, Chiara, 110
Sahlmann, Lotte, 166
Salomone, A. William, 9
Salvatici, Silvia, 212
Salvemini, Gaetano, 34, 41, 46, 64, 217
Sargent, John Singer, 32
Savorgnan di Brazzà, Ascanio, 124
Savorgnan di Brazzà, Detalmo, 18, 95, 215
Savorgnan di Brazzà, Filippo, 109
Savorgnan di Brazzà, Giacinta, 126
Savorgnan di Brazzà, Idanna, 127
Scarrafia, Lucetta, 7
Scattigno, Anna, 210, 221
Schembs, Hans-Otto, 63
Schiff, Paolina, 13
Schweitzer, Albert, 162
Scott, Joan W., 207, 208
Scudder, Vida, 60, 81
Séché, Alphonse, 37
Senape De Pace, Stanislao, 46

Sestito, Maria, 109
Simonetti, Giacinta, 124
Sissi (Elisabeth of Austria), 110
Slocomb, Cuthbert Harrison, 124
Slocomb Day, Abigail. *See* Day, Abigail
Slocomb Savorgnan di Brazzà, Cora, 18, 93
Smith, Hilda L., 3
Soldani, Simonetta, 5, 140, 148, 210
Soldi, Manuela, 10
Spirito, Ugo, 36, 40
Stagnitta, Francesco, 69
Stangher, Amelia Inetta, 112–114, 126
Stanton, Elisabeth Cady, 115
Starace, Francesco Paolo, 149, 177
Starace, Giulia, 19, 20, 33, 36, 54, 140, 150, 153, 155, 158, 159, 161–163, 166–172, 175–177, 180, 181, 183–185, 196, 198, 199, 211, 215, 235, 242
Starace, Lucia, 19, 20, 153, 155–158, 185, 214, 239
Staschcit, Ulrich, 60
Steiner, Rudolf, 16, 20, 23, 154, 165, 166, 168, 170, 177, 179, 183, 199, 200, 215, 235
Stoltz, Marguerite, 71
Suttner, Bertha von, 121, 123
Sutton of Molesey, Caroline, 139

T

Tacchini, Alvaro, 64
Talamo, Edoardo, 85
Taricone, Fiorenza, 3, 5, 6, 9, 72, 134
Tarr, Carrie, 2
Taverna, Lavinia, 10, 65, 72
Tchaikovsky, Modest Ilic, 38
Tea, Eva, 37
Tedesco, Luca, 45, 47
Tennyson, Alfred, 98
Testi, Arnaldo, 214
Thane, Pat, 219
Tims, Margarethe, 3
Tittoni, Antona, 10
Tittoni, Tommaso, 10
Tomassini, Francesca, 81
Tomei Finamore, Rosmunda, 74
Toppazzini Tondello, Mariangela, 94
Travaglini, Carlo, 83
Traversi, Bice, 10
Troysi, Lucia, 139
Turati, Filippo, 41, 150
Turton, Amy, 160

V

Van Hook, James C., 182
Van Molle, Leen, 3, 134
Vannucci, Giovanni, 163
Vannutelli, Elisa, 42
Varikas, Eleni, 5, 212
Vezzosi, Elisabetta, 213, 214, 221
Villari, Pasquale, 64, 68, 217
Vivarelli, Roberto, 44
Vollaire, Christiane, 183, 186
von den Steinen, Cordelia, 63
von den Steinen, Wolfram, 66

W

Wakefield, Edward W., 135
Warriner, Elizabeth C., 123
Webb, Beatrice, 39
Webb, Sidney, 40
Weil, Simone, 200, 229, 233
Willson, Perry, 2, 13, 14, 209, 218, 219
Wilson, Woodrow, 53
Wollemborg, Alina, 42

Z

Zambrano, María, 233

Zanotti Bianco, Umberto, 32, 35–37, 44, 45, 51, 52, 54, 64, 65, 67, 72, 73, 164, 165, 170
Zarri, Gabriella, 221
Zunz, Olivier, 7